The Gardening from Which? Guide to

GARDENING
WITHOUT CHEMICALS

The Gardening from Which? Guide to

GARDENING

WITHOUT CHEMICALS

EDITED BY ALISTAIR AYRES

EDITOR, *GARDENING FROM WHICH?*

PUBLISHED BY
CONSUMERS' ASSOCIATION AND HODDER & STOUGHTON

Which? Books are commissioned and researched by
The Association for Consumer Research
and published by Consumers' Association
2 Marylebone Road, London NW1 4DX
and Hodder & Stoughton
47 Bedford Square, London WC1B 3DP

Designed by Linda Blakemore

First edition 1990

Copyright © 1990 Consumers' Association Ltd
British Library Cataloguing in Publication Data
Ayres, Alistair
    The Gardening from Which? guide to
    gardening without chemicals
    1. Gardening
    I. Title   II. Consumers' Association
    III. Which? books
    635
    ISBN 0 340 52796 X

Typeset, printed and bound in Great Britain by
Jarrold Printing, Norwich

CONTENTS

Below Growing flowers among your vegetables can attract beneficial insects such as hoverflies
Facing page What better way to control snails than a friendly thrush?

CONVERTING TO A NO-CHEMICAL GARDEN

Unlike giving up some other things, not using chemicals can give you a lot more pleasure from your garden. It should give you a much better insight into how plants interact with the soil and the many creatures that live in and visit your garden. And, as a result, you should be able to grow much better plants.

You no doubt have your own reasons for not wanting to use chemicals. It may be out of concern for the environment, to encourage wildlife to the garden or your worry about the possible effects of chemicals on the health of your family or pets. If you grow fruit or vegetables, you may want to be sure that the produce you eat is free of all chemical residues.

Whatever your reasons, the aim of this book is to help you achieve a healthy, good-looking and productive garden without reaching for the sprayer. No doubt some of your plants may occasionally succumb to pest and disease attacks, but as you will learn from this book there are lots of alternative ways to deal with them other than relying on garden chemicals.

There are many good gardening reasons for using techniques which eliminate the need for chemicals even if you don't want to stop using them completely in your garden.

CONVERTING TO A NO-CHEMICAL GARDEN

The garden illustrated here is destined to have lots of pests, diseases and weeds – partly because of the way it has been designed and partly because of the choice of plants.

To maintain such a garden would rely heavily on garden chemicals to deal with crises and to keep it healthy and productive. But with a few modifications, the same garden would be far less work to maintain and you could successfully give up using garden chemicals. To find out how you could change this garden, turn over the page.

KEY TO PROBLEMS WITH THE GARDEN

1 Neglected fruit trees. Crossing and overcrowded branches lead to disease problems and shade the fruit. Broken and split branches allow entry to fungi and bacteria. Fallen fruit left to rot provide a source of infection for the following year's crop.

2 Poor access to vegetable plot for weeding. Plants in rows too close together as not properly thinned after sowing.

3 No organic matter added to the soil. No attempt at crop rotation, leading to problems with diseases such as club root, onion white rot and pests such as potato eelworm.

4 Grass struggling under shade of the tree. Lots of moss.

5 Young specimen tree competing with grass growing right up to the stem.

6 Grass cut too short, causing bare patches due to scalping and weed problems.

7 Roses need regular spraying to prevent blackspot and mildew. Fallen leaves provide a source of re-infection for next year.

8 Bare soil between shrubs encourages weeds.

9 Weeds a problem in gravel path, as gravel just placed on soil, not consolidated on a hardcore base.

10 Shade-loving plants like astilbes struggle in a hot sunny position.

11 Fine-grass lawn needs fertilising to keep it in good condition.

12 Old herbaceous plants starting to die back in the centre and need dividing.

13 Sun-loving plants become weak and straggly in the shady corner.

14 Disease-prone plants like Michaelmas daisies need preventative spraying with a fungicide.

15 Hostas need protection from slugs and snails.

16 Hanging basket of nasturtiums can become plagued with blackfly.

17 Moisture-loving plants like fuchsias in small pots on a hot patio weakened by regular wilting and as a result become more vulnerable to pest and disease attacks.

18 Inadequate ventilation in greenhouse can lead to problems with fungal diseases.

19 Pots and seed trays reused without being washed and disinfected.

20 Greenhouse soil contains diseases as tomatoes have been grown there over many years.

21 Plant debris provides a hiding-place for pests.

Sophie Allington

CONVERTING TO A NO-CHEMICAL GARDEN

The garden illustrated here is the same one as on the previous page. Parts of the garden have been modified to make them less prone to pest, disease and weed problems and so make it easier to maintain without using any chemicals.

KEY TO GARDEN IMPROVEMENTS

1 Fruit trees pruned to open up the centre and let in more light and air. Diseased branches cut back to healthy wood. Grass cleared around base of fruit trees to reduce competition for water and nutrients. Ground mulched with black polythene covered with a shallow layer of bark chippings to improve appearance.

2 Wild flowers introduced to grass between fruit trees to encourage predatory insects such as hoverflies.

3 Compost heap constructed to recycle plant waste.

4 Vegetable plot divided into beds. Soil improved by digging in manure. Crop rotation system adopted and lime added to soil. One bed raised to improve drainage and reduce disease problems with early sowings. Sweet corn and outdoor tomatoes grown through a black polythene mulch. Squares of carpet between courgettes prevent weeds and keep the fruit clean.

5 Crown of tree raised to let in more light. Struggling grass under tree replaced with tough ground-cover plants like *Pachysandra terminalis* 'Variegata' and *Liriope muscari*.

6 Cutting height on mower increased to 2.5cm (1in). Short clippings left on lawn to avoid having to apply fertiliser. Grass removed over a 90cm (3ft) circle around young specimen tree. Bare soil covered with black polythene cover with a topping of bark chippings.

7 Roses removed and replaced with a pond and mixed border to attract wildlife.

8 Border mulched with bark chippings and ground cover planted between well-established shrubs.

9 Gravel path replaced with paving. Polythene used below ballast material to prevent weeds.

10 Moisture-loving plants replaced with drought-resistant ones like lavender, *Sedum* 'Autumn Joy' and purple-leaved sage.

11 Fine lawn containing fescues and bents replaced with a hard-wearing fine-leaved ryegrass such as 'Hunter'.

12 Herbaceous perennials lifted and divided to rejuvenate them. Invasive plants like solidagos and short-lived perennials like lupins replaced with plants that can be left to grow permanently in the same position without being divided, like acanthus and peonies.

13 Sun-loving plants in shady corner replaced with shade-tolerant perennials such as astilbes, hellebores and bergenias.

14 Hostas moved to a tub placed on a rough-surfaced paving slab, where they will be less vulnerable to slug attack than they were in the ground.

15 Nasturtiums in basket replaced with single-flowered trailing geraniums and the grey-leaved trailer *Helichrysum petiolare*.

16 Fuchsias moved to larger pots (which won't dry out so quickly) and moved to light shade. Pots of drought-resistant plants like marguerites, echeveria and houseleeks could be used in sun-baked spots.

17 Roof vents fitted to greenhouse together with automatic vent openers to improve ventilation control and reduce disease problems.

18 Soil in greenhouse replaced with mixture of manure, sand and fresh garden soil.

19 Pots and trays washed and sterilised before reuse.

20 Plant debris collected. Healthy material put on compost heap, and diseased plants, weeds that have seeded and perennial weed roots bagged up to take to the rubbish dump.

CONVERTING TO A NO-CHEMICAL GARDEN

There are lots of myths about gardening without chemicals. For example, if you have read books or articles on organic gardening you may have been led to believe that the essential starting-point is to have a lorry-load of manure dumped outside your front door. In reality, you probably won't need to improve your soil at all to grow ornamental plants – providing that you choose plants that like the soil conditions. Even on heavy clay soils that are prone to waterlogging, there is quite a range of trees, shrubs and herbaceous plants that will grow perfectly happily without any trace of manure (see page 101).

It is only when you want to grow plants which like different soil conditions than exist in your garden that you need to put effort into soil improvement. Even then you don't need to do it all at once. With a vegetable plot, for example, you can just dig in organic matter to one-third each year, following a crop rotation scheme. In the meantime, brassicas, for example, will still give good crops on a heavy compacted soil providing you feed them.

There are no doubt lots of questions that you would like answered about gardening without chemicals. Some of the most frequently asked are dealt with below. Hopefully, you will find the answers to your other questions within the rest of the book.

Q DOES GIVING UP CHEMICALS MEAN MORE WORK?

A In a *Gardening from Which?* survey, gardeners who were using organic growing methods all said that gardening without chemicals took up no more time than it did when they had used chemicals.

A carefully planned no-chemical garden needs a lot less maintenance than a conventional plot. Particularly if you grow vegetables, building up the soil fertility requires time and effort. But using preventative measures such as mulches, pest barriers and disease-resistant plants means that, in the long term, you should spend a lot less time doing routine tasks like weeding, watering, spraying and heavy digging.

Q DO FRUIT AND VEGETABLES TASTE BETTER WHEN GROWN WITHOUT CHEMICALS?

A In *Gardening from Which?* tests on a limited range of vegetables, tasters could not distinguish between the ones that were grown organically and those that were grown using artificial fertilisers. However you grow it, you are likely to find that fresh garden produce tastes better than shop-bought. But the knowledge that what you are eating is totally free from chemical residues is probably a big bonus for many people – especially as organically grown produce commands a premium in the shops. Some sprays, such as malathion, can taint the flavour of certain crops.

Q DO I REALLY NEED TO GIVE UP USING ALL CHEMICALS?

A It's up to you. If you plan your garden carefully and choose plants that like the conditions so they are all growing vigorously, there is no reason why you should need to spray more than the odd garden plant. The problem with using pesticides, even natural ones derived from plants, is that nearly all of them can kill beneficial creatures along with the pests.

If you don't want to stop using chemicals in your garden altogether, you can certainly cut down on their use. For example, instead of applying a lawn weed-killer as an all-over treatment, just spot-treat individual patches of weeds. Where practical, use non-persistent insecticides like pyrethrum, which breaks down into harmless substances after a few hours. If aphids are your main problem, spray with primicarb which will get rid of the aphids without harming bees, lacewings or ladybirds (though it will kill ladybird larvae).

Think twice before using soil insecticides as these will kill ground beetles and other beneficial creatures as well as pests like wireworms. Never use any chemicals where there is the slightest risk of them contaminating ponds and streams – even minute quantities can kill fish and amphibians.

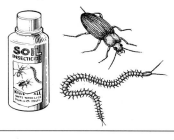

Q WHAT CAN YOU DO WITH GARDEN RUBBISH THAT'S NOT SUITABLE FOR COMPOSTING?

A Tree branches, weeds that have seed, perennial weed roots and plants infected with pests and diseases can be a problem to get rid of – especially if the dustmen won't take away garden rubbish.

A good bonfire may seem the ideal solution, but smoke from a typical bonfire often contains carbon monoxide and other more noxious fumes in small quantities. So, as well as being a nuisance by creating a lot of smoke, a bonfire can also be a potential health hazard.

If you must have a bonfire, minimise the pollution it causes by saving all the material until it's quite dry and ideally use an incinerator. A hot fire which burns quickly and completely will give off much less smoke and fumes than a damp, smouldering fire. Don't use a bonfire as an excuse to get rid of broken seed trays and plastic flowerpots. At all costs, avoid burning PVC, as it can give off highly carcinogenic fumes, such as dioxin.

Time the bonfire to cause least annoyance to neighbours, and keep a bucket of water handy to douse any large flames.

Ashes from a bonfire contain potash and can be used as fertiliser. However, they must be used while still dry as the nutrients are quickly washed out by rain.

Q ARE SOME PESTICIDES WORSE THAN OTHERS?

A All pesticides sold to gardeners in Britain have to be approved by the Ministry of Agriculture, Fisheries and Food (MAFF). Approval is only given by MAFF if it is satisfied that a product is safe if used as directed on the packet. However, some pesticides on sale in Britain – most notably gamma HCH (lindane) – are banned for amateur use in other countries due to concerns about their safety. In theory, none of the chemicals you can legally buy should pose a health risk to you or present any major risk to the environment as a whole (by building up in the food chain, as was the case with DDT, for example). However, using pesticides can upset the balance in the garden environment. It has been shown that the indiscriminate use of chemical sprays can actually lead to a pest and disease problem.

DISPOSING OF CHEMICALS

If you give up using garden chemicals, what do you do with all the bottles of half-used chemicals in the shed?

For small amounts of liquid chemicals, the recommended method of disposal is to dilute them as instructed on the label and pour the solution on to an unused part of the garden, such as a gravel path or bare soil next to a garage or shed. Don't dispose of chemicals near ponds, streams, ditches, marshes or places frequented by pets or wildlife. And don't pour them down the drain, as some chemicals are extremely persistent and could find their way into rivers and watercourses.

Small amounts of solid chemicals and empty containers can be put in the dustbin, but tighten lids firmly and wrap glass bottles in newspaper.

If you have large amounts of chemicals to dispose of (or banned or withdrawn chemicals which contain ioxynil or chlordane), take them to the office of your civic amenity waste disposal site, where they will be disposed of safely. Contact the Waste Disposal Unit of your local authority to find out about opening hours. It's important that you leave chemicals at the office – if you just dump them on the tip, children could get hold of them, with potentially serious consequences.

If you are disabled and cannot get to the disposal site yourself, your local Waste Disposal Unit should be able to arrange for the collection of unwanted chemicals.

Q WON'T PESTS AND DISEASES BECOME MORE PREVALENT?

A A survey undertaken in a typical suburban garden in Leicestershire revealed that there were over 2500 different species of insects. Of these, only a handful were serious garden pests. Aphids alone are preyed on by over 100 different species of insect, as well as blue tits and swifts.

Pests should not become a serious problem, as, along with the non-chemical control methods, there are plenty of predators to take care of them. Aphids will build up quickly early in the season, but if you grit your teeth and accept some damage, the predators should get the upper hand.

Pests are likely to be more numerous when you stop using chemicals only if you have been using chemical sprays throughout your garden for a number of years – in which case it may take a year or more for natural predators to recolonise your garden.

Diseases are most commonly a sign that a plant is not growing vigorously (due to lack of water, nutrients, light, etc.), so if you sort out the cultural problems, diseases are likely to be much less prevalent than when you used the sprayer. If plants are naturally susceptible to diseases every year, like some rose bushes, you would be much better off replacing them in any case.

Q ARE ARTIFICIAL FERTILISERS REALLY HARMFUL?

A Plants can only take up nitrogen in the form of soluble nitrates. It makes no difference to the plants whether the nitrates come in an immediately available form from a manufactured inorganic fertiliser or whether the nitrates are the result of microbes in the soil acting on a fertiliser containing only plant or animal material.

Any excess nitrates are washed away by rain water and irrigation and can end up in rivers and streams. Concern about the levels of nitrates has called into question the use of chemical fertilisers in agriculture. But it's unlikely that sprinkling a few handfuls of Growmore on your flowerbeds or your vegetable plot will have any impact on the environment.

The condition of the soil is far more important than what fertiliser you use. If your soil contains plenty of organic matter, it will retain moisture and nutrients. On free-draining soil with little organic matter, nutrients such as nitrates are quickly washed out. It's only when you apply chemical fertilisers continually without ever adding any bulky organic matter that you are likely to see a depletion of earthworms and other soil organisms.

Timing can be important too. If you use artificial fertilisers like Growmore (where the nitrogen is readily available to plants) in spring, when plants are putting on a lot of new growth, the plants are likely to use up most of the nitrates. But if you were to apply Growmore in autumn, a lot of the nitrates are likely to be washed out through the soil. Exactly the same is true of quick-acting organic fertilisers like dried blood.

Use organic fertilisers if you want to, but don't dismiss using Growmore as a stopgap until you have built up the soil fertility using organic matter as it is a cheap and effective all-purpose fertiliser.

Q WHAT ABOUT FINITE RESOURCES LIKE PEAT?

A If your main reason for not using chemicals is one of concern for the environment, there are other measures you can take in relation to your garden. There is no real reason to use peat in your garden – it's a poor mulch and there are plenty of other widely available organic materials for improving the soil. Peat-based multi-purpose composts are very good for sowings, but new composts based on bark, coconut fibre, and processed sewage slurry are becoming more widely available and are likely to supersede peat-based composts.

Expensive garden furniture and conservatories can be made from teak or oroko, which may have been felled from virgin rainforests. Manufacturers who get their hardwoods from properly managed plantations are entitled to display the Friends of the Earth 'Good Wood Guide Seal of Approval'. If you cannot find this, consider alternative naturally durable timbers such as western red cedar.

CHAPTER TWO

ORNAMENTAL PLANTS

It's a lot easier to grow a beautiful display of ornamental plants without using chemicals than it is to grow a pristine crop of vegetables. You can avoid most problems with pests, diseases and poor growth by choosing your plants wisely. This chapter helps you to choose the right plants for your garden and advises you on how to keep them healthy.

Most of the annuals, perennials and shrubs commonly grown in gardens are generally trouble-free. They may suffer the odd aphid attack or have their leaves chewed by caterpillars, but, provided the plants are growing well, they should survive without any need for treatment. Serious damage by pests or diseases is often a secondary symptom of a plant that is growing poorly – because it's in the wrong position or it's not getting enough water or nutrients.

To reduce problems, use the following guidelines.

AVOIDING PROBLEMS

■ SUN OR SHADE?
Most plants have a preference for a sunny or partially shaded position, and it pays to check this out before planting. If you grow a sun-loving plant in a shady position it will become weak and leggy and very vulnerable to pest and disease attack. Similarly, the foliage of shade-loving plants may become scorched in a sunny position and be prone to wilting in hot weather.

■ SOIL
There are quite a few plants that will grow on any soil, but some need an acid or neutral soil and won't be able to take up essential nutrients like iron and magnesium when grown on chalk – azaleas, rhododendrons and skimmias, for example. Drainage is generally the most critical factor, and relatively few plants (see page 105) survive waterlogging in winter. Free-draining soils tend to dry out very quickly, so avoid plants that need plenty of moisture, like clematis or ligularias, particularly in sunny positions. Shrubs need a minimum planting depth of 30–45cm (12–18in), so dig a pit and fill it with compost before planting on shallow soils.

■ TROUBLE-FREE PLANTS
Some plants are particularly prone to pests and diseases and rarely do well unless sprayed regularly. For example, many bush roses suffer badly from blackspot, mildew and aphids, and larger Michaelmas daisies are very prone to mildew. Think twice before growing them.

■ HOW INVASIVE?
Plants that spread rapidly, like the infamous stone crop (*Sedum acre*), or self-seed everywhere, like sisyrhinciums, can soon become weeds in a border and smother more choice plants.

■ HOW LONG-LIVED?
Some herbaceous perennials need to be divided every year or they become overcrowded and unhealthy – the larger Michaelmas daisies and solidagos (goldenrod), for example. They also take lots of nutrients out of the soil. Avoid such plants if you want a trouble-free border.

PLANTS FOR A TROUBLE-FREE BORDER

The border illustrated contains plants that require very little upkeep. None of the perennials needs staking, and the shrubs don't require pruning other than to cut back the odd wayward branch. All the plants are well behaved. Providing you give them enough space to start with, none of the perennials should need dividing for five years. Some, like agapanthus, acanthus and peony, can be left almost indefinitely.

The plants chosen are not prone to diseases like mildew and rust and should not suffer any serious pest damage, though it would be wise to guard against slugs (see page 60).

All the plants are illustrated in flower for purposes of identification. In reality they would not all flower together – flowering times are given below.

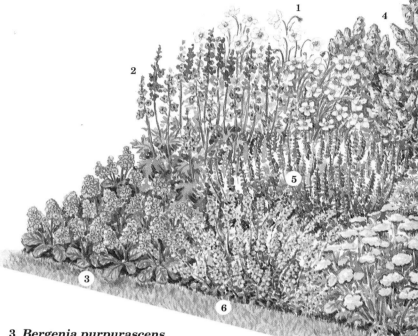

THE PLANTS

1 Anemone japonica 'White Queen' (Japanese anemone) Flowers Aug–Oct. 120×43cm (4×1½ft). Established plants resent being moved, so start with young plants. Although they can take a year or two to settle in, they need little attention. They gradually spread by underground runners, but any unwanted plants are easily pulled out.
2 Delphinium 'Belladonna Hybrids' Flowers Jun–Aug. 90–135×60cm (3–4½×2ft). The flowers are smaller and more widely spaced along the spire than the typical delphiniums, but they are longer flowering, longer-lived and don't need staking. Look for 'Blue Bees' (light blue) or the taller 'Lamartine' (deep blue).

3 Bergenia purpurascens Flowers Apr–May. 30×60cm (1×2ft). Leaves turn red in winter. Good in sun or shade on any soil.
4 Syringa persica (Persian lilac) Flowers May. 180×180cm (6×6ft) after 10 years. Compact, trouble-free lilac. May take a year or two to flower.
5 Salvia superba Flowers Jul–Oct. 90×45cm (3×1½ft). Has erect violet-flowered spikes. Very reliable and long-flowering. Good forms are 'Lubeca' and 'East Friesland'.
6 Diascia rigescens Flowers Jun–Oct. 45×45cm (1½×1½ft). Gives non-stop pink flowers throughout the summer at the front of the border. Despite its delicate appearance, it's very hardy, but it needs a well-drained soil.
7 Aster × frikartii 'Moench' or **'Wunder von Staefa'** Flowers Jul–Oct. 90×45cm (3×1½ft).

These modern Michaelmas daisy hybrids are almost faultless. The lavender-blue flowers appear about a month earlier than traditional types and last until the first frosts. They don't need staking and are not prone to mildew.
8 Achillea 'Moonshine' Flowers Jun–Aug. 60×45cm (2×1½ft). Much less invasive than taller achilleas. Cut it back after flowering for a second crop of leaves and flowers and to prevent flopping.
9 Chrysanthemum maximum 'Snowcap' Flowers Jun–Aug. 45×45cm (1½×1½ft). Old-fashioned white daisy flowers over neat mounds of green foliage. Unlike some white flowers which are very prone to browning, 'Snowcap' stays pure white all summer.

10 *Weigelia florida* **'Variegata'** Flowers May–Jun. 150×180cm (5×6ft) after 10 years. Outstanding trouble-free foliage shrub.

14 *Sidalcea* **'Elsie Heugh'** Flowers Jun–Sep. 120×45cm (4×1½ft). A trouble-free alternative to hollyhocks, with spikes of clear pink flowers. Pinch back shoots as growth starts to encourage bushy plants, which should not need staking. Cut plants right back once flowers fade to get a second flush of flowers. Most named varieties are worth growing.

11 *Acanthus spinosus* (bear's breeches) Flowers Jun–Aug. 150×90cm (5×3ft). Happy in any soil, but flowers best in sun. Plant deeply in spring and in cold areas protect with a thick mulch in its first winter. *A. spinosissimus* is smaller.

12 *Agapanthus* **'Bressingham Blue'** Flowers Jul–Sep. 75×45cm (2½×1½ft). Improved and hardy form of the blue African lily.

13 *Dianthus* **'Doris'** Flowers Jun–Jul and Sep. 45×45cm (1½×1½ft). Very free-flowering, double pink and red flowers on stiff stems. Best on well-drained soil.

15 *Iris pallida* **'Dalmatica'** Flowers Jun. 75×15cm (2½ft×6in). Upright leaves can make a good contrast to other flowering plants.

16 *Juniperus communis* **'Hibernica'** (Irish juniper) 300×75cm (10×2½ft). Good in sun or light shade and on all but waterlogged soils.

17 *Hemerocallis* **'Hyperion'** (day-lily) Flowers Jun–Aug. 100×45cm (3×1½ft). Canary-yellow, scented flowers.

Attractive grassy leaves.

18 *Paeonia mlokosewitschii* Flowers Apr–May. 75×75cm (2½×2½ft). Like all peonies, the flowers are short-lived, but it's worth including for its glaucous leaves and its spectacular seed pods. It resents disturbance and needs no staking.

19 *Geranium wallichianum* **'Buxton's Blue'** Flowers Jul–Sep. 20×60cm (8in×2ft). Blue flowers have a white centre.

ORNAMENTAL PLANTS: ROSES

Below 'Arthur Bell', another cluster-flowered rose with good disease resistance. See also page 133
Bottom Rosa rugosa 'Alba'

BUSH ROSES

There are hundreds of varieties of bush roses, and they vary a lot in their resistance to diseases. Sadly, many of the widely available varieties are also the most disease-prone.

■ LARGE-FLOWERED (HYBRID TEA)

Large-flowered roses on the whole tend to be worse than cluster-flowered roses when it comes to disease resistance. For many years 'Peace' was one of the most reliably healthy roses you could buy, but it is now showing susceptibility to black-spot in some areas. However, there are some good newcomers which should escape disease problems in most years. These are 'Cheshire Life' (rich orange), 'Silver Jubilee' (salmon-pink shaded with creamy-peach) and 'Sunblest' (golden-yellow). The old favourite 'Grandpa Dickson' (yellow with pink edges as it ages) is also still worth growing.

■ CLUSTER-FLOWERED (FLORIBUNDA)

Among the best for disease resistance are 'City of Leeds' (salmon-pink), 'Evelyn Fison' (red), 'Queen Elizabeth' (pink) and 'Trumpeter' (orange-red).

SHRUB ROSES

Within shrub roses, there are three major groups – modern shrub roses, wild roses and old garden roses. If you don't want to use chemicals in your garden, it would be as well to forget the old garden roses, as many of them are very susceptible to blackspot and mildew.

MODERN SHRUB ROSES

This group contains a ragbag of varieties including: larger, bushier versions of large and cluster-flowered types; Polyanthas such as 'The Fairy', which are much smaller; and hybrid damasks, which are strongly scented and have been developed from old varieties. Disease resistance varies with variety. Some worth considering are 'Penelope' (creamy-pink hybrid musk), 'Fred Loads' (trusses of large, fragrant semi-double vermilion flowers) and 'Fountain' (a bright red cluster-flowered type).

WILD ROSES

These are the best for disease resistance, and there are many good ones for the garden. Recommended are: *Rosa rugosa* and its varieties, which flower from June to September, have attractive hips and good autumn foliage colour; *Rosa rubrifolia* (*R. glauca*), which is worth growing for its greyish-purple foliage; and *Rosa moyesii* 'Geranium', which has spectacular bottle-shaped hips.

ENGLISH ROSES

If you like the appearance of old-fashioned roses but don't want the disease problems, the solution is to plant English roses. These have been bred since the 1960s, but they have the shrubby habit, strong scent and rosette-like flowers of old roses. The difference is that they flower all summer and have good disease resistance. Good varieties to look out for are 'Graham Thomas' (yellow, compact habit) and 'Mary Rose' (bright pink, branching habit).

ROSE DISEASES

■ **Blackspot** tends to appear first on older leaves as round black spots, which may join up. The leaves yellow and die, and a severe attack can defoliate the plant. Remove and dispose of all affected leaves as soon as you see them. Pick up fallen leaves in autumn and winter to prevent spores overwintering. In spring apply a mulch around bushes before new foliage appears to prevent spores in the soil being splashed on to the plant.

■ **Mildew** appears as a white deposit on young leaves, stems and buds, which it stunts and eventually kills. Even if not serious, it ruins the appearance of the bush. Prune out affected shoots and keep plants well watered in dry weather.

■ **Rust** appears as orange spots on the undersides of leaves, later turning black. If severe, leaves turn brittle and drop, and the whole plant can be killed if not treated. Treat as for blackspot to minimise problems in future years. Rarely occurs north of the Midlands.

CLIMBING ROSES

With climbing roses, there is a better choice of varieties with good disease resistance than other types. However, some of the varieties on sale are not that hardy. *Rosa banksiae* 'Lutea' and 'Wedding', for example, both have good disease resistance but are prone to frost damage and need a sheltered, sunny position. The other drawback is that many varieties flower for around only three weeks in June or July.

The following climbers flower for most of the summer and have good disease resistance and scent: 'Compassion' (pink to apricot), 'Dublin Bay' (red), 'New Dawn' (pearl-pink), 'Phyllis Bide' (pale yellow and pink).

When buying climbers, look for at least two shoots of pencil thickness or more. With climbing sports of bush roses (these all have 'climbing' in their name), the shoots must be at least 45cm (18in) long. If pruned too hard, they may refuse to climb.

ROSES TO AVOID

The following roses are all particularly prone to blackspot, mildew and rust, and they are not worth growing unless regularly sprayed throughout the growing season.

■ **Bush roses**
'Bettina' – lacks vigour, prone to blackspot and rust
'Blue Moon' – generally disease-prone
'Chicago Peace' – prone to blackspot
'Dearest' – prone to blackspot and rust
'Elizabeth of Glamis' – weak variety, prone to diseases and die back
'Fragrant Cloud' – prone to blackspot and mildew
'Lilli Marlene' – very prone to mildew
'Message' – poor weather resistance, prone to mildew
'Mischief' – prone to blackspot and rust
'Orange Sensation' – prone to blackspot and mildew
'Pascali' – spindly variety, prone to diseases
'Pink Peace' – not very free-flowering and prone to mildew
'Prima Ballerina' – not very free-flowering and prone to mildew
'Red Devil' – flowers ruined by a shower of rain
'Tenerife' – poor weather and disease resistance
'Uncle Walter' – prone to blackspot and mildew

■ **Climbing roses**
'Altissimo' – prone to blackspot
'Bantry Bay' – prone to blackspot
'Casino' – prone to blackspot
'Dorothy Perkins' – prone to mildew
'Emily Gray' – prone to mildew
'Climbing Ena Harkness' – prone to blackspot and mildew
'Excelsa' ('Red Dorothy Perkins') – prone to blackspot and mildew
'Climbing Fragrant Cloud' – prone to blackspot and mildew
'Guinee' – prone to blackspot, mildew and rust
'Leverkusen' – prone to mildew
'Minnehaha' – prone to mildew
'Climbing Sam McGredy' – prone to blackspot
'Paul's Scarlet Climber' – prone to blackspot and mildew
'Schoolgirl' – prone to blackspot
'Climbing Super Star' – prone to mildew
'Swan Lake' – prone to blackspot
'Zephirine Drouhin' – prone to blackspot

ORNAMENTAL PLANTS: PLANTS THAT CAN CAUSE PROBLEMS

The following lists include plants that are widely available which could cause problems if grown in certain situations.

◼ PEST- AND DISEASE-PRONE PLANTS

Antirrhinums – rust, when grown in warm, sheltered positions
Aster novii-belgii (Michaelmas daisy) – mildew. Avoid un-named varieties
Aquilegias – mildew
Hollyhocks – rust
Chrysanthemums – leaf miner
Honeysuckles – mildew, aphids
Hostas – slugs, snails
Nasturtiums – blackfly, cabbage caterpillars
Ornamental almonds – peach leaf curl
Ornamental cherries and plums (*Prunus* species) – canker, silver leaf (prune carefully during dry weather in summer to minimise risks)
Philadelphus (mock orange) – blackfly
Stransvaesia – fire blight
Sweet peas – mildew, aphids, pollen beetle

◼ INVASIVE PLANTS
In beds and borders
Achillea millefolium 'Cerise Queen'
Achillea ptarmica
Achillea ptarmica 'The Pearl'
Alchemilla mollis (lady's mantle)
Allium (ornamental onion)
Aquilegia alpina and *A. vulgaris*
Artemisia ludoviciana
Euphorbia cyparissias
Euphorbia griffithii 'Fireglow' (on light soils)
Geranium macrorrhizum (on light soils)
Hypericum calycinum (rose of Sharon)
Lamium galeobdolon (yellow archangel)

Lamium maculatum (dead nettles)
Mentha (mints)
Oenothera missouriensis (evening primrose)
Papaver orientale (oriental poppy)
Physalis franchetii (Chinese lantern)
Polygonum affine
Polygonum bistorta 'Superbum' (on moist soils)
Polygonum campanulatum
Solidago sp. (golden rod)
Vincas (periwinkle)
In rock gardens
Acaena (New Zealand burr)
Ajuga (bugle)
Aubrieta (seed raised)
Arabis 'Spring Charm'
Campanula portenschlagiana, C. poschaskyana
Cerastium tomentosum (snow-in-summer)
Iberis sempervirens
Polygonum vacciniifolium
Sedum acre 'Aureum'
Waldsteinia ternata

◼ SHORT-LIVED PLANTS
Alyssum saxatile
Anthemis tinctoria
Aquilegia vulgaris 'McKana Hybrids'
Arabis
Aster
Delphiniums
Gaillardia
Gentiana verna (spring gentian)
Lupins (all parts poisonous)
Oenothera missouriensis (evening primrose)
Potentilla warrenii

◼ SHRUBS/TREES WITH INVASIVE ROOTS OR SUCKERS
Kerria japonica (Japanese kerria)
Populus (poplar)
Rhus typhina (stag's horn sumach)
Robinia pseudoacacia (poisonous)

Salix (willow), except dwarf species
Symphoricarpos albus (snowberry, poisonous), *S. albus* 'Laevigatus', *S. orbiculatus* (coral berry)
Syringa vulgaris (common lilac)

◼ SHRUBS NEEDING ACID SOIL
Acer japonicum
Acer palmatum
Azaleas
Calluna vulgaris varieties
Camellias
Cornus kousa
Daboecia
Enkianthus campanulatus
Erica australis
Erica cinerea varieties
Erica tetralix
Fothergilla
Gaultheria
Hydrangea serrata
Kalmia
Leucothoe fontanesiana
Pachysandra
Pernettya mucronata
Pieris
Rhododendrons
Skimmia

◼ LARGE TREES
Could cause problems with excessive shade and roots competing with other plants for nutrients and moisture.
Acer negundo (box elder)
Acer platanoides (Norway maple)
Aesculus hippocastanum (horse chestnut)
Alnus (alder)
Cedrus atlantica (Atlas cedar)
× *Cypressocyparis leylandii* (Leyland cypress)
Eucalyptus gunnii (cidergum), if not regularly coppiced
Picea abies (Norway spruce)
Populus (poplar)
Prunus avium (wild cherry)
Salix × *chrysocoma* (weeping willow)
Tilia × *europaea* (common lime)

CHAPTER THREE

LAWN CARE

A thick, healthy lawn will not only look good, but will also resist invasion by moss and weeds and be less prone to pests and diseases. And by following the simple advice in this chapter, you will find how easy it is to keep your lawn in top condition . . . without depending on chemicals.

KEEPING THE LAWN HEALTHY

The key to a healthy lawn is careful maintenance. You can achieve this with just basic tools – a mower, a lawn rake and a fork. There is no need to spend a fortune on specialist tools and chemicals.

Mowing

The secret of successful mowing is to mow often. The most common faults are cutting grass too short and letting it grow too long between cuts. For an ordinary lawn, 2.5cm (1in) is short enough, though a smooth, fine lawn can be cut to 1.5cm (½in). Any shorter and you may scalp the bumps in the lawn, leaving bare areas which weeds can quickly colonise. Closely shorn grass will take longer to recover in dry spells, again giving weeds the upper hand.

An ordinary lawn needs mowing when the grass reaches about 4cm (1½in), and a fine lawn when the grass reaches about 2cm (¾in). Frequent mowing encourages dense growth, but don't mow when the grass is not growing strongly – in a drought, for example.

Raking

Rake (scarify) your lawn lightly with a lawn rake about once a month when the grass is growing rapidly. In autumn rake off any leaves.

Aerating

All lawns benefit from aeration, which allows air and moisture to reach the roots more easily and so promotes growth. It is best done in spring or autumn.

Topdressing

Your lawn will appreciate a topdressing in spring with sand and sifted garden compost. As well as levelling the surface, this will aid fertility, help decomposition of thatch and improve the structure of the soil. If you don't have enough home-made garden compost, try potting compost. Use horticultural or sharp sand, not builder's sand – it can be too fine.

Feeding

You shouldn't need to use a fertiliser if you cut the grass regularly and leave the short clippings on when you mow. Adding extra fertiliser makes the grass grow quicker and require more frequent mowing. If you do decide your lawn needs a tonic, apply blood, fish and bone at 70–140g a sq m (2–4oz a sq yd) in the spring.

TIPS

■ Keep your mower blades sharp and properly adjusted. This will reduce damage to the grass as well as make mowing easier.

■ In dry spells treat your lawn gently. Raise the cutting height of blades, cut less often and don't rake.

■ In wet or cold weather leave well alone. Don't walk on the lawn and don't mow when the soil or grass is wet.

■ Don't bother to aerate if your soil is light and your lawn not heavily used.

■ Rolling is unnecessary on most lawns and can be harmful on a heavy, clay soil. It compacts the soil and can impede drainage.

■ Remove clippings if grass was allowed to grow more than about 5cm (2in) before cutting the lawn.

Below Cutting the grass very short encourages daisies

DEALING WITH WEEDS

Correct **mowing** is the best way to prevent weeds. Don't cut the grass too short. You may scalp the raised areas and weaken grasses such as ryegrass that don't like close mowing. Weeds will then invade. If weeds have flowered, use a grass box to avoid spreading the weed seeds.

When **aerating** your lawn, collect any cores of soil you remove and compost them. If smeared on the surface they suppress grass growth and make perfect seedbeds for weed seeds. Worm casts pose the same threat. **Lime** or alkaline fertilisers like Nitro-chalk encourage earthworms and weeds. Don't use them unless your soil is very acid.

Raking weakens coarse weed grasses and discourages trailing weeds like clover and chickweed. You should rake lightly once a month when the grass is growing vigorously.

Do not scarify if you found speedwell in your lawn. Broken fragments will be spread around and will take root. Get rid of the speedwell first. **Topdress** only with weed-free material. Garden compost can be a source of weeds if your compost heap doesn't get hot enough to kill the seeds.

REMOVING WEEDS

Hand weeding is the best way to deal with weeds if you don't want to resort to chemicals. Make sure you remove every bit or the chances are that they will re-grow. Some lawn weeds, such as dandelions, have deep tap-roots that can be dug out with an old bread knife, while others send runners creeping through the lawn and need to be hand pulled. Tackle the lawn a bit at a time, and scatter grass seed on any bare patches you create.

LIVING WITH WEEDS

Accepting intruders as part of your lawn may be the best solution. Not all weeds are unsightly. Some low-growing weeds blend in well with grass, and others may be an attractive feature in their own right. Clover, for example, is inconspicuous if it's evenly spread throughout the lawn, though odd patches will be brighter green than the rest of the lawn, particularly during dry spells. Daisies can look quite attractive.

DESPERATE MEASURES

If your lawn has more weeds than grass, it's best to start again from scratch. Cut out the old turf and re-sow the lawn. This is best done in late summer or early autumn, when the soil is

REPAIRING BARE PATCHES

Bare patches should be repaired instantly, before moss and weeds have a chance to colonise.

1 Fork the area over lightly to loosen the soil and work in a little compost.

2 Sprinkle grass seed evenly over the area. Use a ryegrass mixture at a rate of 35g a sq m (1oz a sq yd) for general purpose lawns and a mixture of fescues and bents at a rate of 50g a sq m (1½oz a sq yd) for fine lawns.

3 Rake the seed in and water well. Keep the patch well watered until the grass is established. Protect the seed from birds using plastic netting or clear polythene until they germinate.

warm and there is enough rain for the lawn to get established.

Good preparation of the ground is essential. Dig thoroughly and remove any weeds, making sure you dig out the roots. Hoe to kill annual weeds before sowing.

A ryegrass lawn will need three or four months of growing and mowing before it can be used, and a fine lawn as much as six months. If you want faster results, you can buy turf, though it is much more expensive.

Right Lawn cross-section showing moss and thatch

DEALING WITH MOSS

Moss is the most common lawn problem. It may make your lawn look green and lush in spring, but will die in summer leaving ugly brown patches. If left to build up, it produces a layer of dead material that will impede drainage and prevent grass spreading and rooting properly.

To get rid of moss for good, you must make life unpleasant for it. If you just remove it, it will invade again in the autumn and following spring, when the grass is growing slowly.

■ SHADE

Moss loves damp shady places. Reduce shade by pruning back trees and shrubs. If parts of your lawn are permanently shaded, consider replacing the grass with shade-loving shrubs or ground-cover plants like ajuga, ivies, periwinkles or *Lamium maculatum*. Some grass seed mixtures are specially formulated for growing in shady places, but when last tested by *Gardening from Which?* in 1985, these did no better than ordinary mixtures on shady plots.

■ DRAINAGE

Moss thrives in wet conditions. It is also very shallow-rooting and, unlike grasses, grows well on compacted soil. You can improve surface drainage and relieve compaction by aerating your lawn two or three times a year. Use a hollow-tined aerator to remove cores of soil and top-dress with sand, working it into the holes.

Topdressing will also help to fill in hollows where puddles can collect. If you need to walk on your lawn when it is wet – to hang up the washing, say – then consider laying a path or stepping stones. If starting a lawn from scratch, make it on a slight slope to aid drainage. On a heavy clay soil that is prone to waterlogging, you may have to resort to digging a network of land drains if you want a permanent solution. Modern slit drains will cause much less damage and disfigurement if you have to drain an existing lawn. (See page 104 for drainage systems.)

■ SOIL ACIDITY

Finer grasses like a moderately acid soil, but a soil that is too acid favours mosses. Check the pH and correct by applying lime (aim for a pH of around 6).

■ REMOVING MOSS

You may be unwilling or unable to take drastic measures to fight moss. You can't do much about shade from your house and may not want to cut down your favourite tree or to go to the trouble of laying land drains on poorly drained soil. But you can still do a lot to get rid of moss.

Rake out thatch and dead moss in the summer. A spring-tined wire rake is all you need, but if you have a large, mossy lawn you may want to invest in a powered lawn rake.

Re-seed any bare patches and encourage the grass to thicken by regular mowing. If the grass is very weak, you may want to consider feeding your lawn to encourage vigorous growth (see page 119).

KEY TO MOSS PREVENTION

A healthy lawn Moss can't compete with vigorously growing grass. Follow the advice given overleaf to keep your lawn in top condition.

Careful mowing Don't cut the lawn too short. You may scalp bumps, leaving bare patches which moss will readily invade. Mow at least once a week. If you let the grass get too long it provides a moist, shady place in which trailing mosses will flourish.

Feeding Moss can thrive on poorer soil than grass. Topdress with garden compost to improve fertility.

Regular aeration Moss thrives on badly drained and compacted soil. Improve surface drainage by aerating and topdressing with sand. Do not walk on the lawn when it is wet.

Reducing shade Damp, shady places encourage mosses. Prune back over-hanging shrubs and rake off any leaves that fall in autumn.

Regular scarification Give your lawn a light raking regularly in summer to prevent the build up of a thatch which will impede drainage.

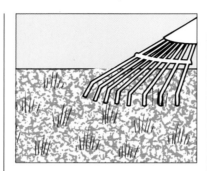

AVOIDING LAWN PROBLEMS

Mow often to encourage dense growth. If you let the grass grow too long, it provides a damp, shady environment, ideal for trailing mosses.

Set the mower blade high – 2.5cm (1in) for general-purpose lawns, 12mm (½in) for fine lawns. This helps to prevent weeds and moss.

Leave clippings on the lawn to nourish it.

Rake lightly every month in summer to prevent thatch building up.

Stay off the lawn when necessary – when it is wet, frozen or covered in snow. If you must walk across it regularly, consider laying a path or stepping stones.

Topdress in late spring with a mixture of equal amounts of sand and sieved, well-rotted garden compost. Use about 1kg a sq m (2lb a sq yd) and brush into the grass.

Aerate or spike once or twice a year, in late spring and/or early autumn, to improve drainage and stimulate grass growth.

PESTS AND DISEASES

	SYMPTOM	CONTROL
PESTS		
Leatherjackets	yellow patches of grass in summer. Swarms of starlings and other birds pecking the ground is another clue. Leatherjackets are the larvae of craneflies (daddy-long-legs)	a few won't do much harm, and in any case by the time the grass turns yellow it's too late to do much about it. The only way to get rid of them without using chemicals is to cover the grass with a plastic sheet, preferably on a warm, humid night, to bring them to the surface – then let the birds eat them, or brush them up yourself
Moles	mounds of earth thrown up; their tunnels may collapse and leave hollows in the lawn	see page 69 for deterrents
Worms	wormcasts on surface of lawn, often smeared by the mower	use a stiff brush or besom to flick casts off before mowing, so that they are not smeared
DISEASES		
Fusarium patch	a common lawn disease, characterised by small brown or orange patches following damp weather. Sometimes the pink, cotton wool-like fungus is visible. It usually attacks in spring and autumn, but can also occur under snow	avoid using nitrogenous fertilisers, especially in autumn, as the lush growth promoted is more vulnerable to disease, and improve drainage where practicable
Red thread	mottled patches of grass in late summer and autumn. Look for pink or coral-red needles of the fungus	sign that grass is not getting enough nitrogen. Apply fertiliser in spring and leave clippings on
OTHER PROBLEMS		
Algae	slime or jelly-like material on soil surface	aerate lawn and apply topdressing of sharp sand
Lichens	dark green, brown or orange growths on bare soil	sign of neglected lawn. See Avoiding Lawn Problems, above

CHAPTER FOUR

VEGETABLES

A healthy, productive vegetable plot *can* be obtained without chemicals. But giving up chemicals without adjusting your growing techniques may be asking for trouble. You also need to adopt good growing practices such as crop rotation to keep pests and diseases at bay, and to use natural barrier methods (see page 58). Your reward will be vegetables to eat that you know are healthy and won't be tainted with chemical residues.

It can take a while to build up soil fertility, so you may want to use some artificial fertilisers at first. And you should be prepared to accept some damage from pests, though there's plenty you can do to discourage them without resorting to pesticides.

GIVING UP CHEMICALS

PESTS

Pests won't necessarily get any worse (or any better) when you give up chemicals. Most pesticides kill pest-eaters as well as the pests and, in theory, if you stop using them, the population of pest-eaters will build up and control pests naturally.

You can use crop rotation to deter soil-borne pests and fight the others by destroying their hiding-places, by hand picking and using barriers and traps.

DISEASES

Crop rotation is the gardener's best defence against *soil-borne* diseases, but good hygiene is also important (see page 32). Good growing conditions, regular watering and resistant varieties are the best defence against other diseases.

WEEDS

Regular hoeing is the best way to deal with weeds. It destroys annual weeds and can constrain perennials.

Other techniques, such as mulching, can help to suppress weeds, and removing all roots when digging the plot will go a long way to controlling perennial weeds.

FERTILISERS

Giving up artificial fertilisers means that you will have to add lots of organic material to your soil. This is hard work, but it will pay dividends. You will need to water less often, and it will improve the soil structure as well as fertility.

To spread the workload, you can improve small areas at a time. The ideal way to do this is to create a system of permanent beds, as described on page 28.

VEGETABLES: CROP ROTATION

THE BENEFITS OF CROP ROTATION

A rotation scheme ensures that crops are not grown in the same plots each year. Related plants are grouped together because they have similar needs and suffer from the same pests and diseases. This has many benefits.

Reduces pests and diseases
Growing related vegetables in different plots each year helps prevent soil-borne pests and diseases from building up.

Makes pest control easier
Grouping related vegetables can make pest control easier.

Saves work
You can save work by grouping vegetables with the same soil requirements. Lime or manure, for instance, need be applied only to a third of the plot each year.

Simplifies feeding and watering
Grouping together vegetables with similar watering and fertiliser requirements makes it a lot easier to supply their needs.

HOW TO INCORPORATE A ROTATION SCHEME

A three-year rotation is the best for most gardeners, and it can be modified to suit even the small-est vegetable patch. Each plot will need preparing annually to suit the crops that are to be planted. A four-year scheme is worth considering for large plots or if you want to grow lots of potatoes.

FILL-IN CROPS

The following vegetables don't usually suffer from soil-borne pests or diseases, so can be fitted in anywhere.

Beetroot
Beetroot is not related to the other root crops but is often grouped with them. It needs a lot of fertiliser but is otherwise undemanding.

Celery, celeriac
These are often grown with peas and beans, which have similar requirements, or with marrows, courgettes and cucumbers. They need a rich, water-retentive soil and frequent watering.

Lettuce
A useful fill-in crop on any vacant land. Lettuce benefits from plenty of organic material, nitrogen and regular watering,

so can be grouped with brassicas.

Marrows, courgettes, outdoor cucumbers
Grow these on well-manured land. They benefit from a rich, water-retentive soil.

Spinach, leaf beet
Requirements are similar to beetroot's and can be treated in the same way.

Sweet corn
A crop that needs fertiliser and lots of sun. To aid pollination, plant in square blocks. It needs water when the cobs are forming.

Left Quick-growing vegetables like radishes can be sown between rows of other crops

FITTING IN WINTER CROPS

Crop rotation would be very simple if you could clear the whole plot in the autumn and start again the following spring. But some crops need to stay in the ground over winter. Late starters are planted out as soon as early crops have been harvested. Be sure to follow the rotation scheme so they will be in the right plot come the spring.

Start autumn-sown peas and broad beans in the potato/root plot as soon as these crops have been harvested. This will be next year's pea and bean plot. Spring cabbage is started in the pea and bean plot, which becomes the next brassica plot. Put over-wintered onions in the potato/root plot so that they will be in the onion plot next year.

▓ THREE-YEAR SCHEME

	YEAR 1	YEAR 2	YEAR 3
PLOT A	Brassicas	Potatoes/roots	Peas and beans/onions
PLOT B	Potatoes/roots	Peas and beans/onions	Brassicas
PLOT C	Peas and beans/onions	Brassicas	Potatoes/roots

▓ FOUR-YEAR SCHEME

	YEAR 1	YEAR 2	YEAR 3	YEAR 4
PLOT A	Brassicas	Onions/roots	Potatoes	Peas and beans
PLOT B	Onions/roots	Potatoes	Peas and beans	Brassicas
PLOT C	Potatoes	Peas and beans	Brassicas	Onions/roots
PLOT D	Peas and beans	Brassicas	Onions/roots	Potatoes

PLOT B

POTATO FAMILY
Soil requirements
The potato family need lots of fertiliser, but no lime. They will benefit from organic material and regular watering when fruits/tubers are forming. Earthing up potatoes ensures the soil is well cultivated for the next crop.
Vegetables included
Potatoes and tomatoes. Sweet peppers, chillies and aubergines are also related but are usually grown in the greenhouse.
Benefits of rotation
Rotation will help to control powdery scab, potato cyst, eelworm and potato blight (which can spread from last year's tubers missed when harvesting).

ROOT CROPS
Soil requirements
Root crops are not demanding. They benefit from some fertiliser but don't need regular watering. Do not apply fresh manure, as this can cause forked roots.
Vegetables included
Carrots, parsley, parsnips, salsify (you can also include beetroot and spinach for convenience).
Benefits of rotation
Rotation helps to prevent violet root rot and parsnip canker.

PLOT A

BRASSICAS
Soil requirements
Brassicas need a fertile, preferably alkaline soil. Dig in plenty of organic material in the autumn or mulch in the spring. Check the pH in the autumn and lime if necessary (wait until spring if your soil is light).

Leafy brassicas may need frequent watering in dry weather, and others at certain stages of growth. Cauliflowers, for example, need water once their curds start to form. Apply fertiliser before planting and during growth – brassicas are heavy feeders.
Vegetables included
Broccoli, Brussels sprouts, cabbage, calabrese, cauliflower, Chinese cabbage, kale, kohl-rabi, swede, turnip, radishes, mustard and rape (both used as green manure), wallflowers, sweet williams and many leafy, oriental vegetables.
Benefits of rotation
Rotation will help to control clubroot and allow brassicas to take advantage of nitrogen 'fixed' by the pea family.

CLUBROOT PROBLEMS
Rotation will help to prevent clubroot building up to really damaging levels, and liming will also help to control it. Severe clubroot requires a different strategy, as it can remain dormant in the soil for at least nine years and will not be eliminated by rotation. Take the brassicas out of your rotation and grow them in the same plot every year, liming it to keep the soil within pH 7.0–7.5. Start the plants in 10–15cm (4–6in) pots, so the roots are well established before being planted out and exposed to clubroot. You should then still achieve a worthwhile crop.

PLOT C

BEANS AND PEAS
Soil requirements
The roots of the pea family 'fix' nitrogen, so they don't require much fertiliser (none in the case of peas). Dig in a lot of organic material like well-rotted manure or compost. Peas and beans will benefit from frequent watering, particularly when the pods are forming.
Vegetables included
Peas, mange-tout, French beans, broad beans, runner beans and green manures such as agricultural lupins, field beans, tares and vetches.
Benefits of rotation
Rotation helps to prevent anthracnose, root rot and, to some extent, downy mildew.

ONIONS
Soil requirements
The onion family like a lot of organic material in the soil. They also benefit from fertiliser worked in to the soil before planting. They do not generally need watering, though leeks need water after transplanting and in late summer.
Vegetables included
Onions, including spring and Welsh onions, chives, garlic, leeks and shallots.
Benefits of rotation
Rotation will help to control white rot and stem and bulb eelworm.

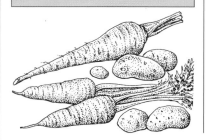

GREEN MANURES IN A ROTATION
Green manures can be grown in a rotation to make use of empty spaces. They are then dug in to improve soil structure or cut and put on the compost heap as soon as the land is needed. In winter they protect the soil surface from pounding rain and prevent nutrients being washed out. Field beans or winter tares are good green manures to grow after lifting potatoes. Dig them in to the plot before planting peas and beans the next year. They add nitrogen to the soil as well as providing organic material.

Summer green manures can help to suppress weeds. Buckwheat can be used anywhere, but grow mustard only in the brassica plot, and lupins, vetches or lucerne in the pea plot.

VEGETABLES: BED SYSTEMS

A good way to manage your vegetable plot is to divide it into permanent beds with paths between them. Then you can do all your work from the paths.

Plan your plots carefully to get the maximum bed area compared to paths. A bed width of 1.2m (4ft) suits most people, but make it narrower if you have difficulty reaching the centre. Paths should be at least 30cm (12in) wide – 45cm (18in) if you want wheelbarrow access.

THE BENEFITS OF A BED SYSTEM

Increase yields
As you don't need to get between rows of crops for hoeing and harvesting, they can be much closer together. You can therefore produce a higher yield from the same area. Permanent beds also make it easy to rotate crops and use pest barriers.

Less digging
You will not be compacting the soil underfoot, so you should not normally have to do any heavy digging once the beds have been prepared.

Fewer weeds
The close spacing of rows in a bed will help to smother weeds and so reduce hoeing.

■ MAINTAINING A BED
Little soil cultivation is needed once you have prepared the beds. Double digging will not need repeating for at least five years. On light soils, just rake or hoe in spring to prepare a seedbed. On heavy soils, lightly fork over in the autumn.

Apply bulky organic material every year as a mulch, or fork it in – at least a bucketful for every metre or yard of bed.

WHICH TYPE OF BED?

■ SHALLOW AND WATERLOGGED SOILS
On shallow and poorly drained soils a raised bed will provide extra rooting depth and improve drainage. You can make permanent edges from railway sleepers, paving slabs or old floorboards. Put the edges in place, then dig over the soil at the bottom of the bed. Fill the bed with equal amounts of organic material and soil or sand.

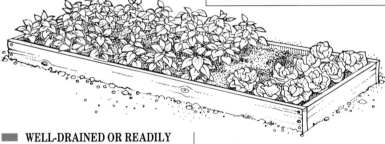

■ WELL-DRAINED OR READILY COMPACTED SOILS
On soils prone to compaction, or on light soils which dry out quickly, you need to double dig, adding a lot of organic material. See page 94 for method.

Try not to mix the more fertile top spit with the bottom spit. Rake the soil into a shallow dome or a flat bed with gently sloping sides.

FERTILISER REQUIREMENTS
As the vegetables are grown closer together than normal, you will need to use a fertiliser if you want to maintain high yields from your beds. Apply an organic fertiliser like blood, fish and bone before planting, and for hungry crops such as brassicas a topdressing of the same fertiliser or dried blood during the growing season. A cheaper alternative is to use Growmore. See the Table on page 31 for application rates.

It is also important to water leafcrops in a dry summer, and peas, beans, outdoor tomatoes and sweet corn when the seeds or fruits are swelling.

■ AVERAGE SOILS
On most uncompacted soils, single digging is all that is needed. Remove perennial weeds like couch grass and bindweed as you dig, collecting all the root fragments. Spread at least a 3cm (1in) layer of organic material over the plot and mix in thoroughly with a fork.

MAKING THE BEST USE OF SPACE

The Table below shows spacings that should give you high yields of average-sized plants. If you are unable to water regularly, a wider spacing is advisable. To fit as many vegetables in as possible, it may be advantageous to stagger some rows of crops so that they are in a triangular pattern. For example, you could stagger rows of lettuces so that plants are 30cm (12in) apart from their neighbours in all directions. Spacing between the rows can then be reduced to 25cm (10in).

PROTECTING CROPS

Dividing your plot into beds can make it easier to protect crops. You can fix hoops made from plastic tubing permanently over the beds and cover them with various materials to protect the crops from pests or frost. If your beds have wooden sides, you can anchor netting or sheets of polythene to them very easily.

AGAINST CATS

Vegetable seedbeds attract cats. Use lengths of wood with a notch in the top to support canes along the centre of the bed to form the ridge pole for a netting tent.

AGAINST FROST

Fix clear polythene or spun polypropylene fibre fleeces over the hoops to protect the crops from frost in the spring and autumn. Polythene sheets can also be used to warm and dry the soil in early spring.

AGAINST PESTS

The hoops can support netting used to protect your crops from pigeons. Deter flying insects such as carrot root fly with a covering of spun fibre fleece.

SPACING GUIDE FOR VEGETABLES IN BEDS

CROP	BETWEEN PLANTS	BETWEEN ROWS
Beans, broad	20cm (8in)	25cm (9in)
Beans, French	8cm (3in)	30cm (12in)
Beans, runner	15cm (6in)	60cm (24in) [1]
Beetroot, early	10cm (4in)	18cm (7in)
Beetroot, main crop	5cm (2in) [2]	18cm (7in)
Brussels sprouts [3]	60cm (24in)	60cm (24in)
Cabbage, summer [4]	30cm (12in)	30cm (12in)
Cabbage, winter [4]	40cm (16in)	40cm (16in)
Cabbage, spring [5]	10cm (4in)	30cm (12in)
Calabrese [6]	15cm (6in)	30cm (12in)
Carrots, early [7]	10cm (4in)	15cm (6in)
Carrots, main crop	2.5cm (1in)	15cm (6in)
Cauliflower [8]	30cm (12in)	30cm (12in)
Celery	25cm (10in)	25cm (10in)
Leek [9]	15cm (6in)	30cm (12in)
Lettuce, crisphead	30cm (12in)	25cm (10in)
Lettuce, cos	20cm (8in)	25cm (10in)
Marrow and courgette	60cm (24in)	60cm (24in)
Onion [10]	5cm (2in)	23cm (9in)
Parsnip [11]	8cm (3in)	20cm (8in)
Pea [12]	10cm (4in)	10cm (4in)
Potato	40cm (16in)	43cm (17in)
Radish	3cm (1in)	3cm (1in)
Spinach	15cm (6in)	20cm (8in)
Sweet corn	30cm (12in)	60cm (24in)
Tomato, bush varieties	40cm (16in)	40cm (16in)
Turnip	15cm (6in)	15cm (6in)

Notes

[1] Distance between double rows of canes. For wigwams, allow 30cm (12in) all round
[2] For baby beets, reduce to 2.5cm (1in)
[3] For small sprouts for freezing, reduce spacing to 40cm (16in)
[4] Reduce spacing to 15cm (6in) for mini-cabbages – smaller heads enough for individual portions
[5] Harvest alternate plants for greens; remainder will heart up
[6] Cut main heads and leave side shoots to develop. For larger main heads, plant 30cm (12in) apart
[7] For baby carrots aim for 1cm (½in) between plants. Alternatively, sow in bands with plants 2cm (1in) apart
[8] For winter cauliflower, increase spacing to 60cm (24in). For mini-cauliflowers (individual portion size), reduce it to 15cm (6in)
[9] For slimmer stems, reduce spacing to 10cm (4in)
[10] Grow salad onions 3cm (1in) apart in bands
[11] For larger roots, increase spacing to 15×15cm (6×6in)
[12] Sow in triple rows with 40cm (16in) between bands. For single picking for the freezer, grow 10cm (4in) in a block

VEGETABLES: CHOOSING THE RIGHT CROPS

Your choice of crops may depend on many factors such as the type of soil and whether you can water regularly. If you are new to vegetable growing, start with the most reliable crops. The Table opposite shows which crops you should find easiest.

If you don't have much space, stick to high value crops like runner beans, tomatoes, lettuces and calabrese. Keep your plot productive all year round by following early crops by overwintered crops. And make good use of catch crops like radishes and beetroot. Extend the growing season by starting plants early in pots under glass and using cloches.

DISEASE RESISTANCE

Plant breeders are continually coming up with new varieties that are less susceptible to disease. If you have the same problem year after year, it's worth trying a resistant variety (see page 135).

CHALKY SOILS

Most brassicas do well on a chalky soil if watered regularly. You shouldn't need to worry about clubroot. Spinach, beet and sweet corn are also reliable. Potatoes may become covered in scabs, particularly the main crop. This will not affect eating quality, though it disfigures the tubers. Choose a scab-resistant variety like 'Pentland Javelin' or 'Maris Peer'. Chalky soils are often shallow and susceptible to drought, so thirsty vegetables like runner beans and leaf crops are not worth growing unless you can water freely.

HEAVY SOILS

Brassicas do best on a heavy soil, provided it is not too compacted or waterlogged. Most other vegetables will grow well as long as you can get on the soil early enough. Carrots and parsnips may be difficult unless you have improved the soil structure by adding lots of organic material. If you want to grow them, choose short varieties like 'Early Nantes' carrots or 'Avonresister' parsnips. Peas generally do poorly.

SHADY PLOTS

Most vegetables grow best in an open, sunny position, and few thrive in even partial shade. If you can't remove the source of shade, concentrate on midsummer crops such as peas, lettuces, summer cauliflowers or radishes.

Some of the more unusual vegetables like endive, kohl-rabi and Jerusalém artichokes do well in shade.

Avoid French and runner beans, onions, marrows, tomatoes and sweet corn, and any crop that needs sun to ripen.

STONY SOILS

Most crops should do well on stony ground as long as the soil is basically loam. Leafy crops are the most reliable. You may have problems with root crops and potatoes because the stones can distort the roots and make digging difficult. Avoid carrots and parsnips. If you must grow carrots, try a round variety like 'Rondo'.

IF YOU CAN'T WATER

If watering is difficult, avoid crops that need watering regularly (see Table opposite – all crops rated *** in the watering column should be avoided). This is most important on sandy and chalky soils, which are both susceptible to drought. You may get away with growing crops that need watering only at key times (rated **) as long as you can water in the critical period.

Avoid celery, cauliflowers, calabrese and late peas. Crops rated * in the table, such as beetroot, broccoli, onions and parsnips, will do best.

VEGETABLE SELECTOR

VEGETABLE	HOW EASY [1]	GOOD YIELD A 1m (3ft) ROW [2]	FERTILISER NEEDS [3]	WATERING NEEDS [4]	SOW IN POTS [5]	PLANT OUT	SOW DIRECT	PROBLEMS
Beans, broad	●●●●	0.9kg (2lb) [6]	*	**	Feb	Mar–Apr	Mar–Apr	blackfly
Beans, French	●●●	0.9kg (2lb)	*****	**	Feb–Apr	May–Jun	Apr–Jun	aphids
Beans, runner	●●●●	6kg (13lb)	*****	***	Mar–Apr	Apr–May	May–Jun	aphids
Beetroot	●●●●	1.5kg (3.3lb)	*****	*	–	–	Feb–Jul	no serious problems [7]
Broccoli, sprouting	●●●	2kg (4.4lb)	*****	*	Apr–May	Jun–Jul	–	[7]
Brussels sprout	●●	1.4kg (3.2lb)	*****	*	Feb–Apr	Apr–Jun	–	[7]
Cabbage, summer	●●●	2.7kg (6lb)	*****	**	Feb–Apr	Apr–May	–	[7]
Cabbage, winter	●●●	3kg (6.6lb)	*****	*	May	Jun	–	[7]
Cabbage, spring	●●	1.8kg (4lb)	**	*	Jul–Aug	Sep–Oct	–	[7]
Calabrese	●●●	1.3kg (3lb)	***	***	Feb–Aug	Apr–Sep	Apr–Aug	[7]
Carrot, early	●●	1.3kg (3lb)	*	*	–	–	Feb–Aug	carrot fly
Carrot, main crop	●●	1.5kg (3.3lb)	*	*	–	–	Apr	carrot fly
Cauliflower, summer	●	2kg (4.4lb)	*****	**	Feb–Apr	Mar–Jun	–	[7]
Cauliflower, autumn	●	2kg (4.4lb)	*****	**	Apr–May	May–Jun	–	[7]
Cauliflower, winter	●	2.3kg (5lb)	**	*	May	Jul	–	[7]
Celery, self-blanching	●	2kg (4.4lb)	**	***	Mar–Apr	Apr–May	–	leaf miner
Leek	●●●●	1.2kg (2.7lb)	****	*	Feb–Apr	Apr–Jul	–	white rot, mildew, onion fly, eelworm
Lettuce	●●●●	3–4 heads	****	***	Feb–Mar	Mar–Apr	Mar–Aug	aphids, mildew
Marrow/courgette	●●●●	2.7kg (6lb)	***	**	Apr–May	May–Jun	–	viruses, slugs
Onion	●●●	1.3kg (3lb)	***	*	Feb–Mar	Apr–May	Mar–Apr	white rot, mildew, onion fly, eelworm
Onion, spring	●●●	0.5kg (1.1lb)	*	*	–	–	Feb–Aug	white rot, mildew, onion fly, eelworm
Parsnip	●●	2kg (4.4lb)	***	*	–	–	Mar–May	carrot fly, canker
Pea	●●	0.9kg (2lb) [6]	none	**	–	–	Feb–Apr	pea moth, pigeons, mildew
Pea, mange-tout	●●	1.7kg (3.7lb)	none	**	–	–	Feb–Apr	pea moth, pigeons, mildew
Potato, early	●●●●	1.8kg (4lb)	****	***	–	Apr–May	–	slugs, scab, blight
Potato, main crop	●●●●	3.7kg (8lb)	****	**	–	May–Jun	–	slugs, scab, blight
Radish	●●●●	0.5kg (1.1lb)	none	*	–	–	Feb–Aug	flea beetle
Spinach	●●●●	1.3kg (3lb)	****	***	–	–	Mar–Jul	leaf miner, slugs
Swede	●●●	1.5kg (3.3lb)	**	*	–	–	Apr–Jun	[7]
Sweet corn	●●	5 cobs	****	**	Apr–May	May–Jun	–	frit fly
Tomato, outdoor	●●	3.5kg (7.7lb)	****	***	Mar–Apr	May–Jun	–	blight, grey mould, viruses
Turnip	●●●●	1.5kg (3.3lb)	**	*	–	–	Mar–Aug	[7]

Notes

[1] Based on survey of *Gardening from Which?* members
[2] Based on *Gardening from Which?* trials or commercial yields
[3] Amount of fertiliser per sq m (sq yd) of bed

	GROWMORE	or BLOOD, FISH AND BONE	or HOOF AND HORN
*	85g (2½oz)	175g (5oz)	35g (1oz)
**	100g (3oz)	210g (6oz)	50g (1½oz)
***	140g (4oz)	300g (9oz)	70g (2oz)
****	175g (5oz)	360g (11oz)	100g (3oz)
*****	210g (6oz)	450g (13oz)	115g (3½oz)

Up to ** = apply all the fertiliser as a base dressing when sowing or planting. * or more = apply half as a base dressing and the rest as one or two top dressings when the crop is growing. If using hoof and horn, also add 35g (1oz) bonemeal and 70g (2oz) rock potash
[4]   *   no need to water
     **   water at key times if dry
     *** water regularly in dry spells
[5] An alternative for brassicas is to sow in a seedbed and transplant the seedlings (for timing see 'plant out' column)
[6] Yield after shelling
[7] Brassicas suffer from many pests and diseases including clubroot, aphids, cabbage root fly and caterpillars (see page 33)

VEGETABLES: DEALING WITH PROBLEMS

◼ HYGIENE

Good hygiene helps to prevent the spread of diseases in your garden. Start with clean pots and sterile compost for raising seedlings. At the end of the season, wash and disinfect all pots, seed trays, canes and other equipment. Also disinfect the greenhouse.

Inspect crops regularly and remove diseased leaves and any badly infected plants. All diseased material must be disposed of, not composted.

Keep the garden clean and tidy. Do not allow piles of dead leaves and prunings to build up. Clear up debris from old plants promptly.

◼ OVERWINTERING PROBLEMS

You can reduce the number of pests in your garden by destroying them and their hiding-places in winter. Winter digging will expose soil pests like onion fly, slugs and wireworms. The birds and the weather will finish them off. Do not leave plants in the ground after harvesting. Dig them up and dispose of or burn infested ones. Mealy aphids and cabbage root fly larvae, for example, may remain in old brassica stems. Other pests like carrot fly larvae can overwinter on roots left in the ground. Onion fly, celery fly and leaf miners can survive on infested leaves.

Overwintering plants can also harbour pests. For example, brassicas may be infested with cabbage white fly. Burn them after harvesting.

Pests like slugs, flea beetles, pea and bean weevils and wireworms may hide near the compost heap, in debris and patches of weeds. Keep the ground clear and cultivate the soil

PEAS AND BEANS

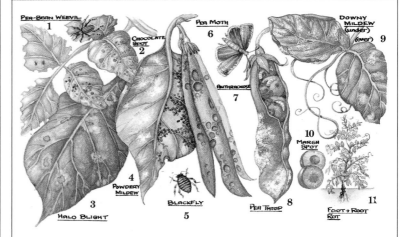

1 Pea and bean weevil
Notched leaves. Yield not affected
2 Chocolate spot
Leaves covered with small, dark brown spots. Destroy badly affected leaves. Next year, lime soil if acid
3 Halo blight
Small, dry brown spots surrounded by a yellow halo affect French or runner beans. Destroy affected plants. Grow on a new site next year
4 Powdery mildew
White mould under leaf, particularly in dry weather. Remove and dispose of affected leaves
5 Blackfly (black bean aphid)
Nip out tips of broad beans when four flower trusses have formed
6 Pea moth
Caterpillar tunnels into pods and eats peas. No cure
7 Anthracnose
Brown, sunken spots on dwarf bean pods. Destroy affected pods. Use a new site next year
8 Pea thrips
Silvery patches on distorted pods. Remove pods if badly affected
9 Downy mildew
Yellow patches on leaves and mauve or

white mould on underside. Destroy affected plants. Rotate
10 Marsh spot
Peas discoloured internally, caused by lack of manganese. Apply fritted trace elements (see page 137)
11 Foot and root rot
Leaves yellow, stem blackened at base and plant collapses at soil level. Destroy affected plants. Avoid poorly drained soil

SAVING SEED

Pea and bean seeds are well worth saving to plant again next year, but don't collect seed from F1 hybrids. They will produce a mixture of plants, mostly not as good as the parents.

Earmark several of the strongest, healthiest plants rather than taking odd pods here and there. Select long, healthy pods full of seed and allow them to ripen as long as possible, removing them before they shed their seed. Spread them out to dry in a well-ventilated place, perhaps in stacking tomato trays. When dry, shell and then clean the seed. Store in a cool, dry place.

BRASSICAS

[Illustrations with the following labels:]

2 POWDERY MILDEW

SLUGS + SNAILS
1

3 BORON DEFICIENCY

5 RING SPOT

4 SOFT ROT (cross-section)

FLEA BEETLE + DOWNY MILDEW

6 SMALL CABBAGE WHITE CATERPILLAR

TURNIP GALL WEEVIL
7

9 BLOWN SPROUTS

11

CABBAGE ROOT FLY (maggots)
8

12 CABBAGE APHID

WHITEFLY
13

CABBAGE MOTH CATERPILLAR
14

WHIPTAIL
15

10

16 MAGNESIUM DEFICIENCY

17 LARGE CABBAGE

18

1 Slugs and snails
Ragged holes in leaves and silvery trails. Protect young plants with cylinders cut from plastic bottles

2 Powdery mildew
White spots, particularly in dry spells. Remove affected leaves

3 Boron deficiency
Cauliflower curds turn brown. Next season, water with borax solution (28g to 17 sq m; 1oz to 20 sq yd).

4 Soft rot
Cauliflower curds brown and rotten. No cure. Destroy

5 Ring spot
Leaves covered in round, 'bull's-eye' spots. Remove and destroy affected leaves. Rotate

6 Small cabbage white caterpillar
Pick off caterpillars

7 Turnip gall weevil
Swollen outgrowths on roots, white grubs inside. Rotate crops

8 Cabbage root fly
Plants stunted with bluish leaves. Small grubs on leaves. Protect new plants with collars made from carpet underlay (see page 58)

brassica collar

9 Blown sprouts
Sprouts open and leafy. Caused by poor soil or a poor variety. Work in plenty of organic material, firm the ground before planting and use an F1 variety

10 Flea beetle
Small, round holes, particularly on young plants. If severe, dust plants and soil with derris

11 Downy mildew
Leaves of young plants turn yellow. White fluffy growth on underside. Destroy affected plants and practise rotation

12 Mealy cabbage aphid
Colonies of grey, waxy insects on undersides of leaves. Pick off badly affected leaves

13 Whitefly
Clouds of small white flies when plant disturbed. Damage usually superficial

14 Cabbage moth caterpillar
Pick caterpillars off. Biological control (see page 65)

15 Whiptail
Leaves of broccoli and cauliflower thin and distorted. No head forms. Caused by lack of the trace element molybdenum. Apply calcified seaweed on acid soil

16 Magnesium deficiency
Leaves yellow between veins, especially on limy soils. Water or spray with a solution of Epsom salts

17 Large cabbage white caterpillar
Ragged leaves. See 14, above

18 Clubroot
Roots swollen. Plants develop red or purple tinge and wilt in warm weather (see page 29)

LETTUCE

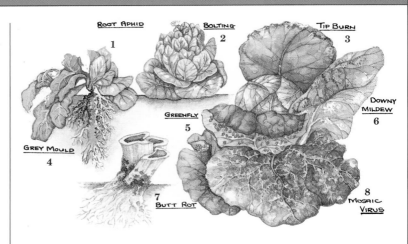

1 Root aphid
Plants stunted, yellow wilted leaves. White, waxy powder on roots. Keep plants well watered in dry spells. Grow resistant varieties like 'Avoncrisp'
2 Bolting
Flower heads form. No heart. Caused by a check to growth or hot, dry weather
3 Tip burn
Brown, dry leaf edges. Caused by sudden loss of water from leaves. No cure, but the plants should continue to grow normally
4 Grey mould (botrytis)
Root rots at soil level. Plant collapses. Destroy if affected
5 Greenfly
Leaves puckered and yellow. Small insects on underside leave a sticky secretion. Spray with soft soap solution
6 Downy mildew
Yellow patches on leaves, white, fluffy growths underneath. Remove diseased leaves. Thin early. Grow resistant varieties
7 Butt rot
Stems hollow and brown and rotten at base. Destroy diseased plants

8 Mosaic virus
Puckered leaves with yellow blotches between veins. Stunted growth. Destroy affected plants

ROOTCROPS

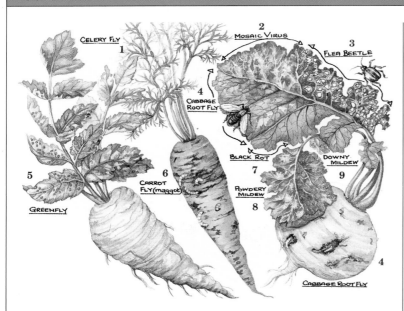

1 Celery fly
White wiggly lines and brown patches on parsnip leaves. Remove and destroy affected leaves
2 Mosaic virus
Leaves mottled or twisted and tinged red. No root damage. Destroy affected plants
3 Flea beetle
Turnip, swede and radish leaves riddled with small holes. Dust with derris if severe
4 Cabbage root fly
Blue/grey patches on swede and turnip leaves. Maggots in roots. Destroy affected plants
5 Greenfly (aphids)
Remove badly infected leaves. Try spraying with soapy water
6 Carrot fly
Carrot leaves reddish and wilting in hot weather. Maggots tunnel into root. Avoid thinning. Use a polythene or other barrier around carrot beds
7 Black rot
Turnip and swede leaves yellowish with black veins. Roots rotten. Dig up and destroy affected plants
8 Powdery mildew
White fluffy growth under swede and turnip leaves. Remove affected leaves
9 Downy mildew
Grey mould on underside of swede and turnip leaves. Remove affected leaves

ONIONS AND LEEKS

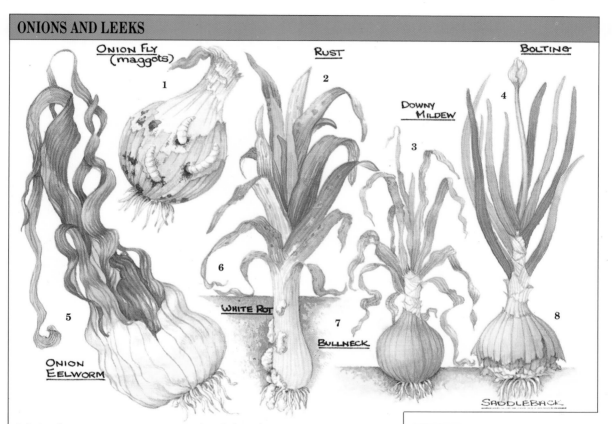

ONION FLY (maggots)
RUST
BOLTING
DOWNY MILDEW
ONION EELWORM
WHITE ROT
BULLNECK
SADDLEBACK

1 Onion fly
Leaves turn yellow and droop. Maggots on roots or inside bulbs. No cure. Destroy

2 Rust
Orange patches, particularly on leek leaves. Bulbs still edible. Destroy affected leaves at the end of the season and choose a new site next year

3 Downy mildew
Leaves grey and shrivelled; they eventually die back. Don't store the bulb. Use up the bulbs as quickly as possible, and grow on another site next year

4 Bolting
Plants produce a flower stalk. No treatment. Cut off stalk and use bulb straight away. Don't try to store the onions, as they won't keep

5 Onion eelworm
Base of plants swollen, leaves distorted and twisted. Destroy affected plants. Don't grow in the same place again

6 White rot
Leaves yellow and wilted. White fluffy growths on bulbs and roots. Destroy affected plants. Don't grow in the same place again

7 Bullneck
Bulbs have thick necks. May be caused by wet weather or too much nitrogen or manure in the soil. Don't store; use straight away

8 Saddleback
Bulbs split at base when lifted. It usually happens in very wet seasons on onions grown from sets; don't store; use straight away

NECK ROT
This is one of the most common diseases of stored onions. After several months in store, the bulb scales soften and brown and sunken lesions are formed around the neck. Soon the rot spreads throughout the onion, and then a grey mould may form on the bulb as a secondary infection. The disease can totally ruin your supplies of stored onions, making them totally unusable. The infection may also come from crop debris.

A three- or four-year crop rotation will help, but not leaving old or infected onions lying around is also important in keeping the disease at bay.

POTATOES

1 Greenfly (aphids)
Rub off or spray with soft soap solution

2 Magnesium deficiency
Yellow between veins. The plants may be stunted. Spray with Epsom salts solution (½kg in 10 litres)

3 Frost
Blackened stems, brown-edged leaves. Protect plants with spun polypropylene fleece

4 Blackleg
Leaves yellow prematurely, stem rots at ground level. Destroy affected tubers. Don't store sound ones

5 Slug damage
Tubers riddled with cavities, large round holes on surface. Lift crops as soon as you can to minimise damage. Don't store

6 Potato blight
Yellow/brown patches on leaves that turn brittle in dry weather and rot in wet weather. White mould on the undersides. Destroy affected plants and tubers

7 Cyst eelworm
Growth poor, leaves discoloured. Half-millimetre cysts on roots. Use crop rotation; grow early or resistant varieties

8 Wireworm
Tubers riddled with narrow tunnels. Lift potatoes as soon as possible. Don't store

9 Common scab
Tubers covered with warts. Potatoes disfigured but edible. Dig in plenty of organic material and water well in dry weather

10 Powdery scab
Round, raised scabs on tubers, releasing masses of brown, powdery spores. Burn affected tubers and don't grow potatoes on same plot for at least three years

11 Spraing
Semi-circular brown marks on tuber flesh, caused by viruses spread by eelworms. Tubers can be eaten if you remove the discoloured part. Use a new plot next year

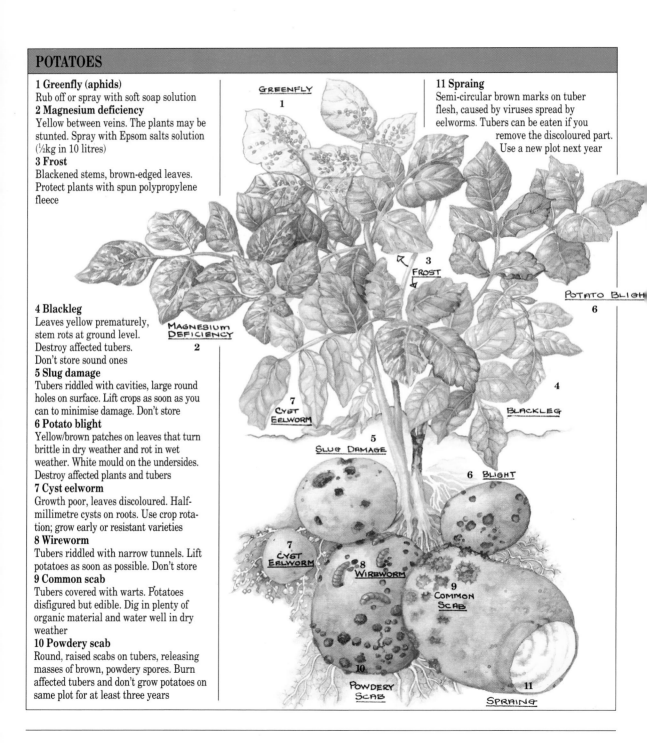

CHAPTER FIVE

FRUIT

Fruit trees and bushes will not crop well if neglected, but if you follow the simple guidelines in this chapter you can be sure of a good harvest.

If you are bothered by pests or diseases, the Troubleshooting sections will help you identify the problem and take the right action.

CHECKLIST FOR HEALTHY FRUIT

1 Pruning
Most fruit is pruned in autumn or winter. Cane fruits are simply cut down to ground level, and trees are pruned to remove dead wood and to open them up. Special pruning may be required for some training systems.

2 Cleaning up
Collect and destroy fallen leaves and fruit – they can harbour pests and diseases.

3 Feeding
Apply an organic fertiliser such as blood, fish and bone in the spring. For soft fruits and dessert apples, use 150g a sq m (4½ oz a sq yd), though strawberries need half this quantity. For other fruits use 300g a sq m (9oz a sq yd). If you are using Growmore, halve these quantities.

4 Watering and mulching
Mulching suppresses weeds and reduces the need to water. First apply fertiliser and water the soil thoroughly. Mulch with chipped bark or well-rotted compost. Strawberries need mulching with straw or polythene to keep the berries clean.

5 Pests and diseases
Looking after your plants well should keep them healthy and able to withstand attack by pests and diseases. Your biggest pest may be birds: the only solution is to net your fruit.

6 Weeds
Perennial weeds should be eradicated before planting. Regular hoeing will control annuals. Weeds and grass compete for water and nutrients, and fruit trees will grow much better if you keep the ground around them clear.

7 Position
All fruits like a sunny, sheltered position. Avoid planting in frost pockets. Plants will do best on a reasonably water-retentive but freely draining soil.

8 Pollination
Most apples and pears are self-sterile and will not crop unless they are pollinated with another variety. You can usually get away with growing one tree in your garden if there are trees in neighbouring gardens. Otherwise, you'll have to plant two or more varieties that flower at the same time.

9 Variety
When choosing varieties, first you need plants that are suitable for the conditions in your garden. Disease resistance, yield and fruit size are also important. And the flavour and the keeping quality of the fruit may also affect your choice.

10 Rootstock
If your fruit trees are not thriving, the rootstock may not be vigorous enough. Try feeding, and keep the area around the tree weed free.

TROUBLESHOOTING: APPLES AND PEARS

PESTS

APPLE APHIDS

Small green or pink aphids build up in spring on young growth. They can damage flowers and fruit and reduce yields.

Try spraying with a soft soap solution. Use permethrin spray as a last resort.

WOOLLY APHIDS

These are colonies of small, grey-brown insects covered with woolly wax. Bark may become galled or cracked, allowing diseases to enter.

Rub off with methylated spirit or cut out small colonies and dispose of prunings.

APPLE BLOSSOM WEEVIL

Look for small, dark brown, shiny weevils. They feed inside developing buds.

Damage not usually severe enough to need controlling.

APPLE SAWFLY

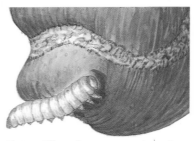

Caterpillars leave curved, corky scars on the fruit and tunnel into it. Many fruits fall off.

Pick up and burn fruitlets as they drop, to prevent infection the following year.

CODLING MOTH

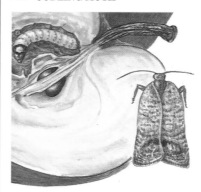

Caterpillars attack apples and occasionally pears, leaving holes in the fruit, which may drop early.

Destroy affected fruit. Use pieces of sacking or corrugated cardboard tied around the trunk and larger branches to attract overwintering caterpillars so you can destroy them. Alternatively, use a pheromone trap. These use an artificial version of the scent (pheromone) that the female moth uses to attract the male. Hang the traps in fruit trees at the end of May (see page 137 for suppliers).

TORTRIX MOTH

Caterpillars feed on developing apples, leaving rough, corky bumps on the skin.

Squash any you can reach, or try biological control using a bacterium that kills caterpillars (see page 65).

WINTER MOTHS

A looping caterpillar that eats the leaves in spring. Wingless female moths emerge from pupae in the soil in autumn or spring and crawl up the trunk to lay eggs.

Put strips of material covered in grease around the trunks 1.2m (4ft) above soil level in October. (Use pbi Boltac greasebands or Synchemicals fruit tree grease.)

PEAR SUCKERS (PSYLLIDS)

Tiny pale green or yellow insects that attack in April and May. Leaves, buds and blossom are discoloured, distorted or blistered and become covered with honeydew and sooty mould.

Prune out badly affected branches.

PEAR MIDGE

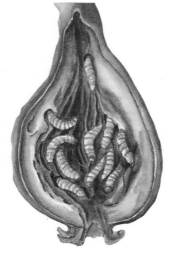

Young fruits swell but don't develop normally and drop prematurely. Look for 4mm-long larvae inside.

Destroy affected fruit and cultivate the soil under trees.

DISEASES

SCAB

Rough brown or black patches on the fruit and young shoots. Leaves develop dark patches and fall prematurely. Most common in wet areas.

The fruit is still edible, though scarred. Rake up and burn leaves in autumn. Prune out affected shoots.

BITTER PIT

Bitter pit is caused by a calcium deficiency. It affects only apples and may not show until after harvest. The symptoms are sunken brown spots on the skin of fruit with discoloured flesh beneath.

Prune apple trees in summer to reduce vigour and improve their cropping potential. On acid soil apply lime to raise the pH to 6.5.

STORED FRUIT

You must choose the right varieties of apples and pears to store. 'Idared' and 'Winston' apples, for instance, are known for their good keeping qualities, whereas 'Fortune' and 'Laxton's Epicure' do not store well.

Pick out only the best fruit. Reject any with bruises or evidence of maggots. Place in polythene bags with a few holes punched in them for ventilation.

Alternatively, you can wrap them in newspaper and store in boxes, but this makes it more difficult to check for rotting ones.

Store in a cool, frost-free place, if possible in a refrigerator. A temperature of between 1° and 4°C (34° and 40°F) should stop the fruit from shrivelling up as the weather gets warmer in the spring.

Check periodically and remove rotting fruit, as this can soon infect the whole lot.

BROWN ROT

The whole or part of the fruit rots. The fungus enters through wounds left by pests.

Remove affected fruit. Control pests (see page 38).

BACTERIAL CANKER

Produces sunken areas on the bark and leaves a gummy, resinous secretion on the trunk and branches.

Cut diseased areas back to healthy wood and seal the wound with canker paint. Remove and dispose of badly affected branches. Badly affected trees are best destroyed.

TROUBLESHOOTING: PLUMS, CHERRIES AND PEACHES

PESTS

■ BROWN SCALE

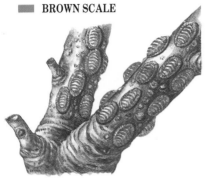

Trunks covered in small, brown scale insects. Can build up on old fruit bushes and plum trees.

Control is not practical on mature trees, but damage is rarely severe unless the tree is badly infested. On young trees you can squash the scales by hand or wipe them off with methylated spirit.

■ CHERRY BLACKFLY

Dark brown aphids colonise young shoots and leaves in spring. Leaves may become distorted.

No effective means of control, but mature trees will recover and the problem won't occur every year.

■ PLUM SAWFLY

Larvae bore into the fruits, which may drop prematurely.
Collect and destroy affected fruit.

DISEASES

■ BACTERIAL CANKER

Gummy secretions on trunk and branches, sunken areas on the bark.

Cut back to healthy wood and seal the wound with pruning paint. Remove and dispose of badly affected branches altogether. Destroy badly affected trees.

■ PEACH LEAF CURL

Leaves twist and blister and fall prematurely. The tree is weakened.

Wall-trained trees can be covered with a polythene sheet between January and late April to prevent the rain washing spores down on to new leaves. Burn infected leaves. Rake up any fallen leaves.

■ SILVER LEAF

Leaves become silvery and may turn brown prematurely. Branches die back.

Cut back affected branches to healthy wood. Destroy prunings. If the trunk is affected, the whole tree should be removed and destroyed.

■ PLUM RUST

Brown, powdery spots on the underside of leaves.
Remove infected leaves and debris and destroy them.

TROUBLESHOOTING: SOFT FRUIT

PESTS

BIG BUD MITE

Black currant buds swell and become spherical. May spread reversion virus (see Diseases).

Prune any affected shoots. Remove the large buds in winter. Destroy badly affected plants.

CLEARWING MOTH

Leaves wilt and the branches become weak and may break off, caused by the caterpillars feeding on the pith. Affects older shoots of currants.

Cut off and burn affected branches.

CURRANT BLISTER APHIDS

Pale yellow or green aphids, producing red or yellow blisters on the edges of leaves.

Little damage, control unnecessary.

SAWFLY

Caterpillars eat the leaves of gooseberries and currants and can completely defoliate bushes. Fruit unaffected, but yields may be reduced next year.

Pick them off or use a biological control (see page 65).

RASPBERRY BEETLE

White/brown grubs found on and in ripening fruit.

Remove and destroy affected fruit.

STRAWBERRY SEED BEETLE

Small patches of flesh eaten out of the fruit. Look for black beetles up to 20mm (¾in) long.

Clear up any debris in the strawberry patch.

DISEASES

AMERICAN GOOSEBERRY MILDEW

Powdery white patches on the foliage. Leaves curl.

Cut back infected shoots and dispose of the prunings.

CANE BLIGHT

Canes wilt in summer, become brittle and easily snap off. They may die in winter or late spring.

Destroy affected canes.

REVERSION VIRUS

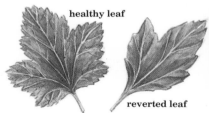

healthy leaf

reverted leaf

New leaves are coarse and nettle-like, with fewer veins. Yields reduced annually.

No cure. Dig up and dispose of bushes. Buy new, certified stock and plant on a fresh site.

SPUR BLIGHT

Often attacks new raspberry canes. Stems develop a purple tinge and turn grey/white in winter.

Destroy affected canes.

SIMPLE PRUNING FOR HEALTHY TREES AND BUSHES

APPLES

Most apple trees need pruning only every four or five years, once established, to deal with overcrowded and overgrown branches and to get rid of dead or diseased wood.

OPENING OUT A TREE

Overcrowded branches may result in small fruit which lack flavour as they do not get enough sun to ripen properly. Prune to create a lot of space between branches and prevent them shading each other. You can do this at any time of the year, though summer is best as winter pruning will encourage lots of new shoots.

Remove vertical branches and any dead or diseased ones. Cut out any that cross or are growing very close to each other. Finally, cut back any wayward branches to give the tree a balanced shape.

Retain branches that are growing near to the horizontal and those required to keep a balanced shape.

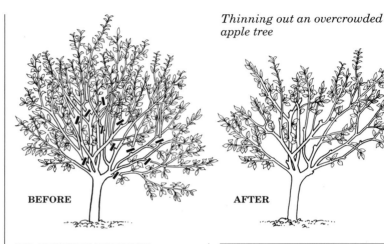

Thinning out an overcrowded apple tree

BEFORE

AFTER

BRINGING THE FRUIT WITHIN REACH

Long branches growing up from the centre take the fruit out of reach. Prune in August or September to reduce the height of the tree.

Remove one or more main branches, or prune them back to a low side branch to bring as much of the tree as possible within reach.

Retain low, horizontal branches and those needed for a well-shaped tree.

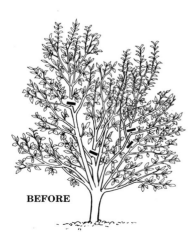

Reducing the height of an apple tree

BEFORE

AFTER

PEARS

Pears produce vigorous branches that tend to grow upwards. They may need pruning every two or three years to keep them in check. Prune as for an apple tree.

REVITALISING AN OLD PEAR TREE

Old trees can become decrepit with lots of twiggy shoots. The fruit may be small and sparse and the tree make little new growth. Prune back hard in winter to stimulate vigorous growth.

Remove dead and diseased wood. Cut back about a third of the branches to half their length.

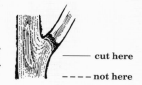

— cut here

- - - - not here

Smaller shoots
On small branches, make a sloping cut just above a bud (or cut flush with a side shoot). Cut cleanly and do not leave stumps or snags that will die back and may rot.

RASPBERRIES

Wait until they have finished fruiting, then cut all the old stems to ground level.

With autumn-fruiting varieties, cut all the stems to ground in late winter or early spring.

BLACKBERRIES AND HYBRID BERRIES

Blackberries and hybrid berries (loganberries, tayberries) can be treated in the same way as raspberries. After cropping, cut all old fruiting stems to ground level. Leave the new shoots; thin the weak ones only if there are too many.

BLACK CURRANTS

Prune every three or four years. Cut about one in three branches right back to the base, removing the oldest branches first.

GOOSEBERRIES, RED AND WHITE CURRANTS

Cut out old gnarled branches and weak shoots using long-handled pruners. If the bush still looks congested, remove complete branches. This can be done at any time of year.

PLUMS, DAMSONS AND GAGES

Plums normally crop well without pruning. You will need to remove only dead or diseased branches and twigs and the occasional over-vigorous branches. Carry out all pruning during dry weather in summer to minimise the risk of diseases entering the cuts. Paint all wounds with a pruning sealant.

Removing dead wood
Plum trees can become clogged with dead twigs and branches. Cut back to live wood in summer.

Cutting down tall branches
Over-vigorous branches may grow too tall for you to reach the fruit. Cut them back in summer. Save work by pruning at harvest time, so you can pick the plums afterwards.

Thinning out a plum tree

Reducing the height of a plum tree

BUYING THE RIGHT FRUIT

You can avoid a number of problems with pests and diseases by choosing varieties of fruit which will thrive in the conditions in your garden. It's also worth looking for plants with disease resistance.

SOIL

In a fertile, well-drained soil, you can grow virtually any type of fruit. But on a poor soil you need to compensate for the poorer growing conditions by choosing a more vigorous variety.

All fruit trees are grafted on to rootstocks with varying degrees of vigour. And it's the rootstock rather than the variety which largely determines the eventual size of the tree. The less vigorous rootstocks form small trees, but they need a good soil and regular feeding.

Apples on rootstock M27, for instance, form weak, unproductive trees unless grown in very fertile soil. On an average soil, apple trees on M9 are more likely to produce healthy trees, and on a poor, dry soil, M26 or MM106 would be the best rootstocks.

Pears on rootstock 'Quince C' are vigorous enough to cope with most conditions, but 'Quince A' is best for poor or dry soils.

On shallow soils overlying chalk, pears are not worth growing. If you want to grow apples, dig a deep pit and fill it with improved soil. Choose one of the more chalk-tolerant varieties like 'Charles Ross' or 'Gascoyne's Scarlet' or an MM106 rootstock.

Sweet cherries can be problematic. If grafted on 'Colt' rootstock, they will grow too big to

ROOTSTOCKS: WHICH ONE?

		HEIGHT OF TREES		FULL CROP	HOW LONG TO FULL CROP?
		After 5 yrs	Ultimate		
Apples	MM106	3.0m (10ft)	5.0m (16ft)	50kg (110lb)	7 yrs
	M26	2.4m (8ft)	3.6m (12ft)	40kg (88lb)	5 yrs
	M9	2.4m (8ft)	3.0m (10ft)	20kg (44lb)	5 yrs
	M27	1.5m (5ft)	1.8m (6 ft)	10kg (22lb)	4 yrs
Cherries	'Inmil'	1.8m (6ft)	3.6m (12ft)	10kg (22lb)	6 yrs
	'Colt'	3.0m (10ft)	5.0m (16ft)	10kg (22lb)	7 yrs
Pears	'Quince A'	2.4m (8ft)	3.6m (12ft)	40kg (88lb)	7 yrs
	'Quince C'	1.8m (6ft)	3.0m (10ft)	35kg (77lb)	5 yrs
Plums	'St Julien A'	3.0m (10ft)	5.0m (16ft)	25kg (55lb)	7 yrs
	'Pixy'	1.8m (6ft)	2.4m (8ft)	10kg (22lb)	4 yrs

net and the birds are likely to get most of the fruit. The rootstock 'Inmil' produces trees of a more reasonable size, but they won't flourish in poor soils. Growing trees in pots is one solution.

When choosing soft fruit, take into account that most types have shallow roots and are vulnerable to drought and waterlogging. On light soils, incorporate organic material before planting and mulch around canes and bushes. On heavy soils, plant on a slight mound to improve drainage.

ASPECT

Fruit crops best on an open, sunny site. A sheltered, south-facing garden is ideal, though most soft fruits grow reasonably well even when the garden is shaded for half the day. Red currants, white currants and

acid cherries even crop reasonably when grown against a north-facing fence or wall. Apples need more sun, and pears crop well only in sunny, sheltered spots.

If you live in one of the colder parts of the country or have an exposed garden, it's worth choosing later-flowering varieties, which stand more chance of being pollinated. For example, the black currants 'Ben Lomond' and 'Malling Jet' flower later than most other varieties.

Cane fruits do not crop well on exposed sites. Wind damages the canes and can discourage pollinating insects.

DISEASE RESISTANCE

For a list of trouble-free fruit varieties which are resistant to diseases, see page 134. When buying soft fruit, look out for certified virus-free plants.

THE GREENHOUSE

No plants are guaranteed trouble-free. Aphids, for example, can attack any soft leaves or stems. But careful choice of plants and good growing techniques should help you to keep the problems in your greenhouse to a minimum.

VEGETABLES

Tomatoes are the favourite greenhouse vegetable. They do suffer from a variety of pests and diseases, but many gardeners grow them year after year without too many problems.

If you have trouble with diseases, try a resistant variety (see page 135). Tomatoes are labour-intensive, but you can save yourself work by growing a bush variety like 'Red Alert' which won't need sideshooting.

Peppers have a reputation for being prone to pests and diseases, but they are really no worse than tomatoes. Good growing conditions should ward off most problems, though aphids, whitefly and red spider mites can attack otherwise healthy plants at any time.

Lettuces are prone to grey mould and downy mildew. Good ventilation will help. Some varieties, like 'Avoncrisp', 'Dolly' or 'Sabine', are resistant to

downy mildew. 'Avoncrisp' and 'Avondefiance' are also resistant to root aphids.

ORNAMENTAL PLANTS

Chrysanthemums, geraniums (pelargoniums) and fuchsias are perhaps the most popular ornamental greenhouse plants. Fuchsias and chrysanthemums are relatively trouble-free, but aphids are often a problem on fuchsias, and chrysanthemums can suffer from rust and leaf miner. Geraniums can attract whitefly and are prone to diseases like grey mould if growing conditions are poor.

Little attempt has been made to breed ornamental plants with pest or disease resistance, but many are relatively untroubled by problems.

For really trouble-free plants, concentrate on old faithfuls that you know are tough and rarely fail, such as the spider plant (chlorophytum), mother-in-law's tongue (sansevieria), and many cacti and succulents.

VULNERABLE PLANTS

Some greenhouse plants are particularly prone to pest and disease problems. Aubergines, for example, give poor yields and are a magnet for pests like aphids and whitefly. Cucumbers can also be troublesome – they are prone to virus diseases spread by aphids. They are attacked by root and stem rots, and if grown in a greenhouse border can suffer from fusarium and verticillium wilt. Whitefly and red spider mite infestations are also more of a problem on cucumbers than on tomatoes.

For details of pest- and disease-resistant varieties of greenhouse crops, see Table on page 135.

GREENHOUSE PROBLEMS

IDENTIFYING THE CAUSE

If any of your greenhouse plants are being nibbled or develop spots or mould, this guide will help to identify the culprit.

1 Yellow leaves
- Nitrogen deficiency
- White rust. Yellow spots on the underside of leaves
- Virus diseases. Yellow mottling, distorted or stunted growth
- Red spider mites. Leaves speckled, turning yellow

2 Holes in leaves
- Capsid bugs
- Caterpillars
- Earwigs. Irregular holes in leaves and flowers
- Slugs and snails. Look for trails
- Woodlice. Nibbled seedlings

3 Mould/mildew on leaves/stems
- Downy mildew. White, downy tufts on undersides of leaves
- Grey mould. Fluffy grey growth
- Leaf mould. Purple/brown mould on underside of leaves
- Powdery mildew. Powdery coating on leaves and stems

4 Dark brown or orange spots
- Rust. Undersides of leaves

5 Green/silvery discoloration
- Thrips

6 White marks on leaves or stems
- Leaf hopper. Tiny white spots on leaves
- Leaf miner. White, wiggly lines

7 Encrustations on stems or leaves
- Mealy bugs. Colonies covered in white, waxy powder
- Scale insects Brown encrustations on stems and leaf veins

8 Wilted plants
- Insufficient water

- Verticillium wilt. Lower leaves turn yellow
- Stem rot. Brown cankers on stem at soil level
- Vine weevil. Maggots on roots

9 Stem rotten at base
- Blackleg. Base soft and black
- Damping off. Seedlings collapse

10 Distorted growth
- Viruses. Leaves mottled
- Capsid bugs. Holes in leaves

11 Infestations of insects
- Ants
- Aphids. Greenfly, blackfly
- Red spider mites. Very tiny, may be webbing, leaves yellowish
- Sciarid flies (fungus gnats). Small flies, white grubs in compost

Left Mealy bugs on a cactus
Below left Stem rot
Below Powdery mildew on begonias

- Springtails. Small, white, jumping insects in compost
- Whitefly. Tiny moth-like flies

12 Frothy deposit on leaves
- Cuckoo spit. From frog hoppers

SEEDLING PROBLEMS
The most common problem with seedlings is damping off. This is caused by soil-borne fungi that make the seedlings collapse at soil level. You can prevent the disease with good hygiene. Sterilise used pots and seed trays with a disinfectant or wash thoroughly with soft soap solution. When planting seeds, only use sterilised compost and sow as thinly as possible. Water from below – damping off fungi can be spread by water splashes from infected plants.

GREENHOUSE DISEASES

MINIMISING THE RISK

There is not a great deal you can do once plants are heavily infected with disease. It's best to reduce the risks at the outset.

WHEN YOU BUY PLANTS
Take care not to bring diseases into your greenhouse on new plants. Check carefully before buying and reject weak, sickly plants and any with signs of pests or diseases.

COMPOST
You should never try growing a second crop of tomatoes (or tomato relatives, which include aubergines, peppers and potatoes) in the same growing bags or compost due to the risk of soil-borne diseases. You could, however, use the compost for cucumbers, a winter salad crop or for strawberries.

WATERING
Water carefully from the bottom, or using a watering can without a rose to avoid splashing.

Splashes can spread disease spores from plant to plant.
To avoid problems with grey mould (botrytis) and downy mildew, reduce watering and remove capillary matting in the autumn to keep humidity low. Open vents whenever possible and allow space between plants.

DEALING WITH DISEASES

DISEASE	SUSCEPTIBLE PLANTS	SYMPTOMS	WHAT YOU CAN DO
Blackleg	pelargonium cuttings, sometimes mature plants	base of the stem soft, black and rotten; plant dies	destroy plants. Keep greenhouse clean and use clean containers
Damping off	seedlings, occasionally young plants	seedlings collapse at soil level, usually in spring or autumn	use sterile seed compost and clean containers. Sow thinly
Downy mildew	lettuces, cinerarias, stock seedlings	leaves blotchy with white, downy tufts on the underside	sow thinly, use sterilised compost. Ventilate well. Try spraying with bicarbonate of soda solution
Grey mould (botrytis)	most plants	grey or brown velvety growth on leaves and stems	ventilate well. Remove dead leaves, stems and flowers
Leaf mould (cladosporium)	tomatoes in summer	purple-brown mould on underside of leaves	ventilate well. Sterilise greenhouse and equipment in late autumn
Powdery mildew	wide range of plants	white, powdery coating on leaves and stems	avoid wetting leaves. Ventilate well. Try bicarbonate of soda spray
Rust	fuchsias, carnations, chrysanthemums, pelargoniums and lettuces	small, dark brown or orange spots on leaves and stems in summer	destroy all infected plant material. Keep greenhouse and surrounds weed-free
Sclerotinia	aubergines and lettuces; many others in summer	stem covered with white, fluffy growth. Rots at soil level	use sterilised compost and destroy infected plants
Stem rot	tomatoes in summer	plants wilt. Brown, sunken cankers at soil level	remove diseased plants; sterilise greenhouse at end of season
Verticillium and fusarium wilt	tomatoes and aubergines in summer	plants wilt, lower leaves turn yellow. Cut stems reveal brown streaks with verticillium	best avoided by using growing bags. Keep infected plants alive by spraying with water and shading
Virus	all plants at any time of year	mottled leaves and distorted or stunted growth	destroy affected plants. Control insect pests to prevent spread of viruses
White rust	chrysanthemums	yellow spots on undersides of leaves, turning brown then white	notify your local Ministry of Agriculture office

GREENHOUSE PESTS

HOW TO MINIMISE PROBLEMS

Do not create cosy homes for pests. Store unused pots, trays and compost away from the greenhouse in a shed or garage. Do not let weeds grow in or around your greenhouse – they too provide refuge for pests.

Give your greenhouse a thorough clean-up at the end of each season.

PREVENTING PESTS WITHOUT CHEMICALS

PEST	SUSCEPTIBLE PLANTS	SYMPTOMS	PRECAUTIONS
Ants	most plants in spring and summer	they protect and spread greenfly, mealy bugs and scale insects	trace ant trails back to the nest and destroy it
Aphids	most plants	colonies make sticky mess on leaves/shoots. Transmit viruses	rub off and spray frequently with soapy water. Put ladybirds on leaves
Capsid bugs	many plants, especially chrysanthemums	irregular holes in leaves, which may be distorted	try spraying with soft soap solution
Caterpillars	most plants in spring or summer	large, irregular holes in leaves	pick off caterpillars and eggs by hand. Biological control (see opposite)
Earwigs	many flowers and fruit	irregular holes in leaves and flowers. Look for earwigs at night	trap in inverted pots full of straw. Keep greenhouse tidy
Frog hoppers	chrysanthemums and other ornamentals	frothy deposit (cuckoo spit) on leaves	none, harmless
Leaf hoppers	cucumbers, tomatoes and pot plants	tiny, white spots on leaves. Shed skins of nymphs under leaves	remove infected leaves
Leaf miner	chrysanthemums, cinerarias and tomatoes	white wiggly lines in leaves	remove infected leaves or squeeze the wide end of the mine to kill grub
Mealy bugs	pot plants and vines	colonies of soft-bodied insects covered with white, waxy powder	use biological control or wipe off with methylated spirit
Red spider mites	wide range of plants	leaves speckled, turning yellow. Tiny insects and webbing visible	provide humid atmosphere. Biological control (see opposite)
Scale insects	many pot plants	small encrustations on stems and leaf veins	squeeze small scales between fingernails or wipe off with methylated spirit
Sciarid flies	all plants, especially if grown in soil-less compost	small flies on compost or around plants. White grubs in compost	replace with good compost and don't overwater
Slugs and snails	Many plants	nibbled leaves and slime trails	keep the greenhouse clean and tidy. Use barriers in the border
Springtails	plants in soil-less compost	small, white insects in compost that jump when disturbed	none, but a sign of poorly drained compost
Thrips	many plants	green or silvery discoloration of leaves or petals	ignore small infestations. Destroy badly infected plants
Whitefly	aubergines, peppers, tomatoes, fuchsias, etc.	small, white flies. Make sticky 'honeydew' on which mould grows	biological control or suck them up with a vacuum cleaner
Woodlice	seedlings	nibbled leaves	keep greenhouse clean and tidy
Vine weevils	cyclamen, tuberous begonias and many others	plant wilts. Plump white maggots on roots	destroy affected plants or remove compost, wash roots and repot

Left Red spider mites seen through a magnifying glass

*Left Mealy bug predator
Below Whitefly predator
Bottom Parasitised whitefly scales*

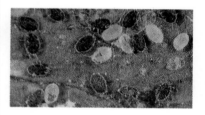

ONCE PESTS STRIKE

If pests attack your plants, there is still a lot you can do to control them without resorting to chemicals.

Space the plants out as much as possible to stop pests spreading. Pick off any pests and their eggs and remove heavily infested leaves and shoots.

Try soapy water for washing off pests like whitefly and greenfly. Use a drop of washing-up liquid in a pint of water (stronger concentrations can damage plants). A sprayer will help to blast pests off the plants, but don't use in direct sunlight as any droplets of water remaining on the leaves can scorch them.

Plants that are heavily infested are best destroyed. At the end of the season, burn all infested plants. It's best to have a good clean-up and start with fresh plants next year if you have had a number of problems with pests.

ORGANIC MYTHS
Marigolds
It is often claimed that whiteflies can be kept at bay by planting African marigolds or tagetes in the greenhouse. Reliable data on 'companion plants' is hard to come by, but an experiment at the University of California showed that whitefly numbers on beans were *higher* when planted alongside marigolds, catnip, summer savoury, basil or nasturtiums than when planted alone.

Traps
Yellow, sticky traps are claimed to trap whitefly. Whitefly are attracted to the colour yellow, but these traps can also catch beneficial insects and biological controls.

BIOLOGICAL CONTROLS

Biological controls use a pest's natural enemies. To be successful, you must keep a close watch for the first signs of the pest and obtain the control as soon as it appears. Release the control evenly over the infested plants, then wait. Keep the greenhouse temperature above 20°C (68°F).

FOR CATERPILLARS
The bacterium *Bacillus thuringiensis* kills caterpillars without harming other insects. It is sold as sachets of dried spores, which are mixed with water and applied as a spray. The bacterium kills caterpillars that eat the sprayed leaves by paralysing their gut. You may have to repeat the treatment if caterpillars persist.

FOR MEALY BUGS
Mealy bugs are eaten by a ladybird, *Cryptolaemus*, whose larvae, which resemble large mealy bugs, are also voracious feeders. The ladybirds are sold as adults or larvae. They thrive in temperatures of 20–26°C (63–83°F) and high humidity.

Release at least one per plant as they search only a small area. Keep the doors and windows closed until they are established to stop adults flying away. *Cryptolaemus* should reduce the pest population considerably in two or three months.

FOR WHITEFLY
A small parasitic wasp (*Encarsia formosa*) can be very effective in controlling whiteflies. It lays its eggs in whitefly scales (larvae) and kills them.

Wasps are supplied in black parasitised scales on a leaf. The wasps hatch out and parasitise more whitefly scales. You must introduce the wasp as soon as you see the first whitefly.

FOR RED SPIDER MITE
Red spider mite is eaten by a predatory mite (*Phytoseiulus*). The mites arrive on pieces of leaf or card which you tear up and distribute among infested plants. It works best at temperatures of over 25°C (80°F).

A RESIDENT TOAD
Before the days of modern biological control, many gardeners kept a toad in the greenhouse to deal with pests. Toads eat insects, grubs, slugs and even earwigs. They need a moist atmosphere and like dense vegetation and secluded corners for hibernation. If you do keep one in your greenhouse, make sure it can get out to find a pond for mating and breeding purposes.

GREENHOUSE HYGIENE

Below left Wash the outside of the greenhouse to improve light
Below Use a plant label to clean between panes; don't forget corners
Bottom Use a label to remove moss at the base

CLEANING OUT THE GREENHOUSE

Your greenhouse must have a thorough clean-out each winter to rid it of pests and diseases. Tackle this job on a mild, dry day. Before you start, remove all the plants to a frost-free place.

Switch off the electricity supply at the mains and cover any electrical fittings with plastic. Remove any greenhouse shading.

Wash the glass inside and out with detergent. Get into all the cracks and crevices in which bugs can hide. Use fine wire wool to clean aluminium glazing bars.

Algae and dirt trapped between overlaps in the glass can be shifted with a plastic plant label or piece of card. For stubborn algae, run bleach down the cracks using a medicine dropper and leave for a few minutes. Flush out using a garden sprayer. Don't be tempted to use bleach for general cleaning – it is very harmful to plants.

A plant label can also be useful for removing moss and dirt trapped in crevices and gutters.

In hard water areas, the inside of the glass may be encrusted with a lime film. Remove this with kettle descaler.

Scrub staging, paths and brick bases with disinfectant solution to remove dirt and algae. Finally, hose down the whole greenhouse.

Sterilise the inside of the greenhouse and any staging with a horticultural disinfectant, diluted as recommended.

Don't rinse the disinfectant off. Leave the doors and vents

open for the greenhouse to dry. After a few days, it may still smell of disinfectant, but it's safe to return the plants.

Before returning the plants, check them for pests and diseases and throw away any infected plants.

WINTER CHECKLIST
- Check the greenhouse for leaks and draughts and seal them with waterproof tape; fit draught excluder to the door
- Repair any broken panes of glass
- Check any heating equipment; for paraffin heaters, make sure the wicks are dry and trimmed
- Check the thermostat setting on electric heaters, using a maximum and minimum thermometer
- Insulate the greenhouse using expanded polystyrene sheets and bubble polythene. Insulate vents separately so you can open them
- Shut down watering systems at the stopcock, but taps in the greenhouse should be left open. Remove capillary matting

If you have been growing plants in the greenhouse border and you've had problems with disease, replace with fresh soil.

If you have used any capillary matting or gravel, wash and sterilise it. Better still, throw it away and start again next year.

USED POTS, TRAYS AND GROWING BAGS
Clean all pots, trays and containers thoroughly before storing them. Scrub off any compost or soil and rinse under the tap. Clay pots may be encrusted with a grey mineral deposit – loosen it by soaking in water overnight.

Sterilise pots and trays using a horticultural disinfectant solution and store them in a garden shed or garage. Soak clay pots in it overnight.

Do not reuse potting compost for greenhouse plants. It may contain pests and diseases, and the nutrients will have been depleted.

Growing bags should not be reused for a second crop of tomatoes or cucumbers because of the risk of soilborne diseases. It is best to discard the bags and use the compost in the garden. You can reuse the bags for a different crop such as lettuces or strawberries, but they will need feeding.

Below right Store gladioli over winter in a frost-free greenhouse

PREPARING PLANTS FOR WINTER

ANNUALS

If you have any annual plants left in the greenhouse, such as cucumbers and tomatoes, put them straight on the compost heap.

BULBS AND TUBERS

Dormant bulbs and tubers like achimenes and gloxinias should not be left in their pots. Lift and clean them and store in the greenhouse in dry peat. Many bulbs and tubers in the garden are not completely hardy and will also need lifting and storing. They need to be kept cool but frost-free, so you will need some sort of heating in your greenhouse during the coldest weather (or take them indoors).

Dahlias

Lift dahlia tubers as soon as the first frosts have blackened the stems. Put them in the greenhouse to dry. Once dry, soil clinging to the roots will fall away (alternatively, you can wash it off after lifting).

Remove thin, stringy roots to leave a firm, fat clump, and cut the old stem down to 10–15cm (4–6in). Stand the tubers upside-down for a few days to drain moisture from the stems.

Pack or cover so they don't dry out. Shallow trays full of dry peat are good for storage. Store in a dry place.

Gladioli

Gladioli corms need lifting as soon as the foliage starts to brown and before the heavy autumn rains. Lift the corms and foliage intact. Cut off the foliage as near to the corms as possible and put the corms on a greenhouse bench to dry.

PREVENTING PROBLEMS WITH WINTER CROPS

■ Keep the humidity down: this reduces heat lost by evaporation and avoids problems with grey mould
■ Avoid splashing water about and be careful not to overwater
■ Ventilate as much as possible without letting the greenhouse get too cold
■ Remove any weeds in or near the greenhouse as these may harbour pests
■ Check plants regularly for pests and disease, and remove any unhealthy ones
■ Do not store pots, trays or old growing bags in the greenhouse: they can provide hiding places for pests such as woodlice and slugs
■ Keep the outside of your greenhouse sparkling clean by washing regularly: this will reduce heat loss by radiation and let in the maximum sunshine

After about two weeks, you should be able to pull away the old corm and cormlets. Air circulation is important, so the corms should be stored in stacking tomato trays or cloth bags.

Many other bulbs, corms and tubers are not completely frost-hardy and are best treated in the same way as gladioli, particularly in cold, wet areas. These include ixia, tigridia pavonia, ranunculus and acidanthera.

TENDER PERENNIALS

Check over perennial plants regularly and remove any dead, drying or diseased leaves and fading flowers.

CHRYSANTHEMUMS

Chrysanthemums are almost hardy but succumb in wet winters. Plants outdoors are best lifted three or four weeks after flowering finishes, in October or November. Cut the stems to about 30cm (12in) and lift in dry weather so there is not too much soil adhering to the roots.

Keep only healthy plants and burn diseased ones. Shake off soil and wash in lukewarm water followed by a weak solution of garden disinfectant.

Pack the stools close together in wooden boxes, working compost in around them to fill in air pockets. Do not bury the crowns. Remove all green growth at soil level. Store in a cold greenhouse (not heated) and water sparingly to keep the compost just moist.

GERANIUMS

Geraniums ideally should be kept only just moist and in full sunlight over winter. They are often overwintered as cuttings, taken in mid-August.

Ventilate as much as possible, but keep the temperature to at least 7°C (45°F). In an unheated greenhouse you will have to cover plants with newspaper on cold nights and move them into the house if a heavy frost is forecast.

FUCHSIAS

Fuchsias are often overwintered as semi-hardwood cuttings taken in September or October. Standard plants should be lifted by mid-October, before the first frost, others just after the first frost. Pack into boxes and surround the roots with damp compost. Water sparingly to prevent the plants from drying out completely.

IMPROVING YOUR GREENHOUSE

Your greenhouse can keep you very busy in the summer, opening and closing vents and watering wilting plants. By following our suggestions, you can reduce your workload and provide a better environment for the growth of strong, healthy plants.

▇ AUTOMATIC VENTILATION
Automatic vent openers open the greenhouse ventilators when the temperature rises above a pre-set level, and close them again when the air cools. This helps to control the temperature without any effort on your part.

Openers that close by gravity are suitable only for roof vents. For side vents and louvres, they must have a built-in spring.

Many small greenhouses have only a single roof vent. This won't provide enough ventilation in midsummer. Ideally, the total area of roof vents should be one-sixth of the floor area – one-fifth if there are no side vents or louvres.

First fit additional roof vents to create a through draught. Louvres are available for most aluminium greenhouses and can be fitted near floor level. For a wooden greenhouse, install a hinged window at bench level or sliding windows at floor level.

You can leave the door open for additional ventilation, but you will need to fit a screen to keep out dogs, cats and birds.

▇ SHADING
Shading is necessary in midsummer to prevent overheating. On dull days, however, plants need as much light as they can get, so the shading must not be too efficient.

Greenhouse shading should be applied outside the glass, on the south and west sides. In *Gardening from Which?* tests shading washes, such as pbi Coolglass and Varishade, which you paint or spray on to the outside of the glass, proved cheap and effective. They wipe off easily in the autumn with a dry cloth. Varishade is more expensive but better because it is transparent when wet, so lets in more light on a rainy day.

▇ HEATING AND INSULATION
Heating your greenhouse will help you make much better use of it. Even if you can keep it only frost-free, it will greatly increase the range of plants you can grow and propagate.

It is expensive to install electricity, but it will enable you to use a thermostatically controlled greenhouse heater which is the most convenient and cheapest way to heat a greenhouse. You will also be able to install an electric propagator and soil-warming cables.

Paraffin and gas heaters are cheaper to buy, but running costs are higher and the greenhouse needs to be permanently ventilated to let out the excess carbon dioxide and water vapour.

The size of the heater you need will depend on where you live as well as the size, shape and location of your greenhouse and the temperature you want to keep it at.

Sheltering and insulating your greenhouse can help to keep it frost-free and reduce heating costs.

To insulate your greenhouse, line it with expanded polystyrene sheets below bench level. Cover the rest of the glass with polythene film. Heat loss can be reduced by up to 40 per cent using bubble polythene and up to 30 per cent using single-thickness polythene.

A windbreak, such as a hedge or evergreen shrub border sited where it won't shade the greenhouse, can also greatly reduce heat loss from greenhouses in exposed gardens.

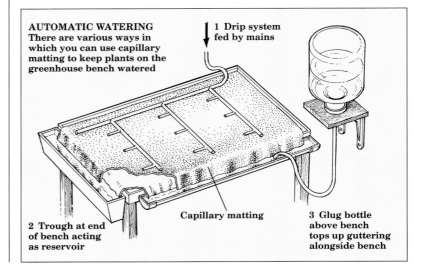

AUTOMATIC WATERING
There are various ways in which you can use capillary matting to keep plants on the greenhouse bench watered

1 Drip system fed by mains

Capillary matting

2 Trough at end of bench acting as reservoir

3 Glug bottle above bench tops up guttering alongside bench

CHAPTER SEVEN

DEALING WITH DISEASES

Rust on a plum tree

Diseases are very difficult to control once plants become badly infected. If you are not going to use fungicides, good garden hygiene and a watchful eye are essential in order to keep your plants healthy. This chapter tells you what steps you can take to prevent diseases from gaining a foothold.

GARDEN HYGIENE

Spores of fungal disease often survive the winter on dead plant material or debris or in the soil, ready to reinfect plants in spring. Remove potential sources of infection by:
- promptly clearing away debris of old plants and not allowing piles of prunings, dead leaves, etc. to accumulate
- washing and disinfecting pots, seed trays and garden canes and other equipment at the end of the season
- disposing of or burning all diseased leaves – not composting them
- removing dead leaves and flowers where practical and pruning out dead or diseased branches from trees and shrubs.

WATERING AND FEEDING

Plants that are growing vigorously are much less vulnerable to diseases. Until you have built up soil fertility by adding manure, apply a general fertiliser like blood, fish and bone each spring. Keep plants well watered or, where this is not possible, space plants more widely apart than usual and use mulches to conserve moisture and keep down the weeds.

HEALTHY SOIL

Many diseases are spread by airborne spores or insects. But some serious diseases like club root of brassicas and white rot of onions remain in the soil. You

can help prevent diseases like these from building up by not growing the same vegetables or bedding plants on the same patch of ground every year. For details of crop rotation schemes, see page 26.

WEEDS

Weeds can provide hosts for pests such as aphids, which spread virus diseases. Some weeds such as sowthistles are very prone to mildew, which can then be spread to garden plants.

MULCHING

Mulching can help stop the spread of diseases by preventing spores which overwinter on plant debris being splashed by rain on to the new plant growth. See page 88 for mulches.

RESISTANT VARIETIES

Some varieties of fruit, vegetables and roses are resistant to certain diseases (see Tables on pages 133–135). Try these varieties if your plants regularly succumb to diseases.

DON'T BRING IN DISEASES
Buying in brassicas or wallflowers, or even accepting them as gifts from friends, can introduce club root to the garden. Walking across someone else's vegetable plot which is infected with club root and then trampling mud on your own plot can also introduce the disease. Wash your boots thoroughly to avoid problems. Inspect all plants for diseases before buying them – see page 122.

Left A shoot badly affected by powdery mildew

DEALING WITH DISEASES

The diseases below all affect a wide range of ornamental and other plants. A number of diseases affect only a limited range of crop plants, and these are dealt with in the relevant chapters of this book. See page 39 for fruit diseases and page 32 for vegetable diseases.

■ POWDERY MILDEW

Powdery mildew appears as a rusty white covering on the leaves and shoots of many plants, but it is particularly damaging on apples, goose-berries, grapevines, cucumber, marrows, peas, swedes, turnips, forget-me-nots, Michaelmas daisies and roses. It often occurs in dry weather when plants are short of water, and it's worse on overcrowded plants. Mulching and watering will help keep the disease at bay. Prune out affected shoots, and as a last resort spray with a copper fungicide such as Bordeaux mixture, which is approved by organic gardeners.

■ DOWNY MILDEW

Downy mildew is a much more serious disease than powdery mildew as it can get right inside the leaves and kill the plant. It has a slightly furry appearance and is worse in warm, damp weather. Remove all affected leaves. If badly affected, either destroy the plant or spray with a copper fungicide.

■ GREY MOULD (BOTRYTIS)

Botrytis is seen as a very grey furry mould on leaves, stems or fruit and is worse in cool, damp conditions. Poor air circulation due to overcrowding, or lack of ventilation under cloches or in the greenhouse, encourages the disease. Cut off and dispose of all infected parts.

■ SOOTY MOULD

This black mould grows on the honeydew dropped by sap-feeding insects like aphids. It is serious only in that it blocks out the light to plants and can be washed off with water.

■ RUSTS

Rusts appear as brown, red, yellowish or black raised spots on the undersides of leaves and on stems. The disease can stunt and even kill plants. Antirrhinums, irises, mahonias, mints, plums, leeks and chives are commonly attacked. There are no reliable controls without using chemicals other than to remove infected leaves. Shrubs and trees in good condition may outgrow the disease. With annuals and perennials, destroy badly infected plants. The exceptions are leeks, which still give reasonable crops if infected, and mints, which can be lifted and dipped in hot water for about 20 seconds to control the disease.

■ LEAF SPOTS

Most plants suffer from at least one fungus that causes spotting of the leaves, but few of these fungi are serious. The one you most need to worry about is blackspot on roses – see page 19.

■ ROTS

Lots of fungal diseases cause the plant tissue to disintegrate. Toadstools on or near woody plants are obvious signs, as is mould on fruit, flower buds, leaves or stored rootcrops and bulbs. With woody plants, cut out infected areas. Root rots of growing vegetables may be due to wet soil, so improve your drainage if possible. Overcrowding and shade can also encourage rots, so thin plants out or prune them to let in air and light. When storing fruit and vegetables, or tubers and bulbs of ornamental plants, inspect them very carefully first. Don't store any that are damaged or have soft patches as these may infect all the healthy ones.

■ SEEDLING DISEASES

The two most common seedling diseases are damping off, which causes the stem to rot at soil level, and grey mould (see previous page) which may come as a secondary infection when seedlings start to damp off. Follow the guidelines below to prevent problems. As home-made compost containing soil or manure, etc. is likely to contain spores of fungal diseases, use a proprietary compost for sowing (to recycle this compost, use it only for established plants – in window boxes, for example). Sow thinly to avoid overcrowded seedlings: if too many come up, thin them out by hand. If you are raising seedlings in the greenhouse, shade them from direct sunlight but give them plenty of ventilation. Try to maintain a steady temperature of around 15°C (60°F) for germination, and a minimum of around 10°C (50°F) when growing on seedlings. If using a propagator, increase the ventilation steadily to harden off the seedlings so they can be moved from the close atmosphere as soon as possible.

Prick out seedlings as soon as they are large enough to handle, being careful not to damage the roots and holding them only by the leaves. Water pots and seed trays from below; overhead watering can spread spores of fungal diseases.

■ CANKERS

Cankers are diseases of woody plants that cause blister-like lesions on the stem. The fungi or bacteria grow

very slowly beneath the bark, killing a slightly larger area each year. If the canker reaches right the way round the branch or trunk, all the growth above the canker will die. Cankers are most common on fruit trees, but also affect ornamental *Prunus* species, weeping willows and roses. The best treatment is to cut out the canker – see page 40.

■ WILTS

There are a number of soil-borne diseases which can cause wilting of plants, especially carnations, chrysanthemums, clematis, cucumbers and tomatoes. Always use sterile compost for seeds and cuttings and destroy badly affected plants. With clematis, plant them about 10cm (4in) deeper than they were in their pots. If the leaves turn black and shoots die, prune them right back to ground level. Often, new healthy shoots will grow the following year. Spring-flowering clematis species are less susceptible to wilt.

■ MALFORMATIONS

Diseases can upset the hormone system of plants and cause abnormal growth. Common examples are club root (see page 33), peach leaf curl (see page 40), crown gall (caused by bacteria) on the stems of trees and shrubs, and witches'-brooms (large bird's nest-like growth on birches and other trees). Malformations are rarely serious on ornamental plants and can be simply cut out if they ruin the appearance.

Above Witches'-broom on Scot's pine, like an upside-down tree

DEALING WITH DISEASES

WHAT HAPPENS TO DISEASE IN WINTER

Spores of disease causing bacteria and fungi can lurk in your garden ready to infect new growth the following spring. Cleaning up the garden in winter can dramatically reduce disease problems.

1 Compost heap Especially in autumn and winter, the compost heap may not heat up sufficiently to kill diseases. Dispose of or burn diseased plants rather than compost them

2 Greenhouse framework can harbour disease spores. Wash out the greenhouse with a soft soap solution

3 Greenhouse borders Disease can build up in the soil, so replace it every few years with fresh soil from the garden

4 Greenhouse vents A poorly ventilated greenhouse, especially if heated by gas or paraffin, will encourage diseases

like grey mould. Improve ventilation and regularly remove dead leaves and flowers from plants

5 Fallen fruit Pick up fallen fruit rather than leaving it to rot

6 Wallflowers (not illustrated) Buying in wallflowers in the autumn could introduce club root to the garden

7 Prunings Don't leave piles of prunings hanging around all winter. Burn or dispose of all infected wood

8 Winter vegetables Pick off dead foliage of overwintering brassicas and clear away debris left by crops that have finished

9 Pots, trays and canes Wash and sterilise at the end of the season

10 Fallen leaves Pick up fallen leaves, particularly around roses and fruit trees, and regularly rake up leaves on lawns

HONEY FUNGUS

If a succession of trees or shrubs start to die in a particular area of the garden, suspect honey fungus. A further sign is clumps of yellowish toadstools appearing around the base of old stumps or affected trees in autumn. To confirm your suspicions, pare off some of the bark from a dying plant. If it's honey fungus, you'll see a white sheath-like layer of fungal growth under the bark and possibly black bootlace-like threads, which may extend into the surrounding soil.

The fungus spreads mainly by these black threads extending underground from the roots of one tree or shrub to infect those of another. To isolate infected plants, dig a trench about 45cm (18in) deep to separate diseased roots from those of healthy plants. Dig out or kill off stumps of dead plants as quickly as possible.

After about two years, you can start to replant the area, but, as insurance, choose species that have some resistance to honey fungus (see list below). In the meantime, you could grow herbaceous plants in the infected area as these are rarely affected.

Honey fungus-resistant plants
Bamboos (*Arundinaria* spp)
Beech (*Fagus* spp)
Box (*Buxus* spp)
Douglas fir (*Pseudotsuga douglasii*)
Elder (*Sambucus* spp)
Eleagnus spp
False acacia (*Robinia* spp)
Hawthorns (*Crateagus* spp)
Holly (*Ilex* spp)
Honeysuckles (*Lonicera* spp)
Ivies (*Hedera* spp)
Larch (*Larix* spp)
Mahonia spp
Rock roses (*Cistus* spp)
Smoke bush (*Cotinus* spp)
Tamarisk (*Tamarix* spp)
Yew (*Taxus* spp)

PREVENTING PESTS

Mealy cabbage aphid

Providing that you are willing to accept some damage to plants, most garden pests can be kept under control without reaching for a sprayer. This chapter tells you both how to prevent pests and what to do if your plants are attacked.

Most gardens teem with potential insect pests, but their numbers are kept in check by the weather and by their own predators, parasites and diseases. However, gardening does disturb this natural balance and pests can get the upper hand. You can help swing the balance in your favour by maintaining the general health and vigour of your plants so they can better resist pest attacks. To do this:

■ Choose plants that do well in your local soil and climate and make sure they are suitable for the position you have in mind in the garden.

■ Improve soil structure, fertility and moisture retentiveness by incorporating bulky organic material, so plants get off to a good start and are better able to withstand pests.

■ Start vulnerable plants off in pots under cover. Young plants of lettuce, brassicas, sweet corn, and annual flowers will withstand pest attack much better than seedlings.

■ Choose resistant varieties of fruit and vegetables – see pages 134 and 135.

REDUCING PEST NUMBERS

There are general steps you can take to reduce pest numbers.

■ Dig over the ground in autumn to expose overwintering pests to birds and frost. This helps to control cutworms, slugs, wireworms and carrot fly, among others.

■ Lift root crops as early as practical to reduce damage by root pests such as carrot fly and slugs.

■ Practise crop rotation (see page 26); this will help control eelworms in potatoes and onions, as well as a number of diseases.

■ Encourage natural predators: birds, hedgehogs, frogs and predatory insects all play their part in controlling pests, and you can attract them to your garden by providing food and shelter.

■ Tidy up, especially in and around the vegetable plot and fruit trees. Remove any debris left after harvesting crops – burn any with signs of pest or disease problems. Pick up and dispose of affected fruit, such as pears with pear midge or plums with plum sawfly grubs, both of which fall early. Keep down weeds and clear up fallen leaves which provide food and shelter for pests.

PREVENTING PESTS: NON-CHEMICAL CONTROLS

There are also a number of measures you can take to prevent pests from ruining your plants.

BARRIERS

Physical barriers, which prevent the pests from reaching their target plants, can be particularly effective at preventing damage to plants. Their success depends on knowing a bit about the habits of the pests. For example, carrot flies tend to fly close to the ground when seeking carrot plants on which to lay their eggs. A physical barrier of around 45–80cm (18–30in) around blocks of carrots can therefore keep your carrots virtually free from this pest.

There are a range of different barriers you can use to control different pests.

FLEECE

Fleece made from spun polypropylene is a lightweight material that you can spread over vegetable crops from seed stage up until harvest time. It was primarily developed to protect crops from frost and to speed crop development in the same way as cloches. But as it lets through both water and light it can be left permanently on the plants. On vegetables it should prevent pests such as aphids, cabbage caterpillars, cabbage root fly and carrot fly. You could also use it on fruit bushes, wall-trained fruit trees and on flower seedlings while they are getting established to prevent attacks from flying pests when they are most vulnerable – for example, when the buds or fruitlets are developing or when plants have a lot of soft growth.

Use sections of plastic bottles at least 10cm (4in) tall to keep off slugs

PLASTIC BOTTLES

Rings cut from plastic bottles are very effective at preventing slug attacks (see page 61) and will also protect seedlings from cutworms. If you use the dome from the top of the bottle as a mini-cloche over young seedlings, this will also prevent them being attacked by virtually all above-ground pests.

POLYTHENE

Polythene barriers will prevent low-flying insects like carrot flies from attacking crops. Bell-shaped cloches made from polythene and coat-hanger wire can also be used like plastic bottles to protect larger plants, such as herbaceous perennials, when new shoots emerge in spring.

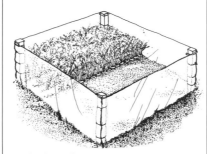

Polythene barriers 45–80cm (18–30in) high can prevent carrot fly damage

CONFUSION TACTICS
One method advocated to keep aphids off young vegetable plants is to lay silver foil between the rows. The theory is that the aphids see a reflection of the sky and don't bother to land. How effective this would be in practice is difficult to say. But it's an interesting idea for anyone who likes experimenting in the garden.

Squares of carpet underlay around young brassicas will deter cabbage root flies from laying eggs

CARPET UNDERLAY

Cut into 15cm (6in) squares and fitted around the bases of plants, this will protect brassicas from pests such as cabbage root fly which lay their eggs in soil near the stem. Ground beetles also like sheltering under collars of carpet underlay, where they will eat other soil pests.

CORRUGATED CARDBOARD

Tying corrugated cardboard around the trunks of apple trees in late summer will attract codling moth caterpillars. This can then be removed and burnt and will help prevent 'maggots' in your apples the following year.

Grease bands prevent caterpillar damage to fruit trees

GREASE

Fruit tree grease placed around the trunk of fruit trees and other deciduous trees about 1.2m (4ft) above ground level will prevent the wingless female moths from climbing into the trees to lay their eggs. The females emerge from pupae in the soil in autumn or spring, so put the grease or grease band in place by October. Fruit tree grease can also be used to prevent other wingless pests gaining access to woody plants, such as ants which protect aphids (see page 62). Another use for grease is to control flea beetles on stocks, wallflowers or young brassicas. These pests tend to dart about above the plants. To catch them, coat a piece of wood with grease and wave it about over the plants.

MIXED PLANTINGS

A lot of folklore exists about plants which are said to deter or inhibit pests. Climbing nasturtiums trained into apple trees, for example, have been claimed to control woolly aphids, and onions grown next to carrots have been said to deter carrot fly. It is quite possible that lots of these plant associations appear to work because they

coincide with years when the pest is absent or at a low level. In controlled experiments where pests are known to be active, companion plantings like these have shown to be of little benefit.

However, mixed plantings do have their virtues. Growing a wide range of plants all mixed together, rather than neat rows of the same plants, should make it harder for pests to find their hosts. It will also slow down their spread from plant to plant. If you also include some of the flowers that attract predatory insects (see page 79) in your mixed plantings, this will help in controlling the pests.

HAND PICKING

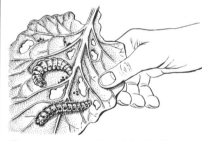

Large pests can be picked off by hand

Although not the most pleasant of jobs, running your fingers along aphid-infested shoots can be an effective control. Similarly, if you have a prize plant such as a citrus tree in a pot which becomes infected with scale insects, carefully squashing them all with your thumb nail is a good way to get rid of them. Any large slow-moving insects can be controlled by hand picking if you have the stomach and the patience for it.

Hang codling moth traps in apple and pear trees in May

TRAPPING

Many trapping techniques, such as grapefruit skins for slugs, are not effective simply because they have little impact on the total pest population. But some, like pheromone traps for codling moths, are very effective. These use synthetic female moth hormones to lure the males to a sticky trap before they can mate.

If you are converting a grass area to a herbaceous border or vegetable plot, it may be worth planting a crop of potatoes before you attempt to grow anything else. The potatoes will attract wireworms and other soil pests which are prevalent in grassland. They can then be lifted and destroyed, along with the pests, after about a month.

BIOLOGICAL CONTROL

You can buy natural predators for most greenhouse pests (see page 49). For outdoor use, there is a bacterium (*Bacillus thuringiensis*), the spores of which are made up into a spray solution for killing caterpillars (see page 65). You could also practise your own biological control – by moving ladybirds on to aphid-infested plants, for example.

PREVENTING PESTS: SLUGS AND SNAILS

Below Garden slug
Bottom left Bourguinat's slug
Bottom right Field slug

Snails, and more especially slugs, are pests because gardeners tend to create conditions that encourage breeding and survival. Plants thrive when protected from drought, frost and wind; so do slugs and snails.

KNOW YOUR ENEMY

There are 25 species of slugs in the British Isles, but fortunately only seven can be considered garden pests. These are found in gardens nearly everywhere throughout the UK, but some species are more common in certain localities.

Although we have nearly 100 species of snails, they are much less of a problem. There are in fact only four species that regularly cause damage in gardens, and in general these tend to be restricted to chalky soils, partly because they use lime for their shell.

The **garden slug** (*Arion hortensis*), which grows to 4cm (1½in) long, is the most serious pest because of its great numbers. It is easily identified by the bright yellow or orange colour of the sole of the 'foot', and attacks plants both above and below the soil. It is a serious pest of maincrop potatoes.

The larger **black slug** (*Arion ater*) can reach 20cm (8in) long. It is not always black; you may find grey, reddish, yellowish or even rare albino forms. Young specimens, up to 2.5cm (1in) long, are always straw-coloured with distinctive dark eye tentacles. This species is not usually numerous enough to be a serious pest, but being so big even a single adult in the wrong place can dispose of a large number of seedlings.

Bourguinat's slug (*Arion fasciatus*) is similar in size and appearance to the garden slug and outnumbers it in some areas, such as the Midlands. You can easily identify it by the striking porcelain-white colour of its 'foot'.

The **field slug** (*Deroceras reticulatum*) is another common species. It grows to only 4cm (1½in), but occurs in large numbers. It is light brown in colour with darker brown mottling.

This species spends most of its time on the surface, and damages plants above or just below soil level. When prodded, it exudes a characteristic chalk-white slime, which makes it easy to identify.

Keeled slugs (three species of *Milax*) spend most of their time under ground. They are recognised by a ridge of skin or 'keel' running along the middle of the back. Mostly brown or black in colour, and up to 7cm

(2½in) long in the largest species, they are covered by a very 'tacky' slime. They remain below the soil surface and damage the underground parts of plants, especially bulbs, root crops and potato tubers.

The **garden snail** (*Helix aspersa*) is the largest and most widely distributed snail. The shell may be 3cm (1¼in) across when mature.

The two so-called **banded snails** (*Cepaea nemoralis* and *Cepaea hortensis*) have smaller shells, up to 2.5cm (1in) across, which are very variable in colour.

The **strawberry snail** (*Trichia striolata*) is noticeably smaller, with a distinctly flattened shell, which is 1.5cm (⅝in) across and pale brown.

WHAT YOU CAN YOU DO

If you can tolerate some damage, most established plants will grow out of danger from slugs and snails. The following will help minimise plant losses.

■ CULTURAL METHODS
Clear dead leaves and other plant remains. Don't leave pots, stones or rubble lying about, as these provide shady refuges for slugs during the day.

More effective measures are any gardening activities that expose slugs and snails, or their eggs, to drying or freezing conditions. So digging, especially if followed by frosty weather or drying winds, can help to reduce their numbers. Digging will also expose them to birds.

■ RESISTANT VARIETIES
In some cases it is possible to minimise the damage by choos-

---

THE LAST RESORT
If your garden is overrun with slugs and snails, you may feel that there is no solution but to use a slug killer. However, instead of using one containing methiocarb or metaldehyde, which may affect animals higher up the food chain, try an aluminium sulphate-based slug killer. This should prove harmful only to slugs and snails and can also kill the eggs if watered on to the soil. If you are worried about aluminium salts ending up in your food, use aluminium sulphate around only ornamental plants.

---

ing to grow plants or varieties that are less susceptible than others to slugs. Among maincrop potatoes, for example, 'Pentland Dell' and 'Pentland Ivory' suffer less from slugs than 'Desirée' and 'Majestic', which in turn are more resistant than, say, 'King Edward'. As a further precaution, harvest potatoes as early as you can to minimise damage.

■ PLASTIC BARRIERS
To protect individual seedlings and young plants, rings cut from plastic bottles are extremely effective. These should be 10cm (4in) high and pushed about 2.5cm (1in) into the ground. You can either leave the ring in place or remove it once the plant has become established. Make sure you don't trap a slug inside when positioning the ring.

INEFFECTIVE CONTROL METHODS

■ TRADITIONAL REMEDIES
Slugs have sensitive skins and don't like crawling over certain surfaces. For this reason, ash, soot, crushed eggshells, sharp sand and lime spread around

---

vulnerable plants have long been recommended as slug deterrents. The problem is that these barriers are easily broken down by rain.

In *Gardening from Which?* trials, slugs were able to find their way through barriers of sharp sand and lime despite frequent topping up. In addition, lime must be kept away from plant stems or it will scorch them, and on alkaline soils it could make the pH too high for healthy plant growth.

■ BEER TRAPS
Plastic cups sunk into the soil and half-filled with beer are sometimes recommended as slug traps. The theory is that the slugs are attracted by the smell of the beer and fall in and drown. In *Gardening from Which?* trials, an average of 8 slugs a week were caught by this method, while a typical garden contains 50 slugs or more for every square metre. What is worse, traps flush with the ground are likely to catch more beneficial creatures than slugs: along with the 8 slugs caught during the trials, 98 ground beetles, 16 earthworms, 4 spiders, 34 harvestmen and 1 centipede fell into the beer traps in one week.

■ OTHER TRAPS
Other methods of trapping, like grapefruit halves, won't harm beneficial creatures, but unless you cover the whole garden with them they won't catch enough slugs to make any difference.

■ BARK MULCHES
In *Gardening from Which?* trials these were found to increase slug damage.

PREVENTING PESTS: APHIDS

Aphids give birth to pregnant females, so their numbers can build up very rapidly. Natural enemies in the form of predators, parasites and diseases will eventually control their numbers, but this may be too late to prevent damage to your plants.

THE PROBLEMS THEY CAUSE

Large infestations can distort and stunt plants, ruining flowers before they open and preventing fruits from developing. Some species, most notably root aphids, can cause wilting by blocking the flow of sap.

Aphids pucker and roll leaves to give themselves some protection from the weather and their enemies. This ruins the appearance of plants. Each aphid sheds its skin four times before becoming an adult. These piles of dead skins, together with the honeydew aphids secrete, forms a sticky mess on leaves. In turn, the honeydew is colonised by sooty mould, which blocks out light to the leaves and makes plants look unsightly.

Aphids feed on sap, and some species spread viruses as they move from plant to plant. Typical viral symptoms are

yellow mottling or flecking on the leaves and distortion of the leaves and flowers. Even small numbers of virus-carrying aphids can do serious damage to susceptible plants.

HOW TO CONTROL THEM

■ If aphids are not causing serious damage, the best thing you can do is nothing. Leave it to the ladybirds, hoverflies, lacewings, predatory midges, parasitic wasps, birds, spiders and fungal diseases that prey on aphids (see page 77 for how to encourage natural predators).

■ Aphids prefer soft young shoots, such as those produced by heavy pruning or excessive use of nitrogen fertilisers. You can avoid problems by choosing plants that don't require heavy pruning – shrub roses instead of bush roses, for example – and avoiding fertilisers like dried blood on fruit and ornamentals.

■ Aphid swarms are attracted by single isolated plants or monocultures. Mixed plantings are less vulnerable to attack than neat rows. Roses, for example, may escape serious attack if grown in mixed borders rather than in separate beds.

■ Members of the rose family are particularly prone to attack by aphids. This rose family includes apples, cotoneasters, cherries, pears, plums, pyracanthas, raspberries and strawberries. Where practical, inspect susceptible plants frequently, especially the growing tips and undersides of the leaves. Small colonies can be kept in check by squashing them between thumb and forefinger. Spraying with a soft soap solution may also control small infestations.

■ Most vegetable aphids overwinter on trees and shrubs, where they are difficult to get at, and move on to vegetables in the summer. Start vegetables off early so they stand a better chance of becoming well established and able to withstand aphid attacks. Covering vegetables with spun polypropylene fleece may also prevent serious aphid damage.

■ Where possible, grow resistant plants. For example, *Philadelphus coronarius* 'Variegatus' and *Weigelia florida* 'Variegata' are both similar foliage shrubs. However, while the *Philadelphus* can be plagued by blackfly, aphids rarely bother the *Weigelia*. For resistant lettuces and raspberries, see opposite.

APHIDS AND ANTS

Common black ants and red ants farm aphids for their honeydew, and in return will aggressively protect them from ladybirds and other predators. If you see this happening on your roses, shrubs or trees, smear a ring of fruit tree grease around the base of the stem to block off access for the ants. This will work only on isolated plants which are not near walls or fences.

Right Rosy leaf-curling aphid
Far right Woolly aphid

APHID SPOTTING

Different plants have different aphids which attack them. Some are serious pests and are worth trying to control; others are not worth worrying about.

APHIDS ON ORNAMENTALS
Beech Long, dark green, woolly aphids can severely disfigure new shoots on beech hedges.
Chrysanthemums/asters Several aphids, including the leaf-curling plum aphid, attack herbaceous plants from May onwards. They distort young growth, produce honeydew (which is colonised by sooty mould) and spread viruses. Control if attacks are severe.
Conifers (especially pine, larch and spruce) Small, dark aphids (or adelgids) can cause severe needle drop in April and May and disfigure plants by covering them with waxy wool.
Bulbs and corms White aphids attack tulip bulbs and corms and stunt young shoots. They overwinter in the scaly leaves.
Greenhouse and pot plants Can be attacked by lots of different aphids. Some may stunt or distort the plants and spread virus diseases.
Roses Large green or pink aphids start to build up on buds and young shoots from May until late summer, disfiguring buds and reducing growth. They are worse on soft growth.
Climbers (especially honeysuckles) Leaves and flower buds are covered with dense colonies of blue-green aphids which can distort growth and reduce flowers during spring and summer.
Shrubs Most shrubs and trees, particularly ornamental cherries, viburnums, pyracanthas and cotoneasters, are attacked. Damage is usually serious only on young plants.

APHIDS ON VEGETABLES
Beans Young stems become smothered by black bean aphids, especially in June and July. Plants will survive even if the aphids aren't controlled, although they will be stunted and the crops reduced. Pinching out the tips of broad beans after flowering may reduce damage.
Brassicas (all except turnips) Dense clusters of grey mealy cabbage aphids can distort and pucker leaves and may kill plants in hot, dry weather. Destroy old brassicas, on which they overwinter.
Carrots Small, green, willow-carrot aphids cause leaves to become discoloured and distorted in May and June and may spread viruses.
Lettuce Shiny, pale or bright green aphids (which overwinter on currants and gooseberries) attack lettuces in May and June outdoors and at other times under cloches. They usually cause superficial damage only, though they can spread virus diseases. Roots may also be colonised by whitish waxy aphids in July to September. Severe attacks cause wilting and even death. Grow resistant varieties like 'Avoncrisp', 'Avondefiance' or 'Sabine'.
Potatoes Large green or pink, very active aphids can appear in large numbers from April onwards, especially in hot, dry years, and distort the foliage. Smaller green aphids spread viruses but are more difficult to spot. Control where possible.

APHIDS ON FRUIT
Apples Small green or pink apple aphids hatch out in spring and build up until early summer on young growth. They may damage flowers and fruit and reduce yields. Purplish-brown aphids covered in fluffy white wax overwinter on the bark and form colonies on damaged areas, causing knobbly galls and upright over-vigorous shoots. Remove woolly aphids by painting them with methylated spirit.
Cherries Dark brown aphids (cherry blackfly) colonise young leaves and shoots in spring and can devastate young trees if unchecked. Green aphids that overwinter on the stems cause the young leaves to curl as they develop in spring.
Plums Small brownish aphids that overwinter on plum trees can cause severe leaf curl in spring and introduce plum pox virus. Long, green, grey-mottled aphids live in large masses on leaves and shoots from June to August. They do little damage, but honeydew and sooty mould disfigure the trees.
Currants Pale yellow or green aphids produce blisters on the edges of leaves (red on red currants, yellow on black currants), but do little real damage.
Raspberries Large shiny yellow-green aphids and small powdery green-grey aphids cause leaves to curl and spread virus disease from April onwards. Grow resistant varieties such as 'Malling Orion', 'Malling Delight' or 'Malling Leo'.
Strawberries Whitish aphids that survive all year on strawberries occasionally build up in sufficient numbers to damage leaves and distort flowers. But even small numbers, which may not be obvious, spread virus diseases. Control where possible.

PREVENTING PESTS: CATERPILLARS

All caterpillars eat plants, but most feed on weeds and wild plants, causing very little damage. It's only the extreme minority that chew away at garden plants, giving caterpillars a bad reputation. With the exception of cabbage whites and gooseberry sawflies, all the offenders are moth caterpillars. All the caterpillars that do serious damage to flowers, shrubs and trees are illustrated on this page (see Chapters 4 and 5 for fruit and vegetable caterpillars). Other caterpillars that you find in the garden are likely to be harmless.

ANGLESHADES MOTH

Attacks a wide range of herbaceous plants, particularly chrysanthemums brought indoors to flower. The green or brown caterpillars feed at night, hiding under leaves by day. Batches of 50–100 eggs are laid on leaves.

Squash caterpillars or spray with *Bacillus thuringiensis* if damage is serious.

BROWN TAIL MOTH
Attacks a range of trees including hawthorn, cherry, rose and brambles. Most common along southern and eastern coasts of

England, occasionally found further inland. The caterpillars often occur in sufficient numbers to defoliate individual trees and shrubs. They cover their feeding area with silk webbing and can cause a painful 'nettle' rash when touched. Caterpillars overwinter in small webbing 'tents' and start feeding on new growth in spring before pupating inside silken cocoons in June or July. Prune out and destroy overwintering caterpillars or pupae. Spray young caterpillars with *Bacillus thuringiensis*.

BUFF TIP MOTH
Attacks roses, trees and shrubs in August and September. Damage is severe but usually limited to a few branches. Small clusters of eggs are laid on the undersides of leaves in July. Caterpillars pupate in the soil in autumn. Hand pick and transfer to wild plants.

CARNATION TORTRIX MOTH
Attacks many outdoor shrubs and greenhouse and pot plants. Eggs are laid on leaves in batches of up to 200. Caterpillars feed on shoot tips, buds and flowers and draw leaves together with silk threads. They can be

found all year in a heated greenhouse. Look for brown patches on leaves, caused by caterpillars feeding on the undersurface. Squash caterpillars or spray with the bacterium *Bacillus thuringiensis*.

CUTWORM
These live in the soil, feeding on lower leaves and seedlings at night, from May to September. The name cutworm covers several species of moth caterpillars, but they are all similar to the large yellow underwing illustrated. Winter digging will destroy some. Protect individual plants with rings cut from plastic bottles pushed 2.5cm (1in) into the soil. Alternatively, sow early or start seeds in pots.

■ LACKEY MOTH

Attacks fruit trees, roses and many other trees and shrubs. Caterpillars hatch in spring, and cover branches with webbing 'tents'. Eggs are laid in bands of 100–200 from August to Septem-

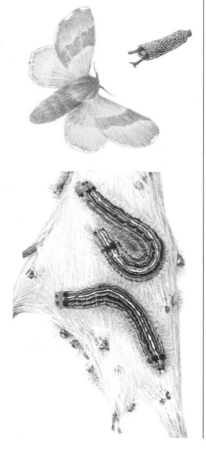

ber on twigs. Cut out and destroy overwintering eggs. Spray with *Bacillus thuringiensis* in spring and early summer.

■ MAGPIE MOTH

Attacks gooseberries, currants, trees and shrubs, mainly in April and June. Caterpillars overwinter and start feeding in spring. When well fed, they pupate and emerge as adult moths between July and August. Eggs are laid singly or in small groups on the underside of leaves. Hand pick or spray with *Bacillus thuringiensis*.

■ SWIFT MOTH

Caterpillars feed on roots, bulbs and tubers of many plants. Symptoms are holes eaten by white grubs. Good weed control helps, as the moth rarely lays eggs on bare soil.

■ VAPOURER MOTH

Attacks trees, shrubs and herbaceous plants from May to August. Eggs are laid on cocoons in which females overwinter on plants. Don't touch caterpillars – their hairs contain an irritant. Destroy cocoons and eggs.

■ WEBBER MOTH

Attacks hawthorn, privets and other shrubs. Leaves large holes in hedges, which are covered in webbing. Spray with *Bacillus thuringiensis*.

CATERPILLAR CONTROLS

Most caterpillars are easy to control, either by hand picking or by spraying with the bacterium *Bacillus thuringiensis*. This is available as a dry powder which you mix up like a normal spray. See page 137 for brands. The organically approved pesticides, pyrethrum and derris, will also control most caterpillars.

PREVENTING PESTS: GENERAL

Aphids, snails, slugs and caterpillars are by far the most common and most serious pests of garden plants, but there are many others which can occasionally damage plants. Pests specific to fruit, vegetables and greenhouse plants are dealt with in the relevant chapters. All the pests listed on these two pages attack ornamental plants, and some are common on all types of plants.

Where no effective non-chemical control exists, suitable pesticides approved for organic gardeners are given (see Box). If a pesticide is mentioned under a particular pest, this denotes that it has government approval for that purpose. It does not necessarily mean that it will be an effective treatment.

■ **Capsid bugs** Attack wide range of ornamentals, and most tree, cane and bush fruit. Telltale signs are small ragged holes in leaves close to veins. Seriously damage buds, leaving fruit and flowers distorted. No effective non-chemical controls, as it is too late to do anything about it once the damage is seen. If plants have a history of capsid damage, routine spraying with pyrethrum when plants in bud and, for fruit, after flowering may help. However, capsids move about a lot and may not be caught by a contact insecticide.

■ **Chafer grubs** Attack roots, causing seedlings and recent plantings to wilt and die. Look in the soil for large white grubs with six legs near the front. Common on gardens which have been recently reclaimed from grassland. Dig over the soil in winter to expose the chafer grubs to birds.

■ **Frog hoppers** Attack carnations, lavender, rosemary and many other ornamentals. Look for conspicuous froth ('cuckoo spit') with fat green insect inside. They do little real damage – dislodge with jet of water.

■ **Leaf cutter bees** Cut circular pieces out of rose leaves. Not serious: the habit is confined to short nest-building period in early summer. No treatment needed.

■ **Leaf hoppers** Attack rhododendrons, roses and many other ornamentals. Cause slight mottling on leaves; can carry viruses. No effective non-chemical control. Try pyrethrum or soft soap sprays if damage serious.

■ **Leaf miners** Attack chrysanthemums and hollies. On hollies you can see large yellow spots on leaf with grub inside; on chrysanthemums miners form tunnels which appear white or brown. Pick off and burn affected leaves.

■ **Leaf-rolling sawflies** Attack roses and other shrubs. Leaves rolled up; grub may be inside. Not usually serious, but pick off and burn affected leaves. Cultivating ground under bushes exposes overwintering grubs to predators.

■ **Lily beetles** Attack lilies and relations. Bright red beetles eat plants, causing extensive damage. At present, found only in and around Surrey. Hand pick and squash.

■ **Millipedes** Feed mainly on dead plant matter, but can kill seedlings and young plants by

Top Leaf damage caused by capsid bugs
Centre Lily beetle
Bottom Curled up rose leaves caused by the rose leaf-rolling sawfly

Below Spotted snake millipede
Centre Whitefly on Brussels sprout
Bottom Thrips

eating their roots. See page 76 for how to recognise them. Keep rubbish and debris, under which they hide, to a minimum. If these and other soil pests are a serious problem, start seeds off in pots rather than sowing direct into the ground.

■ **Narcissus flies** Attack daffodils. Other bulb flies attack ornamental alliums and edible members of the onion family. White grubs eat out centre of bulb. Check bulbs before planting, rejecting any that are soft. Lift and dispose of infested bulbs.

■ **Red spider mites** Attack wide range of plants, but especially damaging on conifers, particularly dwarf spruces such as *Picea albertiana* 'Conica'. Leaves become mottled, turn brown and fall off. Tiny fawn-coloured mites and fine webbing may be visible under a hand lens. In dry weather spray plants with water daily. Derris or soft soap insecticides may help, but had little effect on red spider mites on greenhouse crops in *Gardening from Which?* trials.

■ **Scale insects** Attack wide range of shrubs, fruit trees and vines. Small numbers can be squashed with your thumb nail. With larger infestations, wipe down stems with a sponge or cloth to detach them. You will probably need to repeat this several times.

■ **Slugworms** Attack mainly roses, cherries and pears. Eat upper surface of leaf, causing transparent areas. Effects mainly cosmetic. Pick off if seen.

■ **Thrips** Affect gladioli, roses and other flowers, causing brown speckles and distorted petals. No non-chemical methods effective. Try pesticides approved for organic gardeners if a serious problem.

■ **Whitefly** Ornamentals attacked include azaleas, rhododendron and viburnum. Also a problem on brassicas and greenhouse plants. Small white insects swarm above plants when shaken; honeydew and sooty mould on leaves. Unlikely to do serious damage outside the greenhouse (see page 49). Hose down plants to wash off honeydew and sooty mould.

ORGANICALLY APPROVED PESTICIDES

A small group of pesticides is acceptable to organic organisations like the Soil Association and the Henry Doubleday Research Association if used only occasionally.

The insecticides derris and pyrethrum are natural products in the sense that they are extracted from plants. However, pyrethrum products nearly always contain a chemical called piperonyl butoxide, a synergist which acts on the pyrethrum to make it much more effective.

Derris and pyrethrum are short-lived, remaining fully active for only a few hours, so cannot accumulate in the environment, and are unlikely to harm people or animals even in large quantities. On the other hand they are non-specific and can kill a wide range of insects including bees, hoverflies and ladybirds. They are also poisonous to fish, frogs, toads and tortoises, and must never be used near fishtanks, ponds or water courses.

Soft soap (made from natural fatty acids) is less toxic, though it should still be kept away from fish. It kills soft-bodied insects by destroying the protective wax coating on their skins, and is unlikely to harm adult ladybirds or hoverflies, though it may kill their larvae. It can also scorch tender new shoots or plants, so it should be used with care. Test it on a small area before spraying all your plants.

Organically approved pesticides all work on contact, so you must spray or dust them direct on to the pest, or on to plants which the pests will visit within a few hours. Pests arriving the next day, or hatching out of eggs, will need a further application. Pests which are highly mobile and visit a large number of plants, such as leaf hoppers, are difficult to kill with organically approved pesticides, as are those that feed inside the plant.

In *Gardening from Which?* trials, pyrethrum managed to control light infestations of aphids and reduce heavy ones; soft soap helped control light infestations but did not have much effect on heavy ones; and derris proved little better than spraying the plants with water.

PREVENTING PESTS: LARGER ANIMALS

As well as insects, birds and mammals can do considerable damage in the garden. So what can you do when pets and wildlife start getting out of hand?

■ BIRDS

Birds, particularly bullfinches, can ruin fruit crops and the flowers on ornamental cherries by pecking off the buds. The only preventive measure is to cover fruit bushes and wall-trained trees with fine netting, secured firmly to the ground on all sides. With large free-standing trees, all you can do is to net selected branches to make sure that you get at least some fruit.

Pigeons are the biggest problem in the vegetable plot. Cover brassicas with a 10cm (4in) mesh netting to protect winter and spring crops. You need only suspend it over the vegetable plot, as pigeons tend not to approach cabbages from above. With beans, erecting a netting frame over the plants is the only sure way to keep pigeons off. Repellents and scarers have very little lasting effect on birds.

Among flowers, cotton stretched between small sticks will deter birds from landing to peck off the flower heads. Use weak cotton, not thread, so there is no danger of ensnaring the birds. Yellow flowers seem to be pecked in preference, so choosing other colours, particularly for crocuses and polyanthus, may help.

■ BADGERS

Badgers have very fixed habits and will follow exactly the same routes every night. If their route extends through your garden, they will demolish fences, hedges and any other obstacles you put in their way. There's nothing you can do, as badgers are protected animals. The sensible solution is to keep the badger's path clear.

■ CATS

Cats generally like well-cultivated soil to dig in and soft plants in sunny positions to lie on. Protect new seedbeds with netting and push small sticks among vulnerable plants to deter cats from lying on them. Keeping seedbeds moist may also deter cats, as they generally like dryish soil.

If your own cat is causing the problem, try planting some catmint in a sheltered spot. Hopefully, it will lie on that in preference to other plants. Also try providing it with a toilet area of fine soil, ash or sand in a concealed area.

If neighbours' cats are regularly fouling your garden, a well-aimed jet of water from an old washing-up liquid bottle will make them think twice about doing it next time.

Avoid gravel and bark on unplanted areas if you have a cat problem, and protect children's sandpits with a lid.

■ DOGS

You should be able to train your own dog not to foul your garden. And once it's passed puppy stage, it should not wreck plants.

In the meantime, erect a temporary netting fence around the most vulnerable plants or parts of your garden. If you do see a dog urinating on your plants or a bitch urinating on the lawn, soak the affected areas with water to prevent damage. As dogs tend to take the line of least resistance, a fairly low fence or hedge is often sufficient to steer them around your choice plants.

■ DEER

Deer can do a lot of damage. The only sure way to keep them out is a solid fence at least 2.5m (8ft) high. In some cases a slightly lower fence, above head height of the deer, may be sufficient as deer tend not to jump into areas they can't see. If fencing is impractical, try tracing the owner of the deer to take action. The Land Registry is a good starting point.

FOXES

The main nuisance caused by foxes is upturning dustbins. The solution is to buy a sturdy bin with a lid that locks in place and, ideally, secure it to the wall. Alternatively, you could construct a roofed enclosure for the bin with a secure fastening on the door.

GREY SQUIRRELS

Squirrels strip bark from young trees, dig up bulbs, devour soft fruit, eat food put out for birds

and steal stored crops from garden sheds. You can protect young trees with tree guards or wire netting. With regard to the other problems, there is nothing you can do which will be effective in the long term.

MICE, RATS AND VOLES

To protect seeds, a layer of holly or gorse over newly sown beds may help. Alternatively, start large seeds, such as peas and

HEALTH RISKS FROM DOGS AND CATS

Both cat and dog faeces carry a health risk and should be disposed of without direct handling. Pick them up with a newspaper or a plastic bag turned inside out over your hand and either put them in the dustbin or incinerate them. Don't put cat or dog faeces on the compost heap.

Two parasites affecting dogs and cats can also cause illness in man. *Toxocara* is a roundworm which is carried by about one in five dogs and cats. Eggs from the worms are passed out in the faeces and can survive in the soil for several months. If you eat the eggs, they will hatch out in your stomach and the minute worms will work their way round your body.

Normally there are no ill effects, but worms could damage brain, liver or lung tissue, or cause partial or total blindness if they invade the retina.

Toxoplasma gondii is a microscopic parasite also transmitted in the faeces (and probably saliva too). It generally causes no symptoms in man, but it can sometimes cause sickness and high temperature – rather like glandular fever and, in exceptional cases, can cause brain damage, and even death. Another danger is damage to the eyes or brain of the developing foetus if a pregnant woman is infected.

The risk of disease resulting from cat and dog faeces is low, but the damage that could occur is so severe that care should always be taken.

beans, in pots indoors. You can buy live traps to catch mice and voles without harming them, but you need to release them at least half a mile away from your garden to ensure they don't return. Chocolate or peanut butter are the best bait for mice; carrots or apples for voles. If you have a rat problem, contact your local council, which will arrange to deal with them professionally.

MOLES

There are no sure ways of getting rid of moles without resorting to poisons. But the following method is worth a try. First locate the mole's main runs.

These will be about 20–25cm (8–10in) below the surface, often running towards a hedge or water source. The shallower tunnels are feeding tunnels, and these may be used only once. To test for a main run, block the tunnel or remove all the molehills and wait for fresh activity. When you have located a main run, push long brambles or rose briars down into it. If this fails, try mothballs at intervals along the run.

RABBITS AND HARES

To keep rabbits out of your garden, you need 1.2m (4ft) wide 2.5cm (1in) wire mesh. Bend over the bottom 15cm (6in) at right-angles and bury it so that there is 90cm (3ft) above the ground. For hares, an additional trip wire 15cm (6in) above the fence is also needed. The fence needs to be placed all round the garden and should be checked regularly for damage. In winter remove snowdrifts. If you want only to protect young trees, individual tree guards (which come in the form of a plastic spiral) work well.

PREVENTING PESTS: WINTER ACTION

If you know where pests overwinter, you can often control their numbers so as to reduce the problems in the following growing season. The illustration below points out potential trouble spots, and the captions will tell you what you can do about them. But remember that your plants will be invaded by flying pests from surrounding gardens.

1 Onion fly, beet leaf miner, slugs, cutworms, wireworms, bean seed fly and carrot fly will overwinter in the soil. Dig the soil in winter to expose some of them to the weather and birds.

2 Eelworms also live in the soil. Follow a proper crop rotation system.

3 Carrot fly larvae may spend the winter in roots left in the ground. Dig up all roots and burn infested ones.

4 Mealy aphid and cabbage root fly larvae may remain in brassica stems left in the ground. Dig them up and burn them, and cultivate the soil.

5 Cabbage whitefly are possible on overwintering brassicas. Burn severely infested plants after harvest.

6 Slugs, flea beetles, pea and bean weevils and wireworms are likely to be found near the compost heap, in patches of weeds, and among debris left lying around. Keep the ground clear of weeds and debris, and cultivate the soil.

7 Onion fly, celery fly, carrot fly and leaf miners may survive on infested leaves or the compost heap. Burn, don't compost, infested plants.

8 Aphids that feed on crops can overwinter on hedgerows and ornamental plants. There's nothing you can do except keep a lookout for them.

9 Cabbage white butterfly pupae sometimes overwinter on walls or fences. Keep a lookout and destroy any that you find.

10 Apple/pear sucker eggs or adults, red spider mite eggs, tortrix moths, scale insects and aphid eggs can all be found on the bark of fruit trees. Codling moth caterpillars hide in loose bark. Dispose of winter prunings to help reduce numbers.

11 Apple blossom weevils hide in dead leaves. Clear dead leaves away.

12 Leaf-eating caterpillars (winter moths) can survive in soil beneath the tree. Use grease bands to stop them climbing the tree. Pear midge larvae can also be a problem, but these are best controlled by collecting and destroying infested fruit.

13 Aphids and capsid bug eggs and scale insects may be on the bark or old branches of currant bushes. Winter pruning, providing you dispose of the cut stems, can help get rid of them.

14 Big bud mites live in black currant buds. Prune out and burn shoots with large buds.

15 Remove and destroy any strawberry plants affected by eelworm.

CHAPTER NINE

GOOD AND BAD BUGS

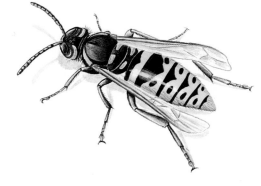

Ladybirds are good . . .   *. . . but are wasps bad?*

Insects and other creepy-crawlies are commonly mis-understood. While bees and ladybirds are generally regarded as the gardener's friends, other insects and their larvae are too often dismissed as pests. This chapter looks at the role of insects in the garden and tells you how to distinguish between the pest eaters and the pests.

A garden without insects would be a pretty sterile place. Think of how the gentle buzzing of bees and the chirping of grasshoppers add an extra dimension to a sunny day in the garden. And the colour and movement of butterflies and moths, and dragonflies and damselflies can really bring alive the flowers.

If there weren't any insects, other wildlife like hedgehogs, frogs, toads and certain birds would not come at all as they would find little to eat.

Many insects also help you with the gardening – even some of those you regard as absolute pests. For example, you may curse wasps when they eat your fruit or buzz around your head. But you may be more understanding towards them when

you realise that they have spent most of the summer catching caterpillars and grubs.

THE ROLE OF INSECTS

■ POLLINATION

Without insects, many garden plants would not produce fruits or berries, or set seeds. It's not just bees that pollinate flowers; many kinds of flies, beetles and wasps also take an active role. Even if you use non-persistent pesticides approved for organic gardeners, these can still kill pollinating insects. To minimise the risk of harming these insects, don't spray plants in flower. Also confine any spraying to the evening, when bees are less active.

■ RECYCLING NUTRIENTS

Many insects and other small creatures that live in the soil feed on dead plant tissue. Even pests like millipedes and wire-worms help with this as well as feeding on the roots of live plants. Several species of beetle specialise in burying dung and dead animals (such as insects, worms, etc.). The activities of all these creatures play a vital role in returning nutrients to the soil.

■ CONTROLLING PESTS

For every pest there are usually at least two or three predators. It has been estimated that if all the cabbage white caterpillars were left to themselves and never sprayed or controlled by man, only three per cent would ever survive to maturity – such is the effectiveness of natural predators and parasites. Aphids arrive in plagues in spring, but there are rarely as many about in the garden by midsummer. A bad year for aphids nearly always turns out to be a bumper year for their predators.

GOOD AND BAD BUGS

LADYBIRDS

The familiar red ladybirds with black spots are easy to recognise. But apart from faint spots, the larvae bear no resemblance to the adults, looking more like tiny armour-plated trains with legs at the front. Like the adults, the larvae are carnivorous and eat aphids and other soft-bodied insects. A single larva can eat 500 aphids, and when it grows into an adult it can eat even more. As well as the larvae, you may find batches of small yellow ladybird eggs or the grey pupae (which don't move) on the leaves of roses and other shrubs. If you do come across them, leave them well alone.

The most common ladybirds are red with either two or seven black spots, but there are many other kinds which you may think are not ladybirds at all. For example, they may be black with red spots, black with yellow spots or yellow with black spots. There is even a small, all-black one which feeds on fruit tree spider mites. But if you study them carefully, you'll see that they all have the typical ladybird shape.

Ladybirds can swarm in a hot summer, and this can lead to panic stories in the press of ladybirds driving people off beaches, etc. They can emit a bitter fluid from their leg joints which repels predators, but don't worry – they can't harm you.

GOOD BEETLES

There are over 250,000 species of beetles, so it isn't always easy to identify them. However, very few do any serious damage in gardens, and it's best to regard all adult beetles as friends. Many are harmless, like the conspicuously horned stag beetle which lives on dead trees. And quite a few busy themselves by eating slugs and soil pests. The most beneficial beetles that you are likely to find in the garden are ground beetles and rove beetles.

■ GROUND BEETLES

The big black beetles that you often see scurrying across the soil, particularly if you shine a torch around the garden at night, are ground beetles. Most of them, both as larvae and adults, are predators. They catch and eat slugs, other insects and unfortunate earthworms. The adults have long legs and many can't fly. Their wing cases, which may be black, bluish or dark brown, are often fused together, and this may give them added protection as they scramble about the soil. The larvae are long, soft-bodied animals with three pairs of legs and dark-coloured heads. Like the adults, they too have powerful jaws.

■ ROVE BEETLES

Perhaps the best known of the rove beetles is the sinister-looking devil's coach horse, but there are over 1000 British species, many of which are small and inconspicuous. They have small wing cases which, unlike those of most beetles, don't completely cover the abdomen.

eyed ladybird

22-spot ladybird   **7-spot ladybird**

7-spot larva

7-spot pupa

COLORADO BEETLES
These small beetles look similar to black and yellow ladybirds. They are occasionally found in Britain on imported potato crops. They are a very serious pest on potatoes and any sighting should be reported immediately to your local Ministry of Agriculture, Fisheries and Food office.

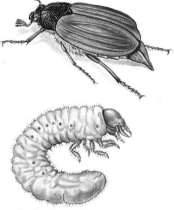

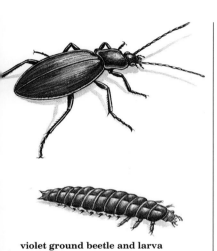

violet ground beetle and larva

devil's coach horse

Nevertheless, they can fly. The larvae are like smaller versions of ground beetle larvae, and both these and the adult rove beetles feed on insects and grubs in the soil.

Years ago the insecticide Aldrin was widely used by commercial growers to control cabbage root fly. Because of this the beetles, being quick moving, picked up a lot of insecticide and perished. As a result, the slow-moving larvae of the cabbage root fly (which was less affected by the insecticide) actually increased because there were fewer predators to keep them under control. In the garden, using soil insecticides could have a similar effect.

BAD BEETLES

The larvae of a few beetles can be serious garden pests.

■ CHAFERS
The most familiar is the May bug, which occasionally crashes into windows. The larvae look like large grubs with legs, and they feed on roots and bulbs.

■ CLICK BEETLES
These brown beetles, about 12mm (½in) long, make an audible click and leap into the air when touched. Their larvae are wireworms, which burrow into root vegetables.

■ RASPBERRY BEETLES
The beetles lay their eggs in the flowers of cane fruits. The eggs hatch out into maggot-like larvae, which burrow into the fruits of blackberries, raspberries and other cane fruits.
Adult beetles can also cause damage to plants.

■ LILY BEETLES
These small red beetles are members of the weevil family, with rectangular abdomens and long snouts. They can deform lilies and prevent leaves from opening. They are found in parts of Surrey, but they may be spreading further afield.

■ POLLEN BEETLES
These tiny beetles are common in sweet pea flowers. They feed on pollen and don't do any serious damage, but they can be a nuisance when cut blooms are brought indoors. To get rid of them, put the blooms in a garage (or somewhere where the light is coming from one direction) and they will all fly off.

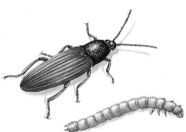

chafer beetle and larva

click beetle and larva

raspberry beetle and larva

lily beetle

pollen beetle

■ STRAWBERRY BEETLES
These are relatives of the ground beetles, but are quite small. There's little you can do to control them other than remove all the debris from your strawberry bed each year.

Right *Adult hoverflies feed on nectar and are attracted by single and flat-topped flowers*

HOVERFLIES

Hoverflies are true flies which mimic bees or wasps to fool potential predators that they have a sting (which they don't). It's very easy to distinguish hoverflies because, unlike bees or wasps, they have only one pair of wings and can remain virtually static in flight.

Most of the bee and wasp mimics are beneficial and have larvae which feed on aphids. The larvae have soft bodies and are usually light coloured, though sometimes they are green or brownish. They are about 12mm (½in) long with a very small head and no legs and have the curious ability to change their shape. You can generally find them on leaves wherever there are aphids.

The black sheep of the family as far as the gardener is concerned is the narcissus fly, whose larvae feed on daffodil bulbs.

LACEWINGS

Lacewings are delicate, greenish insects with long antennae, golden eyes and two pairs of large membraneous wings. They often come into the house on warm summer evenings, and some people mistake them for winged aphids, though they are really not very similar if you study them.

Both the adults and larvae feed on aphids by sucking out their body fluids. The larvae are slightly hairy, and dead aphids often stick to them. For this reason they are often difficult to see as they may look like a mass of zombified aphids on your plants.

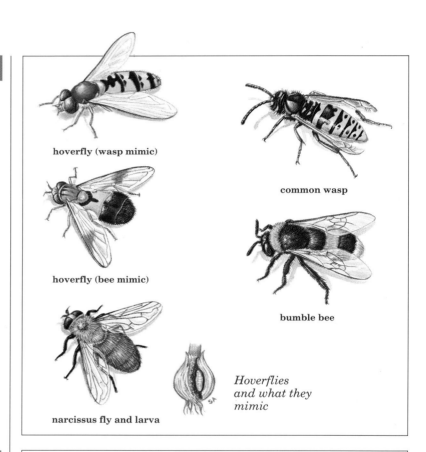

hoverfly (wasp mimic)

common wasp

hoverfly (bee mimic)

bumble bee

narcissus fly and larva

Hoverflies and what they mimic

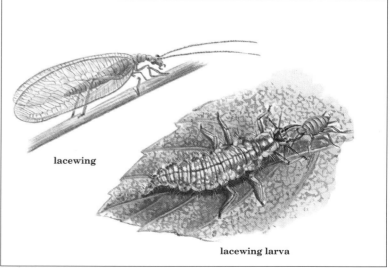

lacewing

lacewing larva

WASPS

Besides the familiar wasp, which eats both caterpillars and fruit, several small wasps are common in gardens which are parasitic on other insects. As you can see from the pictures, they don't look at all like ordinary wasps. Parasitic wasps have two pairs of wings, mostly with a dark dot on the forewing, and a long body with a definite waist.

They lay their eggs inside a larva or adult insect by means of a sharp ovipositor. The resulting wasp larvae then feed inside the insect, ultimately killing the host.

Caterpillars are most commonly parasitised by braconid wasps, and up to a hundred can emerge from a single caterpillar. Other types are parasitic on aphids, laying a single egg inside the host's body. You may see straw-coloured dead aphids with a hole in their body on the leaves of garden plants.

Although you might not like their methods, these insects are mostly working on your side in the battle against pests.

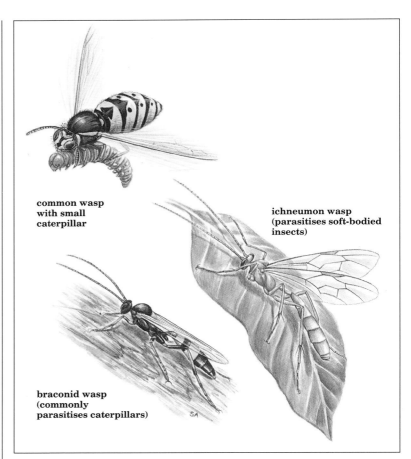

common wasp with small caterpillar

ichneumon wasp (parasitises soft-bodied insects)

braconid wasp (commonly parasitises caterpillars)

CENTIPEDES AND MILLIPEDES

Lots of people confuse the two: centipedes are carnivorous and can run very quickly in order to catch their prey; millipedes feed on plant roots so don't need to move about much. One of the easiest ways to tell them apart is to touch them: centipedes usually run away, while millipedes curl up in a ball.

There are also other obvious differences. If you look at them under a hand lens, centipedes

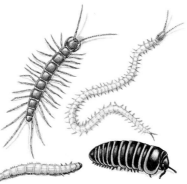

Top, clockwise Centipedes (Lithobius and Geophilus), millipede in defensive response, wireworm

have one pair of legs per segment, while millipedes have two pairs. Centipedes are also usually flatter and less cylindrical than millipedes.

There are two common types of centipede that you are likely to see in the garden. *Lithobius* is dark brown with wide flattened segments; *Geophilus* is pale yellow with thin segments. As they grow, centipedes add on more body segments at the back. Don't confuse them with wireworms, which have only three pairs of legs and grow only to around 1cm (½in).

CHAPTER TEN

ENCOURAGING NATURAL PEST EATERS

The best way to win the war against pests in the garden is to enlist nature's help. For every pest there's usually an army of predators ready to make a meal out of them. Insect-eating birds, mammals, reptiles and insects all have a role to play. They may need a little encouragement to take up residence, however, so it's worth planning for them when you design and plant your garden. The illustration shows some ways in which you can encourage them.

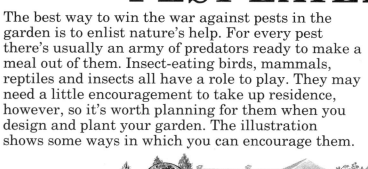

1 Compost heaps are useful for slug-eating slow-worms, which nest there, and for robins, which search for insects in winter.

2 A **pond** is vital for frogs and will attract a whole host of creatures including birds, toads and newts.

3 Piles of **logs** or **leaves** will support a range of insects as well as hedgehogs.

4 Honeysuckle is a popular nesting-site for birds, and the flowers will attract hawkmoths at night.

5 Long **grass** will attract many insects and butterflies.

6 A thick **hedge** like hawthorn provides food and cover for birds.

7 Sunflower and **teasel seeds** are loved by greenfinches and goldfinches.

8 Native British **shrubs** like dogwood, elder and wild rose attract insect-eating wrens and warblers.

9 Nettles attract peacock butterflies, red admirals and tortoiseshells.

10 A **bird table** sited where it can be seen easily is a valuable addition to any garden. Make sure it is cat-proof.

11 Flowers chosen for their nectar, such as buddleia, and sedum, will attract butterflies.

12 Berries on holly, berberis and cotoneaster provide food for birds.

ENCOURAGING NATURAL PEST EATERS: BENEFICIAL INSECTS

GARDEN PRACTICE

We tend to think of insects in the garden as pests, yet the majority are actually beneficial. Many prey on other insects, like aphids, which we are happy to be rid of; others provide food for larger predators like birds, hedgehogs and bats. In many ways, encouraging a healthy insect population is the basis of a well-balanced wildlife garden.

By adapting the way we garden, insects can become friends instead of enemies. Resist the temptation to keep the garden neat and tidy. Most predators like cover, so piles of leaves, sticks and logs are useful. Let hedges and borders get a little overgrown and leave the odd weed among the vegetables.

Slugs and aphids are the most persistent pests, but don't resort to pesticides or slug pellets. It is difficult to eliminate slugs completely, but birds and toads will eat their fair share. You may just have to accept a few slug-eaten leaves or give up growing plants that are particularly susceptible, like delphiniums and hostas.

ESTABLISHING A NETTLE PATCH

Nettles are the staple food of several species of butterfly. Small tortoiseshells, red admirals, commas and peacocks lay their eggs on nettles.

To encourage new shoots, cut the plants back occasionally and apply a nitrogen fertiliser like dried blood at 130g a sq m (4oz a sq yd).

To establish a new patch, look for a clump of new shoots just appearing above the ground in February. Dig out some roots about 10–15cm (4–5in) long, bearing green shoots, and replant in a sunny position.

Sedum spectabile 'Carmen' provides nectar in late summer

Wallflower 'Fairy Mixed' provides nectar in late spring

The only sure way to attract predators is to provide them with their prey. Ladybirds, for example, feed exclusively on greenfly and blackfly and their relatives, and need at least some aphids to ensure their survival.

Don't worry about aphids or caterpillars unless they are actually killing a plant. If you can bear to live with them they will encourage predators to move in and protect other plants.

There's nothing slugs and caterpillars like more than juicy vegetables in a row, so try to mix other plants and flowers in the bed.

A selection of flowers that are rich in nectar throughout the summer should be grown. Butterflies, bees, hoverflies and wasps need open, single flowers for nectar. These need not necessarily be native wild flowers, but avoid highly bred F1 hybrids and double forms. In the winter flowering viburnums like × *V. bodnatense* are a life-saver for insects that emerge from hibernation in early spring.

NECTAR PLANTS

Bees, butterflies, hoverflies and wasps are attracted to plants and flowers that are rich in nectar.

For flowers, choose a mix of showy annuals, like sunflowers and calendulas, with perennials like crane's-bill, and *Sedum spectabile*. Other nectar flowers are stocks, wallflowers, alyssum, poppies, grape hyacinth, sweet williams and aubrietia.

Among shrubs you cannot beat buddleia for all nectar-feeders. Hawthorn, apple and cherry blossom are also useful sources of nectar.

GROUND BEETLE TRAP FOR SLUGS

Ground beetles feed mainly at soil level on slugs and worms. To ensure they stay where they are needed most, it is possible to make a 'pitfall trap'. Dig a ditch around the plot at least 4cm (1½in) deep and line the outside edge with smooth material like lawn edging strip. Make sure the top is flush with the soil outside the plot. As the beetles run across the soil they will fall over the edge. They cannot climb the smooth surface to get out and should turn on slugs that stray into the plot.

COVER FOR GROUND INSECTS

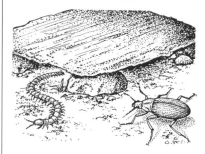

Ground beetles and centipedes are active garden predators. Both hunt at night for their prey, which include slugs, soil grubs, woodlice and, unfortunately, earthworms. During the day they are shy creatures, living under stones, and will scurry away if disturbed.

They require good daytime cover to encourage them to stay. Provide some large stones, pieces of wood, old tiles or propped up slates within the vegetable plot (see illustration above). Brassica collars around members of the cabbage family will also provide shelter for ground-dwelling predatory insects.

Low-growing weeds also offer some measure of cover – weedy cabbage patches have been shown to support more ground beetles, fewer pests and better cabbages than neatly weeded patches. Even a layer of mulch will harbour more insects than bare soil.

There are some 350 species of ground beetles in Britain and over 1000 rove beetles. Both the adults and the grubs (larvae) are predators. Although they usually feed at ground level, they will climb up into plants to eat aphids.

Avoid using soil insecticides, which kill the predators as well as the pests and can actually increase pest problems in some instances.

Ground beetles overwinter in rough grass, so leave an area uncut near the vegetable patch in autumn.

Tolerate a little untidiness in your garden, then with a little luck these ground insects will become permanent residents.

SPIDERS

All our native species of spiders are predators, including their relatives, the harvestmen. They don't always prey on pests, however, and sometimes devour other predators. They certainly do no harm and are beneficial in that they in turn provide food for robins, wrens and other garden friends. The best way to encourage spiders is by leaving the natural debris that builds up under the hedges. Dead leaves and twigs constitute the perfect habitat for spiders and a whole host of insects, which will ensure a healthy population of birds and small mammals.

ENCOURAGING NATURAL PEST EATERS: AMPHIBIANS AND REPTILES

FROGS, TOADS AND NEWTS

Frogs, toads and newts are all useful predators, preying on slugs, flies and other insects. Although frogs and toads will spend much of their life on dry land, they all need water in which to breed.

A pond need not be elaborate, but it should provide the right conditions. Choose a sunny site, away from overhanging trees. The sides should slope to allow easy access for young frogs – and remember that fish will eat some of the tadpoles.

STARTING A POND
Building a pond, even a small one made from an old kitchen sink, will benefit much of garden wildlife. When choosing a site, bear in mind that young frogs and toads need to escape quickly into cover or they may be picked off by birds. Leave some overgrown areas nearby, and make sure the planting comes right up to the water's edge.

A formal pond can be adapted for wildlife, but the ideal shape is one with a deep

A wildlife pond makes an attractive feature as well as encouraging predators such as frogs, birds and bats

centre (at least 60cm/2ft) that won't freeze in winter, and shallow, gently sloping margins. If possible, make a marshy area on one side.

PLANTS FOR THE POND
The best time for planting up a pond is in the spring. Don't line the pond with soil, as this can act as a fertiliser and cause the pond to become rapidly overgrown. Put the plants in large, soil-filled containers (about 20cm/10in square) or purpose-made plastic pond baskets lined with hessian; cover with gravel to keep the soil in place. Lower the plants gently into place but avoid squeezing too many into a small space.

Make sure you include a wide range of species and plenty of oxygenating plants. Algae is often a problem in the first year and must not be allowed to form a thick mat. Pond snails are effective algae-eaters, but also eat the plants.

Submerged oxygenating plants like curl pondweed, water

starwort and hornwort are useful but avoid Canadian pondweed as it tends to be invasive.

Put in plants at all levels. Water violets and flowering rush have their lower stems and roots submerged but their flowers will appear out of the water.

At the edge of the pond plant water forget-me-not, yellow flag iris and water mint (though the last can be invasive). Native marsh marigolds, meadowsweet and purple loosestrife will thrive on marshy areas around the pond.

WHERE TO GET FROGSPAWN
If you have a pond but no spawn, your local wildlife trust may be able to help. It will probably operate a frogspawn swop in spring, putting you in touch with other gardeners who may have too many breeding frogs. Don't take spawn from the countryside, as some species are already in decline. For a list of local wildlife trusts write to the Royal Society for Nature Conservation (address on page 138).

CONSTRUCTING A POND FOR WILDLIFE

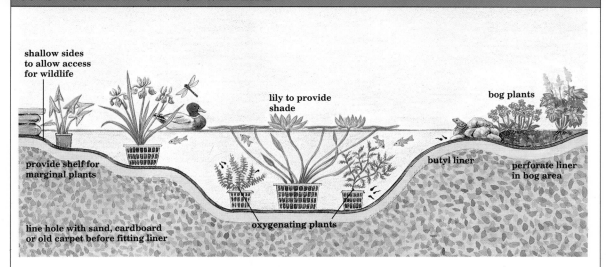

shallow sides
to allow access
for wildlife

lily to provide
shade

bog plants

provide shelf for
marginal plants

butyl liner

perforate liner
in bog area

line hole with sand, cardboard
or old carpet before fitting liner

oxygenating plants

The best way to make a pond is using a flexible butyl liner. These are easier to install than pre-formed models and allow you to choose the exact size and shape you require. To calculate how much liner you will need, use this formula: width=twice depth, plus pond width and 30cm (12in). Length=twice depth, plus pond length and 30cm (12in).

Excavating the pond
Mark out the shape using a rope or washing line. Dig out the soil, making a shelf for marginal plants at 20–23cm (8–9in) below the water level. Remove a 30cm (12in) wide strip of turf around

the edge of the pond to form a shallow trough. Hammer pegs in around the inside edge, making sure they are level, and shovel wet sand around them to form a ridge.

Filling
Line the excavation with wet sand, wet cardboard or old carpet, then use a butyl liner. Weight the edges with bricks or rocks and slowly fill the pond with tap water.

Cut off any surplus liner using a knife or scissors. The grass turves removed earlier can be used to disguise the edge of the liner. To give the pond a head start, add a bucketful of mud and water from an established pond – it will provide a food

source for mini-creatures such as water spiders, damsel and dragonfly nymphs.

The bog garden
A bog garden or marshy area adjacent to the pond is a useful addition for wildlife. It also allows a range of marsh-loving native plants to be grown, such as marsh woundwort. Divide it from the main pond by a raised ridge just below the water level. Hollow out the area to around 20cm (8in) deep and line it as for the pond. Make small holes in the liner and fill with a mixture of soil and coconut fibre instead of water.

A SIMPLE POND FROM A BARREL
Even a half-barrel or ceramic sink sunk into the ground can make a simple pond area. If you can also incorporate a shallow area with rocks, birds will use it to take a bath.

SLOW-WORMS

Although slow-worms, which reach a length of 30cm (12in), look like small snakes, they are

in fact legless lizards. They are distinguishable from snakes because, unlike real snakes, they blink. They are not poisonous and their favourite food is the grey-white slugs that eat vegetables and young perennials. They prefer a sunny garden, and spend their time under flat stones, in dry-stone walls and in the compost heap.

Slow-worms hibernate from October to March and breed from mid-August to mid-September. They may nest and breed in the compost heap, so either provide an alternative site of leaf litter or a wood pile, or avoid turning the compost until the breeding season is over.

ENCOURAGING NATURAL PEST EATERS: MAMMALS

HEDGEHOGS

Hedgehogs are much more common in gardens than we imagine, usually visiting unseen under cover of darkness. They travel large distances searching for food, and several may visit your garden in the course of a night. Hedgehogs are worth encouraging as they eat caterpillars, beetles, grubs and slugs, although not in great numbers.

There are two ways in which you encourage hedgehogs to come into the garden, first by offering a regular supply of food, particularly in the autumn when they are fattening up for their winter hibernation. Tinned pet food is ideal – bread is not good for them.

The second way to encourage hedgehogs is by ensuring that their natural habitats are undisturbed and the garden is free from danger. During the day (and when they hibernate, from November to March) they like to crawl under a garden shed, a thick hedge or into a pile of leaves or logs. Leave these areas alone, particularly in winter. Always check a bonfire before lighting it – a hibernating hedgehog may have climbed in, and many are killed in this way every year.

The garden can be a minefield of potential hazards to hedgehogs. Empty food tins can be lethal, so keep the dustbin well secured. A steep-sided pond has been known to cause drowning, so make sure there is a

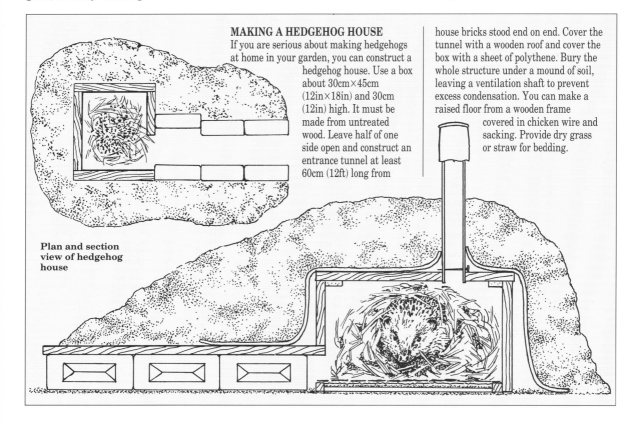

MAKING A HEDGEHOG HOUSE
If you are serious about making hedgehogs at home in your garden, you can construct a hedgehog house. Use a box about 30cm×45cm (12in×18in) and 30cm (12in) high. It must be made from untreated wood. Leave half of one side open and construct an entrance tunnel at least 60cm (12ft) long from house bricks stood end on end. Cover the tunnel with a wooden roof and cover the box with a sheet of polythene. Bury the whole structure under a mound of soil, leaving a ventilation shaft to prevent excess condensation. You can make a raised floor from a wooden frame covered in chicken wire and sacking. Provide dry grass or straw for bedding.

Plan and section view of hedgehog house

shallow shelf or slipway to enable them to climb out again. If you use netting on fruit cages, check it regularly to make sure hedgehogs have not become entangled in it.

Finally, don't use slug pellets if you can avoid them. Hedgehogs can't tell the difference between a poisoned and a healthy slug.

BATS

Many species of bats in Britain are on the decline. They need all the help they can get from householders and gardeners. All British bats eat large numbers of insects, including many pests like aphids and mosquitoes. However, bats are quite difficult to encourage unless they are already resident in the area: one way to find out is to put up some bat boxes and see if any bats roost in them.

Bats are protected by law, and it is an offence to disturb them in any way. If you need to treat loft timbers for woodworm or rot or do any work in the roof which might disturb any bats, you should contact the local office of the Nature Conservancy Council. The Council will give advice if you want to go on offering the bats a home *or* if you want them removed.

Bats live in colonies and have very particular requirements. During the day they need a warm place in which to roost; they feed at dusk. They prefer to live in holes in old trees but have adapted well to human habitations. Pipistrelles and brown long-eared bats are now just as likely to be found in modern houses, hanging from rafters or under loose tiles or fascia boards.

MAKING A BAT BOX

If you decide to put up a bat box, bear in mind that you may need two: one south-facing for the summer, when each female will raise a single young, and one facing north for hibernation in winter. Site the boxes on a tree trunk or under the eaves of the house at least 1.5m (5ft) and preferably over 5m (15ft) above the ground.

A bat box should be made from untreated wood, roughened on the back wall so that the bats can cling on to the wood. The entrance slit should run the width of the box and the lid should be removable for cleaning.

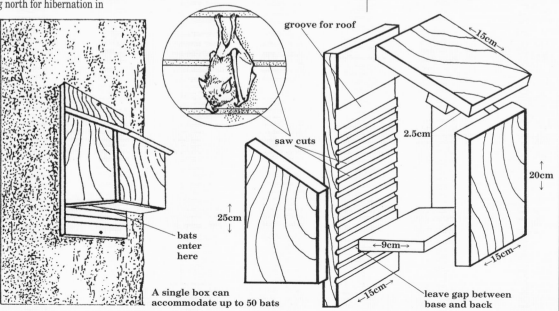

groove for roof

15cm

2.5cm

20cm

saw cuts

25cm

←9cm→

15cm

bats enter here

15cm

leave gap between base and back

A single box can accommodate up to 50 bats

ENCOURAGING NATURAL PEST EATERS: BIRDS

THE MAIN PEST EATERS

Making the garden a haven for birds will ensure that they are always around to keep down the number of pests. Helping them to survive the winter and providing places in which they can rear their young is crucial if they are to take up permanent residence. They, in turn, will forage for themselves all summer long, eating aphids and slugs, keeping pest population down. Although they all have a part to play, the birds listed here are some of the most effective predators.

SONG THRUSHES
Song thrushes build their nests from twigs among dense vegetation. Bushy conifers, hedges, climbers and evergreen wall shrubs provide suitable sites. Allow the plants to get overgrown.

Thrushes feed at ground level on worms, but will eat snails in dry weather when the worms move deeper into the soil. In autumn they eat berries. They are particularly vulnerable to slug pellets and worm killers, so don't use them.

BLUE TITS
Blue tits can be easily encouraged to use a nesting-box, as they naturally nest in small holes in trees. Make sure the box is sited 2–5m (7–16ft) above the ground

Blue tits are specialist caterpillar eaters and swallow up aphids and aphids' eggs. With their sharp needle-like beaks they can even get at leaf miner grubs inside holly leaves. Blue tits can raise 8 to 10 young at a time, so they need a great deal of insect food: don't spray cater-pillars and aphids on sight. In summer there is no better predator for these pests.

HOUSEMARTINS, SWIFTS AND SWALLOWS
You don't really need to encourage these birds – they will find your garden as long as there are plenty of insects. They hunt by sight, homing in on individual aphids and midges. Each adult bird accounts for several thousand flying insects a day.

Housemartins usually make their nests out of mud, beneath the eaves of houses. A large pond with muddy margins will provide nesting material and a supply of insects.

Swallows prefer to nest in outbuildings with open sides. Providing nesting-boxes under eaves may well persuade them to take up residence and return year after year.

PLANTS TO ENCOURAGE BIRDS
As most birds are either insect-, seed- or berry-eaters, it makes sense to grow as many plants as possible that either attract insects or produce large seedheads and berries.

Native British trees support a large number of insects and grubs. For large gardens, oak and willow are the best while smaller gardens can support birch, crabapple and rowan. A mixed native hedge of hawthorn, blackthorn, hazel and dog rose serves two functions for birds: they will build nests there if the hedge is sturdy and thick, and the berries and insects will provide a rich source of food. To encourage a bushy hedge, cut back hard in late winter before the spring nesting season gets under way.

Most birds will eat berries in autumn, so plant berberis, pyracantha, viburnum and cotoneaster; some climbers like ivy and honeysuckle also produce berries. Elder-berries are popular with all garden birds.

Large seedheads like the sunflower are a favourite with greenfinches and you could grow a short row of plants to provide winter food. Goldfinches will go for the seeds of Michaelmas daisies and golden rod. Bull-finches like forget-me-not, wallflower, snapdragon and pansy seeds. You can also collect the seeds of thistle, dock and honesty to make your own bird food.

BIRDS MOST LIKELY TO VISIT YOUR GARDEN	
BIRD	*WHAT THEY EAT*
Blue tit	caterpillars, aphids, leaf miners
Blackbird	worms, berries
Robin	berries, seeds, worms, spiders
Starling	worms, grubs
House sparrow	insects, seeds
Great tit	insects
Hedge sparrow	insects, seeds
Greenfinch	seeds, especially sunflowers
Wren	spiders, insects
Song thrush	worms, snails, slugs

Right Great tit feeding on nuts in winter

FEEDING BIRDS IN WINTER

If you want to encourage birds to eat pests it's best to stop putting out food for them from May onwards. However, regular feeding in winter will help them survive the bad weather when natural food is scarce.

Once you start feeding you must continue, as the birds come to depend on it. Try to put out small amounts twice a day, in early morning and early evening, from November onwards. In winter it's vital to give water when ponds and streams freeze.

The platform of a bird table will be used by ground-feeding birds like blackbirds and thrushes, but scatter food on the ground as well. A hanging feeder will attract tits and finches, which normally feed in trees and shrubs. Fat and peanuts attract blue tits and great tits, while bullfinches and greenfinches prefer seeds. Some grated cheese may entice a wren to feed.

Inevitably, you will attract birds like sparrows and finches that also feed on buds and berries, so it's a wise precaution to protect fruit trees with netting. Overall, the birds you nurture through the winter will become the summer's predators.

BIRDCAKE RECIPE
Ingredients Two parts cake, bread, seeds, nuts, dried fruit, cereal, kitchen scraps; one part melted fat, suet or dripping.
Method Mix well and pour into a suitable mould such as a bowl, yoghurt carton or an empty coconut shell and leave to cool. Tip out on to bird table or hang up coconut shell.

THE IDEAL BIRD TABLE
A bird table is the best way in which to feed garden birds, offering protection from cats and dogs but allowing you to watch the birds easily.

Site the table in an open position with about 1.8m (6ft) space on all sides. This will ensure that cats cannot hide among nearby plants, but that the plants will be near enough to provide cover for some of the shy species.

The best designs have a platform at least 60cm (2ft) square, with beading around the edge to stop the food falling off. Leave gaps in the beading for water to drain away. The post should be smooth and stout, and it's a good idea to put an inverted biscuit tin near the top of the pole to deter cats and squirrels from raiding the platform. The platform should be open-sided so that the birds can watch for danger. It doesn't need a roof; although a roof might keep the food dry it can hinder your view of the birds.

Ideally, the bird table should include a hanging feeder to attract acrobatic birds like tits and finches.

A roof is not essential, but a hanging container for food will add interest

Beading around the edge of the platform helps stop food blowing off the edge

An inverted biscuit tin near the top of the pole will help stop squirrels stealing the food

Right A family of blue tits can consume a lot of aphids and caterpillars

NESTING SITES

The loss of many trees in the storms of 1987 and since have deprived many hole-nesting birds of their natural nesting sites. Likewise, the 150,000 miles of hedgerow lost since the Second World War has forced hedgerow and woodland-edge birds to seek new homes in gardens. In towns as well as country areas, private gardens are the last refuge for some nest-building birds. It is important to create a range of habitats, both man-made and natural, for birds to choose from. Tits and nuthatches will nest in small holes in trees but are easy to attract into nesting-boxes, provided the box is at the right height and safe from cats; in late summer they may abandon the garden for nearby woodland, but are sure to return to feed in winter and to nest the following year.

Robins prefer a more open site and can be found nesting in open-sided outbuildings. They need a special open-fronted nesting-box (see below) situated 1–2m (3–7ft) above the ground. The box should be well concealed by vegetation – on a wall or fence covered with ivy or honeysuckle, for example.

Blackbirds build their own nests from twigs, but you can help by ensuring there are dense hedges or conifers for them to nest in. Thrushes too favour conifers or dense evergreens for nesting. More unusual birds like the goldcrests are attracted by conifers and may build a nest if several tall trees are planted together. Wrens will also use the garden provided there is plenty of ground cover, particularly shrubs and heather. They build their nests low down, from ground level to about 2m (7ft), and favour mature climbers.

Try not to disturb potential nesting sites in spring and early summer. If you are keen to identify birds' nests, the best time to look is in winter. The materials and the shape of the nest, as well as its height above ground, will give some strong clues to the identity of the builder.

MAKING A NESTING-BOX

Follow the diagram to make a nesting-box for small birds like blue tits and nuthatches, using wood about 2cm (¾in) thick.

It is important to make the hole the right size and in the right place. It should be at least 12.5cm (5in) from the floor and measure 25mm in diameter for blue tits, 28mm for great tits and 32mm for nuthatches. If the box is for robins, leave the front open except for a 9cm (4½in) high piece of wood attached at the base.

Fix the box securely to a tree or post facing east or south-east, away from direct sun and rain. The box should be 2–5m (7–16ft) above ground level for blue tits and great tits, 1m (3ft) for coal tits, and 4–5m (13–16ft) for nuthatches.

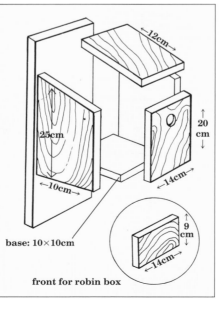

base: 10×10cm

front for robin box

PAPIER MACHE MARTINS' NEST

You can make an artificial nest for house martins out of papier mâché, using a shallow bowl as a mould. Paint the outside with a waterproof paint, and glue to a board. Fix in place with screws.

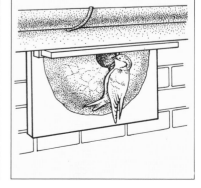

CHAPTER ELEVEN

WEED CONTROL

With a bit of careful planning you can create a virtually weed-free garden without ever resorting to chemical weedkillers.

Many weeds can be dealt with simply by regular hoeing or hand weeding, but to cut down on time and effort it pays to make as much use as possible of mulches and ground-cover plants: their effectiveness will depend on the type of weeds and where they are growing. For advice on dealing with the most troublesome weeds, turn to page 92.

KEEPING WEEDS OUT

Avoid introducing weeds with new garden plants. The compost with plants from garden centres and nurseries often contains weeds, especially hairy bittercress, as well as weed seeds and roots. As a precaution, remove and dispose of the top few centimetres of soil before planting container-grown plants.

Organic materials like manure and compost used as a mulch can also contain lots of weeds and are often better dug into the soil.

If creeping weeds like couch grass and bindweed keep invading from next door, dig every bit out of your soil and then insert a strip of heavy duty polythene at least 15cm (6in) deep along the fence line to stop the invaders. Ideally, also mulch the first 30cm (12in) or so in front of the fence to help prevent any weeds from creeping unseen into your borders.

DEALING WITH WEEDS

Hoeing
Hoeing is a very effective way of dealing with annual weeds. It should be done as soon as possible after they emerge to avoid competition and prevent them from setting seed. Keep the blade of the hoe sharp and run it just below soil level to sever the weeds. Whenever possible, hoe when the soil is dry so that any weed seeds brought to the surface won't germinate.

Some annual weeds produce thousands of seeds per plant. They can remain dormant for many years and germinate when brought to the surface by digging. A no-dig system, as described in Chapter 12, will ensure they stay buried.

Digging
Perennial weeds are best dug up. They are difficult to control by any other method. Many spread by means of creeping stems or roots, and new plants can grow from small fragments, so you have to remove every bit to eliminate the weed completely.

Weeds with deep taproots, like dandelions, will also re-grow unless you carefully lever out at least the top two-thirds of the root. Digging among established plants may be impossible, so you may have to resort to repeated hoeing. You need to be determined and persistent to kill them. Remove new growth every time it reaches 5–10cm (2–4in).

Mulching
Mulching can effectively suppress annual weeds and has other benefits, such as conserving soil moisture. Existing perennial weeds will find their way through or round most mulches, so they need to be dug out first. To find out how to use mulches successfully, turn to the next page.

Ground cover
Ground cover can be invaluable for cutting down the amount of weeding, especially in areas that are difficult to cultivate. It is essential to remove perennial weeds before planting. Advice on choosing and using suitable ground cover plants is given on pages 90 and 91.

WEED CONTROL: MULCHES

USING MULCHES

Mulches can virtually eliminate weeds, or can make the problem much worse. It is important to use them properly and to choose the right mulch for your purpose (see Table).

■ CHOOSING A MULCH

To suppress weeds, all you need to do is to apply material which excludes light. But, depending on the material you choose, a mulch can also add nutrients, protect or warm the soil, conserve moisture or even provide an attractive visual foil for plants. Mulches can also be used to keep ground-level crops like strawberries clean or to protect overwintering plants.

The one drawback of all mulches is that they can provide hiding-places for slugs, so make sure you protect young plants.

The merits and disadvantages of different mulches are compared opposite.

■ BEFORE YOU MULCH

Remove all perennial weeds first, as most will grow through mulches other than old carpet, heavy duty black polythene and woven polypropylene. It's also worth hoeing out annuals. Apply fertilisers and water in before mulching – it is difficult to feed later.

■ APPLYING A MULCH

Mulch in late winter or early spring to control weeds and conserve moisture. If you don't want to have to water in summer, apply the mulch when the soil is thoroughly moist or give it a good soaking beforehand.

Mulch generously, covering 30cm (12in) on either side of

Bark mulches are effective and attractive

rows of vegetables, or 60cm (2ft) around trees and shrubs. Cover the whole of herbaceous borders.

Leave a gap of at least 5cm (2in) around the base of stems if you are using grass clippings,

MATERIALS TO AVOID

Straw can be a cheap mulch for shrub borders on heavy soil. In other situations it can be more trouble than it's worth. It tends to get blown around, it only partially controls weeds, and may actually contain weed seeds. Straw uses up nitrogen from the soil as it breaks down and, if it contains herbicide residues, can even damage sensitive plants like sweet peas and tomatoes.

Grass clippings, manure and particularly garden compost can also contain weed seeds. Although they supply nutrients and help conserve moisture, other mulches are more effective where weed control is the prime concern.

Peat is a poor mulch as it tends to dry out and blow away. As peat is a finite resource, it is best to avoid using it altogether.

manure, partly decomposed compost or straw, all of which can heat up and scorch the plants.

Organic mulches have usually fulfilled their purpose by late summer or early autumn. They can then be forked in or left for the worms to carry under ground.

■ PLANTING THROUGH MULCHES

To plant through a polythene mulch, cut cross-shaped slits and roll back the polythene. Plant using a trowel or dibber.

Planting through a black polythene mulch

MULCHES COMPARED

■ **BLACK POLYTHENE**
Black polythene provides very effective and inexpensive weed control. It's also one of the best mulches for conserving water.

This is an ideal mulch for vegetables like tomatoes and sweet corn, which can be planted through slits, and for fruit trees and bushes. It is not attractive enough to use for ornamentals unless disguised with bark or gravel.

Lay it on smooth, slightly sloping ground to prevent puddles collecting, or make small drainage holes with a fork. Weigh down the edges or push them into the soil.

■ **WOVEN POLYPROPYLENE**
This is more expensive than black polythene but may last for five or more years. It is easier to handle and can be used in the same way as polythene. It stops weeds growing but lets water through.

■ **GRASS CLIPPINGS**
Fresh grass clippings can keep down weeds as long as they themselves are weed-free. If you treat your lawn with weedkiller, do not use clippings from the next two mows.

Use clippings between bedding plants in layers no thicker than 2.5cm (1in), keeping them away from the stems. They can also be useful for vegetables, though you may need to apply fertiliser for shallow-rooted crops to compensate for the nitrogen lost as the grass rots down.

■ **BARK**
Bark chippings are attractive and easy to use, but expensive.

WHICH MULCH TO USE WHERE

ORNAMENTALS

Bulbs	Protect tender bulbs in winter with a 15cm (6in) layer of bark chippings
Herbaceous borders	Use a 5–7.5cm (2–3in) layer of bark chippings or well-rotted manure (if you are sure it does not contain too many weed seeds)
Trees and shrubs	Use a 90cm (3ft) square of black polythene or carpet. Cut a slit to fit around the trunk and disguise with soil or bark chippings. Most beneficial in first few years while the plants are getting established
Rock gardens	Pea-sized gravel or chippings (granite for acid-loving plants, limestone for others), 5–7.5cm (2–3in) deep. Keeps base of the plants dry and leaves off the soil. Controls weeds, conserves moisture and keeps roots cool

VEGETABLES

Vegetables in rows	Use strips of black polythene or carpet between rows
Large vegetables	Plant through black polythene to conserve moisture and control weeds. With potatoes, it also saves earthing up. Alternatively, place squares of carpet around the plants
Winter storage of root crops	Cover rows in November with 10–15cm (4–6in) of straw, then black polythene to keep out the frost and rain and exclude light

FRUIT

Individual trees	Use a 90cm (3ft) square of black polythene or carpet
Bushes or canes in rows	Use strips of black polythene or woven polypropylene. Cut a slit to fit the polythene or carpet around the trunk
Strawberries	Black polythene between rows will keep fruit clean, conserve moisture and control weeds. The only disadvantage is that the mulch can get hot and damage the fruit in very hot weather. Ideally, cover black polythene with a sheet of white polythene to prevent this. Apply after the soil has warmed up

To control weeds, spread the bark at least 5cm (2in) deep and replenish the mulch each spring. They are generally trouble-free, though they may attract fouling cats, and birds may scatter the pieces. Bark can deplete the nitrogen in the top layer of soil, so apply a light sprinkling of hoof and horn before applying bark around shallow-rooted plants.

■ **GRAVEL**
Gravel provides a perfect foil for foliage plants. It can help to suppress weeds, but is more effective if you lay it on top of thick, black polythene. Spike the polythene to make drainage holes and cut slits to plant through. Gravel also conserves moisture.

If you are going to walk on the gravel frequently, remove the top 8cm (3in) of soil and replace it with ballast from a builder's merchant. This stops the gravel working its way into the soil. Plant before laying the gravel, making holes through the ballast.

■ **OLD CARPET**
Carpet is easy to use and very effective at controlling weeds. It may last two or more years. Use a sharp knife to cut slits in it for planting. You won't need to weigh or peg it down.

WEED CONTROL: GROUND COVER

Below left Cotoneaster dammeri
Below right Vinca major
'Variegata'
Bottom Erica carnea 'Vivellii'
with Erica erigena 'Golden Lady'

Ground-cover plants prevent weeds growing by competing for light, water and nutrients. But to control weeds successfully, you must choose the right plants and prepare the ground properly. Ground cover needs little maintenance, and most kinds should last at least ten years before replanting is necessary. How long it takes to establish depends on the vigour of the plants, how closely you plant them and the conditions in your garden. For complete cover in a year, use the 'quick' planting distance shown in the Table opposite.

WHAT MAKES GOOD GROUND COVER

A good ground-cover plant is one that covers the ground quickly and withstands invasion by weeds. But plants that are too vigorous for the situation soon become weeds themselves.

If planting different species next to each other, choose plants of equal vigour, otherwise one will take over and suppress the other.

PREPARING THE SITE

Ground cover will have little or no effect on existing perennial weeds, except to get in the way of effective control. They must be eliminated by digging before you plant.

As the ground-cover plants will take at least a year to form complete cover, be prepared to hand weed among the plants until they are established. To cut down on work, it's worth applying a bark mulch around the ground cover for the first year. Planting in autumn will also give the ground cover a head start against the weeds which emerge in spring.

CUTTING COSTS

To economise, you can plant further apart – see the 'budget' planting distances in the Table.

This will give you cover in two or three years. To cut costs further, you may be able to raise your own plants.

GOOD GROUND COVER SHRUBS

PLANT [1]	FOLIAGE [2]	FLOWERS	QUICK PLANTING DISTANCE [3]	COST A SQ M [4]	BUDGET PLANTING DISTANCE [3]	COST A SQ M [4]
Calluna vulgaris 'Gold Haze' [5]	gold (E)	white, Aug/Sep	30cm	£	45cm	£
Calluna vulgaris 'Robert Chapman' [5]	gold, turning orange/red (E)	purple, Aug/Sep	30cm	£	45cm	£
Cotoneaster dammeri	dark green, glossy (E)	white, Jun	50–60cm	£	60–105cm	£
Cotoneaster salicifolius 'Gnom'	sage green, narrow (E)	white, Jun	45–50cm	££	75–100cm	£
Cotoneaster salicifolius 'Repens'	mid-green, narrow (E)	white, Jun	40–50cm	£	50–60cm	£
Erica carnea 'Myretoun Ruby' [6]	dark green (E)	rose-pink, Feb–Apr	30–40cm	£	40cm	£
Erica carnea 'Vivellii' [6]	light green, turning red (E)	pink or red, Nov–May	30cm	£	40–50cm	£
Erica carnea 'Winter Beauty'	green (E)	rose-pink, Dec onwards	30–40cm	£	60–75cm	£
Euonymus fortunei 'Emerald 'n' Gold'	green/gold edges (E)	—	25–40cm	££	45–60cm	£
Gaultheria procumbens [5]	dark green (E)	white, mainly Jul/Aug	25–30cm	£££	40–60cm	£
Hedera colchica 'Dentata Variegata'	dark green, cream edges (E)	—	60–90cm	£	1.5–1.8m	£
Hypericum calycinum	green (E)	yellow, Jun/Oct	15–75cm	£	30–100cm	£
Juniperus horizontalis 'Glauca'	grey-green (E)	—	30–40cm	£££	45–60cm	££
Juniperus × media 'Old Gold'	golden (E)	—	45–75cm	£	75–100cm	£
Juniperus sabina 'Tamariscifolia'	grey-green (E)	—	45cm	££	75–100cm	£
Juniperus squamata 'Blue Carpet'	blue (E)	—	90cm	£	150cm	£
Pachysandra terminalis and P.t. 'Variegata' [5]	green, white edges (E)	white, Apr	30–45cm	£	40–90cm	£
Rubus tricolor	dark above, white beneath (E)	small, white, Jul	15–120cm	£	60–180cm	£
Sarcococca humilis	shiny, dark green (E)	tiny, white, scented, Feb/Mar	40–45cm	££	60–105cm	£
Vaccinium vitis-idaea	glossy, dark green (E)	white or pink, bell-shaped, May/Jun	30–50cm	££	60–75cm	£
Vinca major 'Variegata'	cream edges (E)	bright blue, Apr/Jun	50cm	£	100cm	£
Vinca minor	glossy, dark green (E)	bright blue, Mar/Jul	50cm	£	100–200cm	£
Vinca minor 'Variegata'	green, creamy edges (E)	purple-blue, Mar/Jul	45cm	£	60cm	£

Notes
Metric conversion 5cm=2in
[1] **Common names**
If you are not familiar with Latin names, the following list may help: *Calluna* and *Erica*, heathers; *Hedera*, ivy; *Hypericum calycinum*, rose of Sharon, Aaron's beard; *Vaccinium*, cowberry, mountain cranberry; *Vinca*, periwinkle
[2] D=deciduous
E=evergreen

[3] **Planting distances**
'Quick' should form complete cover within a year. Some may need thinning out after three years
'Budget' should form complete cover in two or three years, and should need no thinning
[4] £ =inexpensive
££ =moderately expensive
£££=very expensive
[5] Needs acid soil
[6] Tolerates up to pH7.8 but best on acid soils

WEED CONTROL: PROBLEM WEEDS

Field bindweed
This weed twists around garden plants. The roots can go down over 6m (20ft) and creep horizontally, producing new plants as they go. Unwrap the stems from garden plants in spring and dig up the roots. Remaining fragments generally don't re-grow. If you can't dig, cut off the shoots regularly at ground level to control the weed.

Hedge bindweed
This is similar to field bindweed but doesn't root very deeply. The brittle, white stems creep long distances above and below ground. Dig them out, removing every fragment – each one can produce a new plant. Where you can't dig, cut off new shoots repeatedly to weaken the weed.

Brambles
Old plants have deep, woody roots, and prostrate stems can also take root. Cut back the top growth and dig deeply to remove the woody roots.

Chickweed
Chickweed seeds can survive in the soil for up to 40 years, and can germinate at any time of the year. Hoe as soon as seedlings appear. If they become established, dig up the whole weed before it seeds.

Cleavers
Cleavers produces bristly seeds, which attach themselves to clothing and get carried around the garden. It is easy to control by hoeing young plants in winter or early spring. Dig up older plants. The stems are brittle and will break easily if you try to pull them up.

Couch grass
Couch has very vigorous underground stems with sharp points that can bore through the roots of garden plants. The stems can grow several metres in all

directions, bearing buds along their length, and each segment can produce a new plant. You can control couch grass by digging it up, then repeatedly hoeing as soon as one or two new leaves spring up.

Creeping buttercup
Vigorous stems creep along the surface, producing many new plants. One plant can cover 4sq m (40sq ft) a year. Dig out the weed, tracing all the runners. Do not let it seed. Once under control, a mulch should prevent further problems.

Dandelions
Dandelions have a long taproot going down 15cm (6in) or more. Hoeing is useless as each tiny piece of root left behind can produce a new plant. Hand weed before plants have a chance to establish, removing every bit of root. Getting rid of larger plants will need extensive digging. Never let plants seed. Each one can produce over 5000 seeds a year.

Ground elder
White, underground stems creep up to 90cm (3ft) a year in all directions. Dig out and remove every bit of stem – each can produce a new plant.

Hairy bittercress
This annual weed is often introduced into gardens with container-grown plants. Each weed produces around 600 seeds a year, and an explosive mechanism scatters them around the garden. Never let the plant set seed. It is easy to control by hoeing or hand weeding, and a mulch will also suppress it.

Horsetail
Thin, black stems can go down several metres and creep in all directions under ground. Repeated hoeing and digging may eventually weaken the plant. For more effective control, cover affected areas with black polythene or pieces of carpet for a year or two.

Japanese knotweed
The shoots of this weed are so tough they can crack paving-stones. Its stems spread under ground. Control by cutting back to ground level regularly. To remove it requires excavating down to about 1.8m (6ft), but it's worth digging out the edges of the clump to prevent it spreading.

Oxalis – pink flowered
Each plant produces many tiny, fleshy, pinky-brown bulbils – sometimes hundreds – just below ground level. The bulbils can survive for years in the soil. They are scattered about the garden when you hoe, dig or pull up the weed. Disturb the soil as little as possible to avoid spreading them. When the plants are just forming leaves, the bulbils are firmly attached, so dig up the plant carefully.

Stinging nettles
Nettles do not root deeply but produce lots of seeds and send stems creeping along the surface. Cut the plants to ground level and dig out the roots. Fragments left will not grow again.

CHAPTER TWELVE

IMPROVING YOUR SOIL

WHAT TYPE OF SOIL?

You need to know what sort of soil you've got before you can improve it. To identify your soil type, take a small sample, moisten it, then try the tests shown on the right.		**1** Can it be rolled into a ball?	 **2** Does it look polished when rubbed?	 **3** Can it be rolled into a cylinder?	**4** Can cylinder be bent into a ring?
	Texture				
Sand	gritty	no	no	no	no
Sandy loam	gritty	yes	no	no	no
Sandy clay loam	gritty/sticky	yes	yes	yes	no
Clay loam	sticky	yes	yes	yes	no
Clay	sticky	yes	yes	yes	yes
Silt	smooth/silky	yes	slightly	yes	slightly
Peat	dark, fibrous	yes	no	no	no

The ideal soil for most plants is a well-drained, sandy, clay loam. But as few of us are blessed with this type of soil, how can you improve on what you've got?

Clay soils
Clay soils are usually very fertile but difficult to work. They are like concrete in summer and glue in winter. It's best to adapt your gardening techniques and take steps to improve the soil by adding plenty of organic matter and sand – see pages 99–101.

Sandy soils
Sandy soils are easy to cultivate but often have low fertility because nutrients are readily washed out.

The most effective thing you can do is to add a lot of organic matter to increase fertility and improve water retention. Other suggestions for improving this type of soil are given on page 106.

Silty soils
The surface of silty soils is prone to compaction and a hard crust may form, but this type of soil is generally very fertile and moisture retentive. Use green manures and mulching (see pages 88 and 98) to help reduce surface compaction. You will find other suggestions on page 106.

Peaty soils
Peaty soils are warm and easy to work, but often waterlogged and boggy. They may also be short of some nutrients. Advice on dealing with them is given on page 106.

Chalky soils
If your garden is on chalk or limestone, the soil is likely to be very alkaline, and the topsoil may also be very shallow and likely to dry out quickly. It's not worth trying to change the pH,

but you can increase the depth and fertility of the soil by adding a lot of organic material. This will also improve water retention. See pages 102 and 103.

Bad drainage
Clay and peaty soils often suffer from bad drainage. You need to assess how bad it is before deciding how to tackle the problem. Instructions for determining the problem and suggestions for improving it will be found on page 104.

If you can't treat the whole garden
Improving your soil can take a lot of hard work and lorry-loads of manure and sand. A more practical solution is to concentrate on improving selected beds for choice plants. You can still have a flourishing garden if you adapt your gardening techniques to suit the conditions, and choose your plants carefully.

Saving work
You can save a lot of effort by thinking before you dig, or even

adopting a no-dig system. Using deep beds and double digging can help to overcome compaction and poor drainage.

Why does pH matter?
Soil pH is important because it affects the availability of plant nutrients. For example, some plants can't absorb iron on alkaline soils, but most of the major nutrients are less available in very acid soils. The pH depends largely on the amount of lime present. The more lime, the more alkaline the soil.

Most plants grow happily on neutral or slightly alkaline soils, but some will thrive only on acid soils and others do well only in alkaline conditions. For this reason the pH of your soil can affect your choice of plants.

To check your soil pH, see opposite page.

DIGGING

▬ IS IT WORTHWHILE?
Whether regular digging is worthwhile depends on your soil type. Regular digging can break up the natural soil structure created by plant roots and worms, and most light soils need only raking or hoeing. Organic matter can be added as a mulch and left for the worms to carry underground.

On the other hand, if your soil is heavy or compacted, digging can be very beneficial. It will break up the soil, incorporate air, and enable you to mix in organic matter to improve aeration and drainage.

Digging also exposes soil pests to the birds, and you can bury weeds and crop debris (though you will also bring a fresh batch of weed seeds to the surface).

DOUBLE DIGGING
If you have a clay soil, or one that has become very compacted, double digging should help – and it should not be necessary more frequently than every five years.

It helps because it:
- breaks up hard pans
- improves drainage
- provides extra rooting depth

- improves soils that dry out quickly by increasing water retention (assuming you add organic matter).

Dig to one spade's depth. Mix manure with the soil below, loosening it to a second spade's depth. Fill with soil from the next strip, mixing in more manure. Do not mix the upper and lower layers.

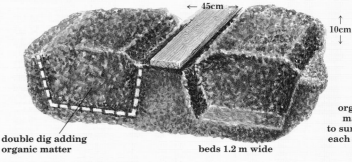

dig this soil into trench already dug (soil from first trench barrowed to fill last trench)

incorporate compost or manure

DEEP BEDS
These are beneficial on shallow and poorly drained soils, especially for early vegetables and root crops. They:

- improve drainage
- raise the temperature of the soil surface in spring
- increase the rooting zone.

← 45cm →

↕ 10cm

double dig adding organic matter

beds 1.2 m wide

add organic matter to surface each year

▬ WHEN TO DIG
Light soils can be dug at practically any time. Clay or loam is best dug in late autumn so that winter frosts can help break up the clods. On heavy soil, this may be one of the few times when conditions are suitable. Never be tempted to dig when the soil is too wet. It's hard work and damages the soil structure.

▬ HOW DEEP?
If you are going to the trouble of digging a compacted soil or clay,

it may be worth double digging. The soil is dug to the depth of two spade blades (about 50cm/20in), which breaks up the soil well and enables you to incorporate a lot of organic matter. It will break up a hard pan and also improve drainage.

After double digging, you shouldn't have to dig again for at least five years. Just fork over the soil in the autumn.

Light soils simply need raking or hoeing to prepare seedbeds.

EARTHWORMS

Earthworms are valuable creatures. They help to build the soil structure, and play a vital role in the production of humus, an important source of plant nutrients. Worms make a system of burrows, which help to aerate and drain the soil. They feed off organic material and carry it down from the surface into the soil, where it can decompose. They also bring humus to the surface in their casts, making nutrients more accessible to shallow plant roots.

The more organic material you add to your soil, the more you will encourage worms. Liming also helps because worms are more active in slightly alkaline soils.

NO-DIG SYSTEM

A no-dig system relies on digging deeply initially and incorporating a lot of organic material. You shouldn't have to dig again for at least five years if you avoid compacting the soil, so:

■ avoid walking on it, especially when it's wet
■ use a plank to spread your weight when working in borders
■ plan your vegetable garden as a system of permanent beds with paths between them.

This system not only saves a lot of work but also preserves the soil structure built up by earthworms and avoids mixing the more fertile topsoil with the subsoil.

ORGANIC MATERIAL

Most soils benefit from the addition of organic material. It will improve the structure as well as fertility, make heavy soils easier to work, and increase water retention in sandy soils.

Organic materials gradually release plant nutrients, though the amount will depend on what you are using – different materials are compared on the next two pages. It also increases the activity of earthworms and other soil organisms, which in turn release more plant nutrients.

Organic materials are usually incorporated while digging. Some need composting first. You can also apply them as a mulch, which earthworms will gradually carry down into the soil.

OTHER BULKY MATERIALS

Other materials like coarse sand or grit can be used to open up the structure of the soil. These improve both aeration and drainage and are particularly useful on heavy clay or compacted soils.

BUYING TOPSOIL

If your topsoil is very poor (perhaps your garden has recently been a building site), you may want to replace it rather than spend years trying to improve it.

This is a mammoth job and very expensive. If you can't afford to do the whole garden, it may still be worth buying enough topsoil to create a few raised beds for choice plants or crops.

Look for suppliers in Yellow Pages. Topsoil varies a lot in quality so it's important to examine it before you buy. Use the simple tests given at the beginning of this chapter to check the soil type.

The structure is the most important feature – you can always improve the fertility. Reject soil that is too sandy or that contains a lot of clay, stones or rubble. It may also be worth testing the pH. You can adjust the pH to some extent, but it is difficult to correct an alkaline soil.

pH AND LIME

You can test your soil pH using a kit available at shops and garden centres.
1 Collect soil samples from different parts of your garden at a depth of about 10cm (4in).
2 Mix thoroughly and leave to dry.
3 Add a small amount to the tube provided.
4 Add chemicals as instructed.
5 Shake, allow to settle then compare the colour with the chart.

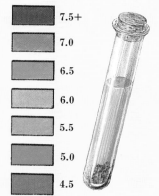

7.5+
7.0
6.5
6.0
5.5
5.0
4.5

Interpreting the results

pH 5 Very acid. Suitable only for lime-haters like heathers and azaleas. Add lime to raise pH.

pH 6 Acid. Suitable for lawns, fruit and lime-haters. For most other plants, lime regularly.

pH 6.5–7 Nuetral/slightly acid. Ideal for most plants. Don't lime.

pH 8 Alkaline. Don't lime. See pages 102 to 103 for choosing plants and dealing with an alkaline soil.

If the soil is too acid

You can increase the alkalinity by using some form of lime. Lime is usually applied in the autumn and dug in; wait until the spring on sandy soils, where the lime is readily leached out.

Clay soils need liming only every five or six years, and sandy soils every two or three years. In areas of high rainfall, lime is rapidly washed out of the soil, so apply it more often.

To raise the soil pH by one unit, use the following quantities of ground limestone. If you are using hydrated lime instead, you need only three-quarters of these amounts:

Clay	850g/sq m	1.5lb/sq yd
Loam	550g/sq m	1.0lb/sq yd
Sand	275g/sq m	0.5lb/sq yd

IMPROVING YOUR SOIL: SOIL IMPROVERS

MANURES

The term 'manures' is used here in a broad sense, to mean any organic material that can be dug into the soil to improve the structure. These bulky materials also increase water retention and some supply nutrients.

FARMYARD MANURE

This is cheap and bulky and contains some nutrients. Raw manure can damage plants so it is best stacked under cover to rot down. Avoid manure with wood shavings, or compost it first. Dig it in during the autumn or use it as a mulch in spring.

POULTRY MANURE

A very concentrated manure, high in nutrients. It can harm plants if applied direct. It is best added sparingly to the compost heap as an activator, or mixed with straw. Wet the heap and leave covered for at least two months – longer if it contains wood shavings.

STABLE MANURE

Stable manure is cheap and bulky and contains some nutrients, but it is best composted first. Raw stable manure can damage plants and usually contains a lot of wood shavings or straw, which can rob the soil of nitrogen as they decompose. Straw may also contain herbicide residues.

Use as a mulch in spring, or dig in during the autumn.

SPENT MUSHROOM COMPOST

Most mushroom composts consist of horse manure with added peat and chalk. Others are based on straw with a chemical activator. Most mushroom composts are likely to contain pesticides. The compost is fairly cheap and contains some nutrients, but is low in phosphate so you may need to supplement it with a topdressing of fishmeal or bonemeal. The chalk it contains is good for acid soils, and can help to deter clubroot from brassicas.

SPENT HOPS

These can work out cheap – or even free – if available locally. Hops are bulky and contain some nutrients, but stack and leave to rot before digging in.

STRAW

Straw is cheap but may contain weedkiller residues that can harm plants. It also can deplete the nitrogen in the soil as it rots down unless you compost it first.

CONCENTRATED MANURES

If you find it hard work shifting cartloads of manure, bagged organic concentrates might appeal to you. But organic concentrates are not bulky enough to improve the soil structure unless added in such vast quantities as to be prohibitively expensive.

Concentrated manures do contain more nutrients than bulky manures, but with many products the levels are very low when compared with fertilisers (where nutrient content has to be stated on the packaging). Many concentrated manures are a bi-product of factory farming so you may object to using them on moral grounds.

FREE SOURCES OF ORGANIC MATERIAL

GARDEN COMPOST

Compost must be made with care to kill weed seeds and diseases. It involves a lot of work and can be tricky to get right (see Chapter 13 for advice on compost-making). It contains a reasonable amount of nutrients.

GRASS CLIPPINGS

Grass clippings can be used as a mulch or dug in. They may use up nitrogen as they decompose. Do not use clippings from grass that has been treated with weedkillers or that contains weed seeds.

If used as a mulch, keep away from plant stems as they can get quite hot as the clippings rot down.

LEAFMOULD

Leafmould is low in nutrients but is a good source of bulky, organic material. In autumn fallen leaves are available in large quantities in towns as well as in rural districts. If you obtain them from your local council from parks and street sweepings, beware of dog faeces, litter and other pollutants.

Do not put lots of leaves on the compost heap. Pack them into a wire cage and leave to rot – it may take about two years. Mixing in some grass cuttings may speed up the process (see also page 114).

NEWSPAPERS

Newspapers rot rather slowly, so do not add large quantities to your compost heap. They can be used for mulching, though the paper will be inclined to blow about unless weighted down. They are also useful for protecting frost-sensitive plants in winter. Cardboard can be used in the same way and rots more readily.

SEAWEED

Washed-up seaweed, often thrown up in large quantities by winter storms, is useful provided it is not contaminated with oil. It contains lots of trace elements and variable amounts of other nutrients. There is usually a reasonable amount of phosphate and potash, but little nitrogen. Before using, wash off the salt or leave the seaweed exposed to the rain for a couple of months to avoid making your soil saline. Seaweed rots quickly so there's no need to compost it.

SAWDUST AND WOOD CHIPPINGS

These will deplete the soil of nitrogen as they decompose. Compost them with a nitrogen-rich activator such as dried blood or poultry manure before use.

NON-ORGANIC MATERIALS

Non-organic materials such as gravel are cheapest if bought from bulk suppliers. Look through the Yellow Pages under agricultural and horticultural suppliers for one in your area. Some garden centres are reasonably competitive and give discounts on large orders. Look out for those offering free delivery.

If minimum orders are too large for your needs, try sharing with friends or neighbours, or join a gardening club or allotment society to make use of bulk-buying arrangements.

CALCIFIED SEAWEED

This is an expensive alternative to garden lime for acid or clay soils. Calcified seaweed is the remains of a type of seaweed that builds up a 'skeleton'. It supplies trace elements as well as calcium.

GYPSUM

Gypsum contains calcium. It helps to improve the structure of clay soils by making the particles clump together. Unlike lime, it does not affect pH, so can be used on alkaline clays.

LIME

Liming makes soil more alkaline. This encourages earthworms which prefer a slightly alkaline pH, and makes some nutrients more available to plants. It also helps to control clubroot in brassicas. Like gypsum, lime can be used to improve clay soils.

Check the pH before you lime. If you make the soil too alkaline plants may suffer trace element deficiencies. Liming is essential on very acid soils (pH less than 5.5) where nutrients like phosphate are locked up.

SAND AND GRIT

Use only coarse, gritty sand for improving soil structure. It's cheaper at builder's merchants than garden centres. Ask for coarse, sharp sand. Take a large pinch and rub it in your palm. If you can't feel the grittiness or separate the particles, don't buy.

HOW MUCH DO YOU NEED?

Manures
Add at least one bucketful a sq m (or sq yd).

Sand
To improve the structure of clay soils, you need 1 cu m (1.7 ton) of grit or sharp sand for every 20 sq m. This is equivalent to a 5cm (2in) layer spread over the surface before digging in.

4 sq m

PEAT AND BARK

Peat and bark can be used to improve soil structure but work out very expensive. They also contain virtually no nutrients and may reduce the amount of nitrogen in the soil as they are broken down. Peat is bulky and has good water-retention capabilities, but it is a natural resource that can't be replaced and there are plenty of better alternatives that you can use.

Bark can open up the soil structure, but needs to be at least partly composted before digging in. It retains little moisture and is better used as a mulch.

IMPROVING YOUR SOIL: GREEN MANURES

Green manures are crops grown to produce bulky material for digging into the soil or adding to the compost heap. They are usually grown on spare land and cut or dug in as soon as the ground is required.

■ THE BENEFITS

■ Addition of bulky material improves soil structure
■ Growing a crop suppresses weeds
■ Covering the soil with a crop prevents it capping (a hard surface crust forming), especially in winter
■ Green manures take up nutrients and this prevents them being washed out of the soil by heavy rain. They are released again as the manure decomposes
■ Growing a crop rather than leaving the soil bare encourages beneficial earthworms and micro-organisms
■ Green manures from the pea family (legumes) add nitrogen to the soil. It is 'fixed' by their roots and released into the soil as they decompose.

■ WHAT TO DO

Rake over the plot to prepare it for sowing. Most green manure seed can be broadcast, but lupins and winter tares are usually sown in drills.

The manure can be left to grow until the land is needed, though should be dug in before it gets woody otherwise it will take a long time to decay. Tall crops can be cut first with a strimmer or shears to make the job easier.

Break up the plants well and mix with the top few inches of soil. You can use a powered cultivator, but make sure you don't bury the manure too deeply – air is needed for rapid decomposition.

GREEN MANURES COMPARED

GREEN MANURE	SOW	DIG IN	NOTES
Clover	Spring or late summer	After 2–3 months	Fixes nitrogen. Summer growth can be cut and used for mulching. 'White' variety competes well with weeds. 'Essex Red' produces masses of roots and leaves
Lupins	Apr–Jul	After 3–4 months	Fix nitrogen. Can be grown on acid infertile soils. A summer crop, so has to be fitted carefully into the rotation and cut when space is needed
Ryegrass	Jun–Oct	Spring	Good for smothering weeds. Extensive roots that benefit soil structure. Provides good soil cover in winter and further growth in spring
Winter tares	Aug/Sep	Spring	Give ground cover in winter. Fix nitrogen

OTHER PLANTS YOU CAN USE AS GREEN MANURE

Agricultural chicory	Sow at any time during the growing season. Can be difficult to get rid of
Alfalfa (lucerne)	As for chicory, above
Buckwheat	Sow May to July. Grows rapidly. Flowers attract bees and hoverflies
Fodder radish	Sow late summer. Grows very fast unless you sow it too late. Avoid if soil has clubroot
Mustard	Sow in summer. Produces lots of leaves in a few weeks. Avoid if soil has clubroot
Quick-growing vegetables	Any spare seeds of quick-growing vegetables like lettuce, turnips or radishes can be grown on to seedling stage as a green manure crop

If digging is difficult on your soil, you can kill the green manure by flattening it and then covering it with a mulch. Earthworms will gradually disperse it into the soil.

■ THE COMPOST HEAP

If the manure has become tough or woody, cut or dig up the plants and compost them. Break them up well before putting them on the compost heap.

IMPROVING YOUR SOIL: CLAY SOIL

Below Azalea mollis varieties thrive on clay providing it's lime-free

IMPROVING THE STRUCTURE

Most soils contain some clay, but problems with aeration and drainage occur when the clay content exceeds a third. The difficulty is caused by the tiny size of the clay particles, which cling tightly together, making digging very heavy work. Water is also attracted to the surface of the particles, which makes clay soils prone to waterlogging in winter and slow to dry out in spring. Clay soil also shrinks and cracks in hot dry weather.

On the plus side, nutrients are not readily washed out of clay, and established plants in clay are less prone to drought than on other soil types. To improve the structure, you need to encourage the particles to clump together in tiny lumps or crumbs. This will improve aeration and drainage and make cultivation easier. There are several ways in which you can do this.

Adding organic material and lime will help to bind the clay particles together chemically. Bulky organic materials will also help to separate tiny clay particles, though the effect will work off as the organic matter breaks down. For a more permanent improvement, dig in gritty sand to decrease the proportion of clay (see page 97).

In addition to these measures, the action of frost, worms, plant roots and digging will all help to break up the clay into more workable sized lumps.

DIGGING THE SOIL
Digging in late autumn, while the ground is still workable, can be very effective, especially if

you get heavy frosts. The timing can be crucial. If the soil is too dry, digging is impossible. If it is too wet, it will stick to everything and you may compact the soil by standing on it.

Stand on a plank to spread your weight as you dig. You may find it easier to use a fork or to dip your spade into a bucket of water between spadefuls to leave a film of water over which the clay can slide.

Applying lime
Lime and gypsum both contain calcium. This is absorbed by the clay and causes the particles to clump together. Liming alone may not significantly improve soil structure and should be used together with organic material.

Gypsum does not affect the pH of the soil, so should be used in preference if the soil is alkaline. Gypsum also reduces the salinity of the soil, so is particularly useful if the soil has been flooded by sea water.

Adding organic material
To improve clay soil, don't waste money on concentrated manures. The bulkier the material the

better. Garden compost is excellent, but you will have difficulty making enough to treat your whole garden.

Other sources of material include farmyard and stable manure and spent mushroom compost. Ideally, manure should be well rotted and crumbly. If you dig in large lumps of raw manure, it can damage plants and produce toxic chemicals as it breaks down. At the very least, make sure you break it into small pieces and mix it in well.

Apply the organic material generously, concentrating your efforts on a small area rather than spreading thinly over the whole garden. The benefits should last for several years. You will need to cultivate only the surface.

MULCHING
Use organic material for mulching if you find it too hard to dig it in. Worms will gradually carry the mulch down into the soil. In a few years the soil near the surface will be a lot easier to weed and cultivate.

Left Primula denticulata – an easy spring-flowering perennial to grow from seed

with permanent paths between them (see page 94). If you make the beds raised and dig in lots of organic matter, this will greatly improve drainage and soil structure, enabling you to grow almost any vegetable.

Seedbeds

Prepare seedbeds with the minimum of cultivation. A light raking may be all that is required if you have dug in well-rotted organic material in previous years. Digging in spring is likely only to compact the soil. Use cloches or cover the seedbed with clear polythene to warm up the soil in spring. Alternatively, raise flower and vegetable seedlings in pots or trays in a cold frame or greenhouse and transplant when soil conditions are suitable.

■ CLAY IMPROVERS

Some clay improvers are claimed to work wonders on clay soil. They contain a variety of materials such as gypsum, seaweed, fertiliser, concentrated manure and perlite.

The organic materials, gypsum and seaweed (which has a high calcium content) should have some effect by making the soil particles clump together. Others, like perlite, open up the soil structure. However, gritty sand and bulky organic matter are likely to prove a lot cheaper and more effective than any of these products.

■ LIVING WITH CLAY

You can achieve a beautiful, productive garden on clay. But to get the most out of it you must select plants that can thrive on this type of soil. See the Table opposite for some suggestions. You can grow almost any tree, as long as the soil is not boggy. If the soil is waterlogged, you will have to be more selective – see the Table on page 105.

You must also adapt your gardening techniques to suit the conditions. Dig in the autumn. In winter the soil gets too wet and sticky and digging may damage the structure.

Borders

Make the best of shrubs and hardy perennials to avoid the need for digging. Many will thrive even on the heaviest clay. They will need weeding occasionally but require very little cultivation once established. In summer they will take advantage of the nutrients and water held in the soil.

If you can apply a 10–15cm (4–6in) mulch over beds each autumn or spring, this should improve the soil sufficiently to grow bulbs and bedding plants without having to dig.

Vegetables

Cultivation is difficult to avoid in the vegetable garden because most vegetables are treated as annuals. Conditions for digging may be ideal for only very short periods, so reduce the area to be dug by creating a system of beds

---

PLANTING IN CLAY SOILS

Shrubs and trees are usually planted in the autumn. But spring planting is better on clay soils as this avoids subjecting young plants to cold, wet conditions before they are established.

Spring planting also allows you to prepare the ground well beforehand. Dig the soil roughly in autumn and leave for frosts to break down the lumps.

In spring prepare a larger hole than usual. Add plenty of organic material and sand, working them well in over an area of, say, one metre in diameter. Add one or two handfuls of bonemeal. (Don't dig a small hole and fill it with manure and sand. Water will drain into it, creating a bog.)

Sit the plant at the same height in the soil as it was originally growing. Tease the roots out before covering. When firming the soil, do not overdo it. Clay is easily compacted. Form a slight mound to allow for settlement.

Water during dry periods until the tree or shrub is established.

PLANTS FOR CLAY SOILS

	HEIGHT × SPREAD [1]	FLOWERS	FOLIAGE	REMARKS
HERBACEOUS				
Acanthus spinosus	120×60cm (4×2ft)	white/purple, Jul–Sep	spiny, dark green	striking foliage
Achillea filipendulina	90×45cm (3×1½ft)	golden yellow, Jun–Aug	grey-green, fern-like	good forms are 'Coronation Gold' and 'Moonshine'
Alchemilla mollis	45×45cm (18×18in)	lime yellow, Jun–Jul	light green, palmate	cut back after flowering
Anemone × hybrida	60–90×60cm (2–3×2ft)	pink/white, Aug–Sep	lobed, green	all varieties are worth growing
Astrantia major	60×45cm (24×18in)	greeny-pink, Jun–Aug	dense, mid-green	dense clumps of foliage, interesting 'papery' flowers
Bergenia cordifolia	45×45cm (18×18in)	pinkish-red, Mar–Apr	glossy, evergreen	many good varieties. Flowers good for cutting
Chrysanthemum maximum	75×45–60cm (30×18–24in)	white, Jun–Sep	dark green, toothed	reliable old favourite, good for cutting. Dead-head regularly
Coreopsis verticillata	60×45cm (24×18in)	yellow, Jun–Sep	bushy, finely cut	daisy-like flowers. Tight upright clumps of foliage
Epimedium × rubrum	23×30cm (9×12in)	pink, Apr–May	reddish, evergreen	cut old foliage in March to reveal flowers and young foliage
Miscanthus sinensis 'Silver Feather'	2×1m (7×3ft)	pink/brown, Sep–Oct	blue-green, white midrib	good focal point for a border. Fountain-like habit
Primula denticulata	30×30cm (12×12in)	lavender, Mar–May	dense green rosette	also white, pink and purple forms. Easy from seed
Pulmonaria	30×30cm (12×12in)	various, Mar–May	some white spotted	attractive foliage. Pink, white or blue flowers
Rudbeckia fulgida 'Goldsturm'	60×45cm (24×18in)	golden yellow, Jul–Oct	mid-green	dazzling flowers with dark brown, conical centres
Saxifraga × 'Autumn Joy'	60×45cm (24×18in)	deep pink, Sep–Oct	pale green	dead flower heads remain attractive all winter
Sidalcea	120×50cm (48×20in)	pink, Jun–Sep	mid-green	tall flower spikes above a clump of attractive foliage
Solidago 'Cloth of Gold'	50×45cm (20×18in)	golden yellow, Aug–Sep	pale green, lanceolate	less invasive than the species
SHRUBS				
Aucuba japonica	3×1.8m (10×6ft)	purple-green, Mar–Apr	shiny, evergreen	most varieties variegated; some have red berries
Azalea ('Exbury' and 'Mollis' varieties)	1–2×1.5–2.5m (3–7×5–8ft)	various, May	mid-green, deciduous	need lime-free soil – some turn orange-red in autumn
Buddleia davidii	1.5–4×1.5–2.5m (5–14×5–8ft)	various, Jul–Oct	mid-green, toothed	fragrant flowers in plume-shaped clusters. Attracts butterflies
Choisya ternata	2×2m (7×7ft)	white, Apr–May	evergreen	fragrant leaves and flowers
Cotinus coggygria	2.5–4×2.5–4m (8–14×8–14ft)	fawn, Jun–Jul	good autumn colour	'Foliis Purpureis' and 'Royal Purple' have dark, purple foliage
Cotoneaster	0.6–3×3m (2–10×10ft)	whitish-pink, May–Jun	mostly dark green	red or yellow berries. Deciduous types have good autumn colour
Euonymus	1.5–4×2m (5–14×7ft)	various, Jun	various	deciduous species grown for autumn colour, evergreens for variegated foliage
Mahonia	1.2×2m (4×7ft)	yellow, Nov–Apr	bold, evergreen	clusters of fragrant flowers
Philadelphus	1–3×1.2m (3–10×4ft)	white, Jun–Jul	egg-shaped, veined	easy to grow. Very fragrant
Potentilla	0.3–1.5×0.9m (1–5×3ft)	various, Jun–Nov	green or greyish	many species and varieties. Long colourful display
Rhododendron (hardy hybrids)	1–3×1–2.5m (3–10×3–8ft)	various, Apr–Jun	large, evergreen	need lime-free soil
Viburnum	1–3×1–2.5m (3–10×3–8ft)	white, period varies	autumn colour	some have fragrant flowers, some colourful berries
Weigela	1–3×1.5–2m (3–10×5–7ft)	white, red or pink, May–Jun	green, purple or variegated	all species and varieties suitable. Small, foxglove-like flowers

Note [1] Height of shrubs is approximate height after 10–15 years in garden conditions. This is only a guide and height can vary widely. Height of herbaceous perennials is ultimate height in favourable conditions.

IMPROVING YOUR SOIL: CHALKY SOILS

INCREASING SOIL DEPTH

The depth of topsoil over lime-stone or chalk can vary enormously, but it tends to be shallow, especially over chalk. A thin topsoil makes it difficult for deep-rooted plants to grow. Plants that like deep, moist soil may also fail because the soil is likely to be free-draining and to dry out quickly.

To increase the soil depth, double dig wherever possible, incorporating organic material. Be careful not to bring more chalk into the topsoil. The roots of established trees and shrubs may penetrate the chalk. Help them by breaking up the ground underneath before planting. Use a pickaxe if necessary.

IMPROVING FERTILITY

Chalk and limestone soils are often deficient in plant nutrients. The high pH favours microbes that help to break down organic material quickly, so you need to apply generous amounts regularly. This will help to make the soil more workable and water retentive as well as increasing fertility.

Garden compost, manure, spent hops and seaweed are all suitable.

Spent mushroom compost is best avoided. It usually contains a significant amount of limestone which will make it more difficult to keep the soil pH down, though it probably won't make matters any worse.

Green manures, like mustard, clover or ryegrass (see page 98), will also add humus and help to improve soil structure. Grow them wherever suitable (in the vegetable patch or in annual flowerbeds over winter, for instance), and dig them in before they set seed.

LOWERING pH

Don't waste effort by trying to make your whole garden less alkaline. Even if you lower the pH of the top few inches of soil, roots will soon grow deeper. And most soils have a buffering action which soon brings the pH back to its former level.

Sulphate of ammonia, aluminium sulphate and flowers of sulphur will make the soil more acid, but they won't have a lasting effect. If you really want to grow lime-hating plants, use containers or raised beds and fill them with lime-free compost.

TRACE ELEMENT DEFICIENCY

Plants grown on alkaline soils are likely to suffer from iron and magnesium deficiency. These trace elements may be present in the soil, but locked up in a form that plants can't absorb.

Iron deficiency results in yellow, sickly leaves (chlorosis). If you apply sulphate of iron, it too becomes locked up.

You need to use sequestered iron. This is held in a form that can be absorbed by plants and remains stable in the soil for several months, though it works out expensive to apply round lots of plants. Follow the manufacturer's instructions.

Magnesium deficiency causes leaves to become pale in the centre, and areas next to the midrib often die. In brassicas the leaves may turn red, orange or purple: on fruit trees the leaves may brown between the veins.

You may be able to solve the problem of magnesium deficiency with Epsom salts. Dissolve 3g in 1 litre of water (½oz in 1 gallon) and apply as a foliar spray. Some sequestered iron products also contain salts of magnesium.

PLANTING PITS

If you want to grow lime-hating plants, and don't want to use containers, digging a planting pit can provide a solution.

Dig a hole large enough to allow for several years of root growth. Make it straight-sided with a flat bottom sloping in one direction. Line with thick polythene (you could dust the hole first with flowers of sulphur to provide added protection). Make drainage holes at the lowest edge. Fill with neutral or acid soil or compost.

Bear in mind that if you live in a chalk area, your mains water may also be alkaline (hard). So don't use it on lime-hating plants. If this is unavoidable, you may need to counteract it by applying sequestered iron (see Trace Element Deficiency, below left).

Digging a large pit may prove difficult on very thin soils, and is not practical for large trees and shrubs. They will soon outgrow the hole and will be prone to being blown over. Don't use a liner near a large tree. The roots will soon break through it.

MULCHES

Most alkaline soils are dry in summer. Water sinks to lower levels, and the top layer in which most plants are rooted tends to dry out quickly.

Weeds compete for moisture, so hoeing helps, but using a mulch is even better (see page 88 for more details). Black polythene is one of the best for conserving water, but it's not very attractive. Where appearances matter, use bark chippings. Water the ground (and bark) thoroughly and apply a layer at least 5cm (2in) thick.

PLANTS FOR CHALKY SOILS

	HEIGHT × SPREAD [1]	FLOWERS	FOLIAGE	REMARKS
TREES				
Arbutus andrachne	4.5×2.5m (15×8ft)	white, Mar–Apr	dark, leathery	tender when young. Strawberry-like fruits
Crataegus × lavallei	4.5–6×3–4.5m (15–20×10–15ft)	white, Jun	glossy, dark green	almost thornless. Orange-red haws Sep–Oct
Cupressus glabra	10.5×3.6m (35×12ft)	yellow, Sep–Apr	evergreen, blue-grey	attractive bark
Juniperus communis	3×1.8m (10×6ft)	insignificant	pointed needles	aromatic, many dwarf forms
Prunus 'Kursar'	7.5×6m (25×20ft)	rich pink, Apr	slender, mid-green	only one of many suitable *Prunus* species
Sorbus vilmorinii	2.5–3.6×1.5–2.5m (8–12×5–8ft)	white, Jun	fern-like, green	red fruits, turning white. There are many other good species
Taxus baccata	4.5×4.5m (15×15ft)	–	black-green needles	most parts poisonous. Red fruits
SHRUBS				
Berberis thunbergii 'Red Pillar'	1.8×1m (6×3ft)	white, red buds, Apr	purple-red	autumn tints. Red fruits. Many other berberis are suitable
Chaenomeles speciosa	1.8×1.2–1.8m (6×4–6ft)	red, Jan-Apr	dark green, glossy	fragrant, green-yellow fruits
Cistus × purpureus	1.2–1.5×1.2m (4–5×4ft)	rose-purple, May–Jul	evergreen, grey-green	many other suitable species. Masses of large single flowers
Clematis alpina	2–3×3m+ (7–10×10ft+)	blue, nodding, Apr–May	dark green leaflets	*C. macropetala* and *C. montana* also suitable
Genista lydia	1.8×1.2m (6×4ft)	yellow, May–Jun	grey-green	bright plant with arching or prostrate branches
Hebe × franciscana	1.2×1.2m (4×4ft)	bright blue, intermittent	rich green	flowers throughout the year. 'Variegata' is a popular form
Helianthemum nummularium	15×60cm (6×24in)	various, Jun–Jul	deep green	flowers profusely. Many good varieties
Lonicera × japonica	7.5–9m/climber (25–30ft/climber)	yellow/white, Jun–Oct	evergreen, light green	vigorous twining plant. Fragrant flowers
Pyracantha coccinea	3–4.5×3–4.5m (10–15×10–15ft)	white, Jun	evergreen, mid-green	spiny. Bright red berries Sep–Mar
Symphoricarpus albus	1.5–2×2–2.5m (5–7×7–8ft)	pink, urn-shaped, Jul–Sep	greyish-green	large white berries Oct–Feb
HERBACEOUS				
Aubretia deltoidea	10×45–60cm (4×18–24in)	purple-rose, Mar–Jun	hairy, green	matt-forming. Many varieties
Campanula carpatica	20–30×30–40cm (8–12×12–15in)	blue-purple, Jul–Aug	mid-green	several varieties with different flower colours
Delphinium elatum	1–1.5×0.45–0.6m (3–5×1½–2ft)	blue, Jun–Jul	palmate, mid-green	many varieties, some dwarf, flowers white/pink/purple/blue
Dicentra eximia	30–45×30cm (12–18×12in)	rose-pink, May–Sep	fern-like, grey-green	graceful, pendulous flowers. There are white and pale pink varieties
Digitalis purpurea	1–1.5×0.6m (3–5×2ft)	purple/red, Jun–Jul	rich green rosettes	tall spikes of tubular flowers. There are several different coloured forms
Gaillardia aristata	60–75×45cm (24–30×18in)	yellow/red, Jun–Oct	grey-green	daisy-like flowers good for cutting. Many striking hybrids
Helleborus atrorubens	25×45cm (10×18in)	deep plum, Jan–Apr	dark green, lobed	long-lasting cut flowers for winter
Hosta crispula	60×60cm (24×24in)	lilac-purple, Aug	green, white margins	excellent ground cover, attractive foliage
Mertensia virginica	30–60×30cm (12–24×12in)	purple-blue, May	blue-grey	foliage dies back in Jul, reappears Feb
Paeonia lactiflora hybrids	75–100×90cm (2½–3½×3ft)	white/pink/red, May–Jul	mid/deep green	large double flowers, often scented
Sidalcea malviflora 'Rose Queen'	75×40cm (30×16in)	rose-pink, Jun–Sep	mid-green	mallow-like flowers in long spikes. Many other varieties

Note [1] Height of trees and shrubs is approximate height after 10–15 years, though this can vary widely. Height of herbaceous perennials is ultimate height in normal conditions.

IMPROVING YOUR SOIL: BADLY DRAINED SOILS

Bad drainage is easy to detect. Puddles and a heavy, sticky soil are tell-tale signs, and moisture-loving mosses and sedges may invade your lawns and borders. But improving drainage can be a major task, so you need to assess the extent of the problem and find the cause before trying to remedy it (see Box).

IMPROVING DRAINAGE

You can improve drainage by digging in lots of bulky material. To open up the soil, spread on a 5cm (2in) layer of gritty sand and dig in. Organic matter will also help (but it doesn't have a permanent effect): add a bucketful per square metre or yard when digging in the sand. In future years apply an organic mulch and leave the worms to work it into the soil.

COMPACTION
This is caused by rain or watering, or by walking on the soil. Digging and breaking up the lumps will help, but the effects will be short-lived unless you take steps to prevent the soil becoming compacted again.

Mulches will stop heavy rain compacting the soil. Keep off the soil, especially when wet. Lay stepping stones in borders and lawns, and divide the vegetable plot into beds with permanent paths between them. In the long term you will need to improve the soil to prevent compaction.

HARD PANS
A layer of hard, compacted soil – a pan – impedes drainage and root growth. It can be broken up by digging and shouldn't re-form for many years.

Pans are usually caused by cultivating the soil to the same depth year after year. This can result from using a powered cultivator, though gardens that used to be agricultural land may have the same problem. Some soils, such as those with a high iron content, can form a natural pan.

INSTALLING LAND DRAINS
Land drains can solve serious drainage problems, but you must be prepared for a lot of work, expense and disruption.

For drains to work, the water must have somewhere to go. Unless you have a handy ditch, start by building a soakaway. Make it 1.8m (6ft) deep and line with unmortared bricks. Fill with stones or rubble. If you hit an impermeable rock such as granite, or you are still digging clay after 1.5m (5ft), abandon the project. The soakaway will not be able to drain. The drains should slope by 1 in 40 (30cm in 12m or 1ft in 40ft). This can be tricky to achieve if the ground slopes less than this or slopes in several directions. Dig a main drain 30cm (1ft) deep and 60cm (2ft) wide. Lay drain pipes (known as tiles) bedded on stones or rubble and refill the trench with soil. Run off side drains in a herringbone pattern at about 60 degrees, every 4.5m (15ft). To help prevent the drains silting up cover the joints with tiles or thick pieces of polythene and cover with rubble or gravel.

HOW BADLY DRAINED?
To find out how bad the drainage is and how easy it will be to improve it, dig a pit 60cm (2ft) deep. Examine the sides of the pit to check for evidence of a hard pan. Cover to prevent rain getting in and leave overnight.

■ If water has seeped into the pit, the water table is high or there are natural springs in the garden. Don't waste time trying to improve drainage. Grow moisture-loving plants and use raised beds for vegetables and selected ornamentals.

If the pit is dry, fill it with water and time how long it takes to drain.

■ **Over 24 hours**: Drainage is very poor and usually indicates a heavy clay topsoil, or a layer of clay subsoil which can prevent drainage altogether. It can also be a symptom of a hard pan in the subsoil. Alternatively, the land could be low-lying so water tends to drain into it.

The topsoil can be improved, but if your problem lies deeper you may have to resort to raised beds or choosing plants that suit the conditions. Drains may be the only solution for lawns.

■ **Up to 24 hours**: You have no major drainage problems. Poorly drained areas are probably caused by surface compaction. If cultivation doesn't improve them, check for leaking drains or concrete left under the soil.

■ **Less than an hour**: Your soil is very free-draining. Any problems are likely to be due to surface compaction or a shallow pan. Remedy by digging.

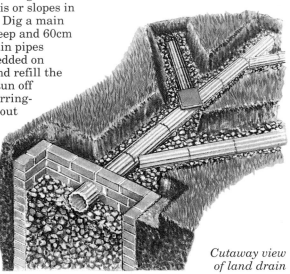

Cutaway view of land drain

TREES AND SHRUBS FOR BADLY DRAINED SOILS

	HEIGHT × SPREAD [1]	FLOWERS	FOLIAGE	REMARKS
TREES				
Alnus glutinosa	9×4.5m (30×15ft)	pendulous catkins, Mar	dark green, heart-shaped	attracts wide range of wildlife. Hates acid, peaty soils
Salix alba 'Argentea'	9×5.5m (30×18ft)	greenish-yellow catkins, Apr	long, silvery	glistening foliage, white stems. To grow as a shrub, cut to ground each year
Salix alba 'Britzensis' (syn. 'Chermesina')	9×5.5m (30×18ft)	green-yellow catkins, May	grey-green	orange/red stems, attractive in winter. Can be grown as a shrub – see S. a. 'Argentea'
Salix matsudana 'Tortuosa'	9×6m (30×20ft)	green-yellow catkins, Apr	mid-green	branches and leaves contorted, attractive in winter. Almost evergreen. Can be kept small by regular pruning
Salix purpurea 'Pendula'	4.5×5m (16×17ft)	purplish-yellow catkins, Apr	blue/grey, narrow	weeping branches. Train main step up a cane
SHRUBS				
Clethra alnifolia	1.8×1.8m (6×6ft)	creamy-white, Aug–Oct	mid-green	tufty spikes of sweetly scented flowers
Cornus alba 'Sibirica'	3×3m (10×10ft)	yellowish-white, May–Jun	mid-green, grey beneath	prune hard in spring to limit size and encourage young, vivid red stems. 'Kesselringii' has purple-black stems. Inconspicuous flowers, white berries
Myrica gale	1.2×1.8m+ (4×6ft+)	brown catkins, Apr–May	grey-green, hairy beneath	attractive, leafy bush with scented catkins
Salix elaeagnus	3×2.5m (10×8ft)	yellow catkins, Apr	fine, grey-green	slender branches with feathery foliage
Salix exigua	3.6×3.6m (12×12ft)	yellow catkins, Apr	long, narrow, silvery-grey	keep smaller by cutting back. One of the prettiest willows
Salix gracilistyla	3.6×3.6m (12×12ft)	yellow catkins, Mar	silvery-grey/green	attractive pussy willow catkins. Foliage turns a pretty yellow in autumn
Salix purpurea 'Nana'	0.9–1.5m (3–5ft)	purple-silver catkins, Mar	small, narrow	very easy to grow. Forms leafy tufts

Note [1] Height and spread are what you might expect from a mature specimen. Use it only as an approximate guide, as local conditions will have a significant effect on growth and height.

Above Cornus alba 'Sibirica' (red stems) and Cornus stolonifera 'Flaviramiea' (yellow stems) Left Astilbe × ardensii

IMPROVING YOUR SOIL: OTHER SOIL TYPES

■ SANDY SOILS

Sandy soils are very free-draining, so they dry out rapidly and nutrients are readily washed out. They are often acidic and infertile. Those containing some clay are also prone to compaction. On the plus side, sandy soils are easy to work at any time of year and are quick to warm up in the spring.

Living with sandy soil

Delay digging until late winter or early spring, otherwise the structure will be lost over winter. Because the soil warms rapidly, you will be able to sow seeds early. Loose seedbeds will dry rapidly. Tread them lightly to settle and reduce drying. You may still need to water to get good germination.

Fertiliser is best applied little and often throughout the growing season. You will need to water frequently, particularly if your garden is exposed or in a drier part of the country. Using mulches will help to retain moisture.

Avoid plants that need a lot of water like shallow-rooting peas and beans. Potatoes may be prone to scab unless you add a lot of organic material.

Try root crops like carrots and parsnips. Deep-rooting trees and shrubs will also do well, though you will need to water until established.

To improve the soil:

■ add organic material regularly to improve water retention, digging in when planting and using it as a mulch

■ test the pH each year and lime if necessary

■ if you want to grow plants that need a lot of water, like runner beans or courgettes, prepare special sites for them, digging in a lot of organic material.

■ PEATY SOILS

Peaty soils are usually found in low-lying areas. They retain water well but are frequently waterlogged because of poor drainage or a high water table. They are usually high in nitrogen but short of potash. If they are alkaline, they may also lack manganese.

On the plus side, peaty soils are warm and easily worked, even after rain.

Living with a peaty soil

Use raised beds, especially for early crops. Firm seedbeds well to prevent them drying out.

Avoid Brussels sprouts. They may produce excessive leaf and blown sprouts. Many sun-loving plants won't thrive because they also need good drainage. These often have aromatic leaves, like myrtle, thyme and rosemary, or silver-grey foliage, like artemesia and *Convolvulus cneorum*. Woodland plants also need a well-drained soil.

Try plants that will tolerate poor drainage (see Table on page 105). As long as drainage is not too bad, crops that need a lot of water, like peas and lettuces, will flourish. Courgettes, parsnips and celery should also do well.

To improve the soil

■ on waterlogged soil, you may have to resort to land drains (see page 104)

■ if the water table is high, land drains will be useless. Use raised beds

■ check pH regularly and lime the soil if necessary.

■ STONY SOILS

Cultivation is difficult on stony soils. Using a spade may be impossible, and your hoe may need sharpening frequently.

Living with stones

Keep digging to a minimum (see page 95 for the 'no-dig' method). You may find it easier with a fork. Rake lightly to remove surface stones when preparing seedbeds.

Don't overdo the raking or you'll bring more stones to the surface.

Avoid root crops like carrots and parsnips. Stones can distort the roots. Potatoes require a lot of digging and are best avoided if cultivation is difficult. Alternatively, try growing them under a black polythene mulch so that tubers form on the soil surface. This avoids earthing up as well as digging up tubers. Most vegetables except root crops should do well as long as the soil is basically loam.

Try planting permanent borders rather than annuals and bedding plants to cut down on digging.

■ SILTY SOILS

Silty soils are generally very fertile and retain moisture well. However, the surface can become compacted if worked when wet. A hard crust or 'cap' may also form if a dry period is followed by heavy rain or extensive watering. This prevents seedlings emerging.

Living with a silty soil

Don't cultivate when wet – you'll compact the soil. To prevent capping, cover seed drills with moist peat and water frequently with a fine spray.

Avoid early sowing in outdoor seedbeds.

Try raising early plants in pots or trays for transplanting. This saves you working wet soil in early spring and also avoids problems with capping. Most plants do well in this type of soil.

CHAPTER THIRTEEN

MAKING COMPOST

Gardening from Which? composting trials

There is an immense satisfaction in creating a heap of perfect, odourless compost from a pile of re-cycled garden or kitchen waste. Some gardeners seem to acquire the knack easily; others – despite years of trying – always end up with a pile of slimy, smelly sludge or a heap that refused to break down. This chapter should ensure that you join the first group rather than the second.

Compost making is often treated as a mystical craft. The principles behind compost making which are explained overleaf should dispel this idea. In the rest of this chapter the practical do's and don'ts will help you put the theory into practice.

To a certain extent, the more effort you put into compost making the better the result. But consider what you are going to use your compost for. If, for example, you want to use it as a substitute for peat in potting composts, it needs to be of the highest quality. But if you are just going to dig it into the ground, any reasonably well-decomposed material is satis-factory, and the effort involved in forming the heap and building up the material in layers is not essential.

It's also worth noting that however carefully you make compost, it's likely to contain weed seeds. For this reason garden compost makes a less than ideal surface mulch.

BASICS FOR SUCCESS

- Use as large a heap or bin as you can fill. The larger the heap, the more heat it should generate, and there should be proportionally less uncomposted material at the edges
- A good mix of materials, maintaining an appropriate balance between carbon and nitrogen
- Conditions in which the compost becomes neither water-logged nor dried out. This may mean covering the heap with polythene sheeting to keep the rain out or watering it if it gets too dry
- Patience to allow enough time for the compost to decompose and mature. This will depend on the time of year and what materials you use. For example, a mixed heap can produce compost in as little as three months during summer. Started in autumn, a similar heap may take seven to eight months to rot down.

BIN OR HEAP

Perfectly good compost can be made in either a heap or a bin. The choice depends on how much material you want to compost and where you want to put it. Heaps are better for larger quantities, but bins look neater. Using a bin should also speed up the composting process.

HOW BIG?

About 1 cu m (35 cu ft) capacity is an ideal size for a compost bin. You can use smaller bins, but the smaller the bin or heap, the greater the proportion of the material exposed at the edges, and this will not rot as well or as fast because it does not heat up as much.

TURN THE COMPOST?

Turning the compost, or taking the heap apart and piling it up again with the outside material on the inside, aerates the heap, giving the aerobic micro-organisms a supply of oxygen and allowing them access to more raw material from the outside. The effect of turning is to start the heating cycle all over again.

The best time to turn a heap is about seven to ten days after it starts to cool.

If you don't turn a compost heap it may become anaerobic and decompose more slowly.

ACTIVATORS

A compost activator can be anything that's rich in nitrogen – manure, dried blood or even human urine.

If you want to compost a lot of woody material, it is worth using an activator, and the cheapest is likely to be poultry manure if you have a local source.

On heaps which contain only soft material, an activator is not essential, but a light sprinkling of soil may help speed up the decomposition.

LIKELY RESULTS

REGULAR TURNING	ACTIVATOR	WOODY MATERIAL	GRASS CLIPPINGS	
■	■			Crumbly, well-decomposed compost with only a thin layer of less well-rotted material at the edges
	■	■		Similar to above but thicker layer of partially decomposed material at edges
■				Well-decomposed but slightly less crumbly than when activator used
	■	■		If you add a lot of prunings without chopping them up, be prepared to wait at least 12 months. The end result is likely to contain a thick layer of partly decomposed material at the edges which can be used to start another heap
			■	If more than a third of the material is grass clippings, the result is likely to be slimy and smelly compost. However, it should be fully decomposed and weed free

MATERIALS YOU CAN USE

In theory you can make compost from anything organic – that is, anything that was once living, or was produced by a living thing. However, some materials present problems – they may be difficult to break down, like woody stems, or attract rats and flies, like scraps of cooked food. But if you follow the guidelines on this page you should be able to produce pleasing compost without too much difficulty.

▬ FROM INSIDE THE HOUSE AND GARDEN

Soft plant materials: dead flowers or houseplants, vegetable waste from the kitchen, lawn clippings or the remains of bedding plants can be turned into compost with few problems.

Woody materials: prunings from shrubs or hedges and other woody matter can be used, but only if chopped into small pieces – chips of less than 4cm (1½in) if possible. You may wish to consider buying or hiring a garden shredder (see page 113) if you have a lot of woody material to dispose of.

Dead leaves: can be added to the compost heap mixed with other materials. If you have lots it would probably be better to compost them separately as leafmould (see page 114).

Household and DIY waste such as newspapers and sawdust: these can be useful if you don't add too much at once and use an activator with them.

MATERIALS TO AVOID

Roots of perennial weeds: for example, couch, bindweed, dandelions.

Seeding weeds or bedding plants: unless your heap generates enough heat to kill them you may spread the seeds around the garden.

Diseased plants (such as those with club root or black spot): these should be disposed of or burned and the ash added to the compost heap.

Lawn mowings from a treated lawn: don't use the clippings from the first cut after using a lawn weedkiller.

Cooked food scraps: these may attract pests such as rats, mice and flies unless well mixed with other materials.

Too much of any one material: especially grass clippings, or woody material that has not been chopped up into small pieces.

COMPOSTABLE MATERIALS CARBON:NITROGEN RATIO

FROM THE HOUSE & GARDEN			WORTH BUYING?		
	Nettles	low:high		Poultry manure	v. low:high
	Pea and bean haulms	low:high		Dried blood	low:high
	Kitchen scraps	well balanced		Farmyard manure (including straw)	low:high
	Lawn mowings	well balanced		Stable manure (including straw)	low:high
	Garden weeds	well balanced		Bonemeal or hoof and horn	low:high
	Old bedding plants	well balanced		Seaweed	well balanced
	Green vegetable remains	well balanced		Straw	high:low
	Potato or tomato haulms	well balanced		Sawdust	high:zero
	Hedge or shrub prunings	high:low			
	Woody brassica stalks	high:low			
	Autumn leaves	high:low			
	Newspaper or cardboard	high:zero			

If you use materials with a high carbon content, try to balance them with materials high in nitrogen, and vice versa. Well-balanced materials contain an ideal carbon to nitrogen ratio of around 30:1.

Weeds, especially nettles: a good source of nutrients, but watch out for weed seeds and remove roots from perennial weeds before adding them to the heap.

▬ FROM OUTSIDE THE HOUSE AND GARDEN
If you want to make a lot of compost you may consider collecting suitable materials from elsewhere.
Manures: poultry manure is very strong and must be mixed with other wastes. Farmyard and stable manures are usually fairly cheap and are already mixed with straw.
Straw, paper and cardboard: all need to be mixed with a nitrogen source to speed up rotting. Cut paper and cardboard into narrow strips before composting and mix them with at least twice as much green material.
Autumn leaves: best used in small quantities and mixed with a nitrogen source. If you collect a lot, compost them separately into leafmould (see page 114).
Seaweed: a good source of nutrients if you live by the seaside and have a ready source available.
Agricultural and shop waste: local growers, food-processors, greengrocers, market stalls and restaurants may have large amounts of vegetable waste which they are only too glad to get rid of.

One of the secrets of making successful compost is to mix different materials together. Every time you use a lot of one material – sawdust, say – you will need to add another material (in this case something like nettles or poultry manure) to balance the carbon and nitrogen ratio. If you try to make compost from lawn mowings alone, or heaps of sawdust and leaves, the results are likely to be unsatisfactory. The processes involved in breaking down plant materials into compost need the right balance of carbon and nitrogen as well as air and moisture.

GROWING COMPOST
Green manuring is the term used to describe a crop grown primarily for digging in to increase the humus content of the soil. It makes use of ground that would otherwise be empty, competes with weeds that would otherwise grow, and absorbs nutrients that are made available for later crops as the plants decompose after they have been dug in. Some enrich the ground in other ways (by fixing nitrogen from the atmosphere, for instance).

As well as digging in green manure crops, you can leave them in the ground for longer and cut them for the compost heap. See page 98 for a list of suitable green manure crops. As well as those listed, you could sow surplus seeds of quick-growing vegetables, such as turnips or radishes, and harvest them at any stage for the compost heap.

COMPOSTING GRASS CLIPPINGS
Grass on its own is notoriously difficult to compost. It can, however, be used quite satisfactorily in a compost heap provided it is well mixed with other materials, but avoid using the first lawn mowings after the application of a weedkiller.

Used in large quantities, grass clippings tend to produce a slimy and smelly result, but they have the advantage of being weed-free and are perfectly usable as a mulch, or to dig into the soil. Various compost 'cauldrons' are available on the market which claim to produce good results from lawn clippings. These are intended to stop the grass clippings drying out or becoming too wet, to protect them from the cooling effect of the rain and to keep the grass aerated by spinning the compost round. However, tests show that they don't perform better than a conventional covered and turned heap. It's best to put your grass clippings on the compost heap, well mixed with other garden and kitchen waste.

Compare the weed growth in compost from a mixed heap (left) with that from grass cuttings only

MAKING COMPOST: BIN DESIGNS

MAKING A COMPOST BIN

Although proprietary compost bins save you construction time, you may find it cheaper and more satisfactory to make your own.
Whatever you use to make the bin, it must be durable, and timber is a popular choice. The one illustrated on the right incorporates many features that you will find useful, and it's within the scope of most gardeners with elementary carpentry skills.

SIZE AND SHAPE
A square or rectangular bin makes construction easy and will be practical to use. The size depends on how much you have to compost, but it's best to make the bin at least 90cm (3ft) in each dimension for good results.

AIR AND MOISTURE
The bin will get plenty of air, so don't leave gaps between the boards as this will allow the material to dry out. It's essential that the material doesn't become waterlogged, so fit a sloping lid.

REFINEMENTS
A double bin, like the one in the illustration below, will help when you have to turn the compost. You can simply fork it from one bin to another, mixing and aerating it at the same time. Or you can fill one bin and leave it to mature while you are filling the other.

SITING
If possible, the bin should be out of direct sun and somewhere reasonably sheltered. Place the bin straight on the ground, not on paving or concrete. This way,

nutrients seep into the soil and are not wasted, and worms and micro-organisms can enter the heap more readily.

You can easily make a bin yourself from wooden planks (treat them with a wood preservative). A design that allows you to slide the front out for access will make removing the compost easier, and a sloping top and lid will keep off the rain and prevent the compost from becoming soggy.
A double bin, like the one below, makes turning the compost easy – you can simply fork the compost out of one bin and into the other.

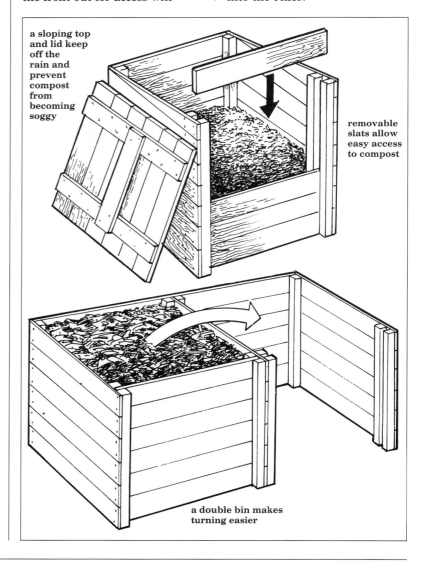

a sloping top and lid keep off the rain and prevent compost from becoming soggy

removable slats allow easy access to compost

a double bin makes turning easier

ALTERNATIVE DESIGNS

Bricks or breeze blocks make a good, durable bin. You could also fit a wooden front and a lid like the one shown on the previous page. With bricks, leave some in the first course unmortared so that they can later be removed for ventilation gaps. With breeze blocks, there is no need to mortar them.

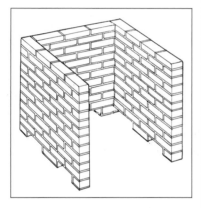

Straw bales will eventually rot, when they can themselves be incorporated into compost, but in the meantime they make useful improvised 'bins', offering good insulation for the compost.

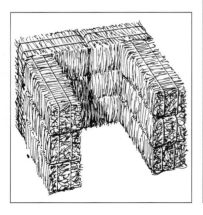

Wire netting can be fixed to a wooden frame. Line with a sheet of polythene or, if two layers of wire netting have been used, pack paper or cardboard between them for insulation.

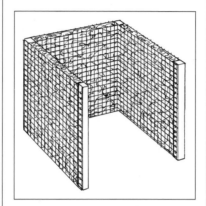

BUYING A BIN

If you decide to buy a compost bin rather than make your own, bear these points in mind when making your choice:
■ **Is it big enough?** The smaller the bin, the more difficult it will be to reach a high temperature to get decomposition going well, especially in the winter.
■ **Is it easy to assemble and robustly made?** Some bins have complicated clips and fastenings, and some are so light and flimsy they are liable to blow away or collapse under the weight of compost.
■ **Does it provide for ventilation and drainage?** Some bins come without lids, or holes to let air in or moisture out.
■ **Will you be able to get at the compost in order to turn it?**
■ **Can the finished compost be removed easily from the bin?**
■ **Is it good value for money?**

COMPOST HEAPS

If you decide to make a heap rather than a bin, build it at least 1m (3ft) square with a layer of coarse material at the base. Build up the heap in level layers, compacting it as you go, and making it slightly pyramidal in shape so that the finished heap is stable. Cover the heap with black polythene to prevent the material from drying out or from becoming waterlogged. When the initial heating has taken place, turn the heap putting the outside material to the inside to give it a chance to decompose.

An alternative idea is to build an elongated heap, adding new material to one end and taking finished compost from the other. Turning will be easier as you need to turn only the new end of the heap.

HOW WELL DID YOU DO?

| *APPEARANCE* | *TIPS FOR IMPROVEMENT* |

Near-perfect compost
If yours has turned out looking like the crumbly well-decomposed compost in this picture, with only a thin layer of partially rotted material around the outside, you can justifiably be proud.

Uncomposted material at the edges
The compost within this heap is nearly as good as that in the first picture, but the heap is far less uniform, and there is too much unsuitable material not fully decomposed around the outside and on top.

Turning would have improved this compost. It is always worth turning the compost in a small bin to make full use of the available capacity. With a large heap it may not be worth the trouble.

Usable compost only at centre of heap
Really good compost is found only at the heart of this heap. However, apart from an uncomposted layer at the top and sides, the rest would be perfectly acceptable for digging into the soil.

Reduce the proportion of woody material. Consider buying a shredder to make woody material more suitable for composting.

Large proportion of uncomposted material
This heap is taking a very long time to break down. It looks as if it contains too much woody material that hasn't been chopped up. Not enough attention has been paid to maintaining the balance between carbon and nitrogen.

Try a more balanced mix of materials. Chop up woody material into 4cm (1½in) lengths and use an activator such as dried blood.

Compost wet and slimy
Although most of the heap is fully decomposed, the result is rather unpleasant, with liquid oozing from the base of a bin of slimy and smelly compost. It is, nevertheless, perfectly usable for digging into soil.

Don't put too many grass clippings on at once. Don't let the heap become waterlogged.

COMPOSTING WOODY MATERIAL

Most waste plant material can be composted satisfactorily. Woody prunings from shrubs and hedges, however, need to be well mixed with other materials, and chopped up small. If the heap contains lots of woody material, add a nitrogen fertiliser such as dried blood as an activator. If your garden has many shrubs it may be worth buying a garden shredder.

COMPOST SHREDDERS

A powered compost shredder will turn prunings and hedge clippings into fine chippings ready for composting or mulching. Wet, fibrous material tends to clog and long grass can jam the blades.

Before buying or hiring a shredder:
■ when you hire, make sure you get full instructions, and ask to see the shredder in operation
■ check the shredder is properly guarded. You should not be able to see the blades from the operating position or touch the blades at all.

When using a shredder:
■ read the instructions
■ wear eye protectors, ear protectors and gloves
■ switch off and remove the plug before leaving or dismantling the machine
■ keep away children and pets
■ never use the shredder unless it is fully assembled
■ never put hands into inlets or outlets
■ never feed with stones, soil, glass, metal, bone or plastic.

WORM COMPOST

Worms are highly beneficial in the garden, and you may like to consider making your own worm farm. To do so:

First construct a bottomless box at least 60cm (2ft) high, about 60cm (2ft) by 90cm (3ft) square – slightly wider and longer than your wheelbarrow. Staple a piece of strong 5cm (2in) mesh chicken wire across the bottom. Then make two holes in the sides of the box near the bottom, and slide two lengths of wood through them. Fix two pieces of metal or wood on the ends to make scrapers.

Finally, mount the whole thing on legs or bricks so that you can push your barrow underneath.

When the box is complete, lay a sheet of soaked newspapers over the mesh floor. Cover this with a thin layer of old compost or manure and a handful of brandling worms (obtainable from a fishing-bait supplier). Put a thin layer of uncomposted material on top and cover it with old carpet or bubble polythene.

Build the wormery up slowly, putting no more than 8cm (3in) of material into the box each week. The worms will work upwards, digesting each layer as they go, and producing precious compost that can be raked into your wheelbarrow.

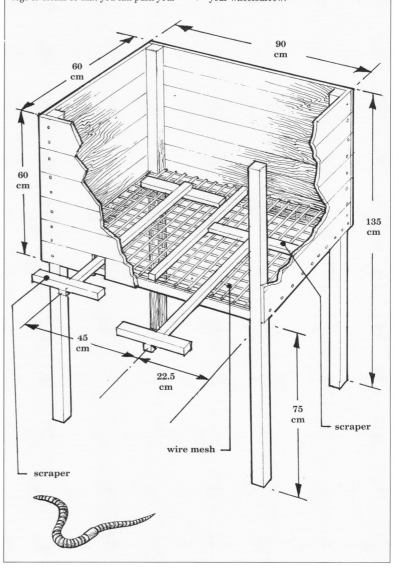

MAKING COMPOST: LEAFMOULD

In a forest, a thick carpet of leaves decaying on the surface suppresses grass and undergrowth and builds up into an ideal soil for more trees. In gardens, leaves can cause problems unless they are collected:

- on lawns dead leaves slowly kill grass by excluding light, and they can encourage worms and lawn diseases
- some plant diseases such as apple and pear scab overwinter on dead leaves and are spread to other plants as the leaves blow around. Fallen leaves can also provide a refuge for diseases such as rose black spot and insect pests, which can re-infest new growth in spring
- wet leaves on paths and steps can be slippery and dangerous.

COLLECTING LEAVES

From parts of the garden where they can't be dug in, it's best to collect all leaves preferably when they are dry, and remove them to a leafmould heap. If you can't collect sufficient leaves from your own garden to make a decent sized heap, you might consider collecting leaves from elsewhere. Thousands of tons of potential leafmould are wasted every year, in parks, cemeteries and public gardens. You might get permission to bring leaves home in plastic bags in the car.

Don't take leaves from woodlands without permission. Beware of contamination with oil or lead, or fouling by dogs, in leaves from streets or parks. Don't use leaves from these sources on fruit or vegetables.

WHAT TO DO

Making leafmould is different from making compost. You don't need to use activators or to aerate the leafmould heap –

though a nitrogen fertiliser and aeration will speed up the process. Because a leafmould heap won't heat up enough to kill weed seeds, try not to collect weeds with the leaves.

Nearly all types of leaves are suitable, but avoid evergreens such as holly and laurel and the needles of conifers. The best leafmould is made from beech or oak leaves. Both contain a lot of tannin which breaks down slowly to release nitrogen.

Choose a sheltered site where nothing much grows, and make a wire netting container about 90cm (3ft) in each dimension. Fix the netting to stout supports driven into the ground.

Fill with leaves and tread them firm as they accumulate, until the enclosure is full. If the leaves are dry, water the heap well to encourage the fungi that rot them down.

The heap should be ready for digging about a year later. If you want it for potting compost, however, it is best left for two to four years, and then chopped down with a spade and sifted.

If you have only small amounts of leaves, pack them into plastic sacks. Seal to keep the leaves moist and you should have reasonable leafmould after two years.

USING LEAFMOULD

You can use leafmould instead of peat or bark as a surface mulch around shrubs, roses, or herbaceous plants, to suppress weeds and conserve moisture – apply a layer at least 2.5cm (1in) thick; double this for weed control.

You can dig it in to help retain moisture in dry soils, or to open up heavy soils. It can also be used in potting composts.

Sieved leafmould is a good topdressing for lawns, especially on dry soils. Apply it when the grass is growing vigorously or after you have spiked the lawn, and brush it in well.

FAST LEAFMOULD

If you are in a hurry, build a heap as above, but in spring turn it into another enclosure and add between a quarter and a third of its bulk of fresh grass cuttings. This will result in leafmould in about half the time. It is important to do this in spring, when the grass clippings are less likely to contain weed seeds, but you can add them gradually over several weeks. What you get is a cross between compost and leafmould.

CHAPTER FOURTEEN

FEEDING PLANTS

Plants feed by taking up nutrients from the soil, so using the right fertiliser will have a big impact on how well your plants perform. Generally, man-made fertilisers will have more effect on the growth of your plants, and they may be cheaper. However, if you have patience, good results can be achieved using organic gardening methods.

These cabbages were grown in adjacent plots and show that improving soil fertility (right) can have a dramatic effect on cabbage yields

WHEN TO USE FERTILISER

Cultivating a garden generally takes more from the soil than it returns to it, and this exhausts the soil quickly, until there aren't enough nutrients to sustain healthy growth or produce good crops. To overcome this, fertilisers are added to boost the nutrient content of the soil – and these can be organic or inorganic in origin. Generally, the result is more immediate with artificial fertilisers. Some organic fertilisers, like dried blood, are also quick-acting, but most release nutrients slowly over a long period of time.

Different plants need different levels of the various nutrients to flourish, and this varies with the time of year. A basic rule for applying all fertilisers is to use them during active growth (usually spring and summer) and to cease feeding during the dormant stage (autumn and winter). There are exceptions – bonemeal releases its nutrients slowly and is often used when planting in autumn.

BUILDING UP FERTILITY

Plants need three major nutrients for successful growth – nitrogen, potassium and phosphorus. Practically all soils contain these nutrients in reasonable amounts.

Some soils are more likely than others to be short of these elements (see Improving Your Soil, pages 93–106). For that reason you need to understand your soil as well as the specific needs of your plants, for best results. A light, sandy soil or a chalky soil, for example, will benefit from bulky organic material such as well-rotted manure as well as a source of nitrogen that is released relatively slowly. Nitrogen applied in conventional fertilisers can be quickly washed out of free-draining soils. Peaty soils often need extra phosphorus and potassium, and the plants may need additional traces of copper or boron to overcome natural deficiencies.

Clay soils generally hold nutrients well, and benefit most from improved soil structure – achieved with plenty of organic material, for example, rather than fertilisers.

FEEDING PLANTS: ORGANIC FERTILISERS

WHAT'S AVAILABLE

Fertilisers are usually classed as 'organic' or 'inorganic', although there are many proprietary fertilisers that are a blend of both.

Organic fertilisers are derived from animal or plant wastes, while inorganic fertilisers are either derived from natural mineral sources or manufactured using chemicals. The latter are usually quick-acting and will provide a rapid boost to plants. Organic fertilisers tend to be slower-acting and more expensive.

▬ BALANCED FERTILISERS

Balanced fertilisers contain all three essential major nutrients (nitrogen, potassium and phosphorus) and can be used all round the garden as a general spring feed. Blood, fish and bone is commonly used as general fertiliser, though it contains little potassium unless this is added by the manufacturer. Check the N:P:K ratio on the packet – if the K value is less than 1.0, apply rock potash at 30g a sq m (1oz a sq yd) to supplement the blood, fish and bone. Clay soils are rarely short of potassium so there's no need to use rock potash.

▬ NITROGEN FERTILISERS

Nitrogen is the element most likely to need replenishing, as it is used up rapidly.

Nitrogen in the soluble form used by plants is readily washed out of the soil by rain.

Nitrogenous fertilisers are most useful for promoting leaf and stem growth, and give foliage a good dark green colour. Use them to boost leafy crops, such as cabbages, during the

growing season, and for greening and encouraging the growth of lawn grasses.

If nitrogen is lacking, your plants will be stunted, have pale foliage, and be vulnerable to pests and diseases. Fruiting may be prevented or delayed. And without enough nitrogen your

plants won't be able to make full use of the potassium and phosphorus either, even if they are in plentiful supply.

Dried blood and hoof and horn are both good sources of nitrogen. Dried blood releases its nitrogen into the soil quite

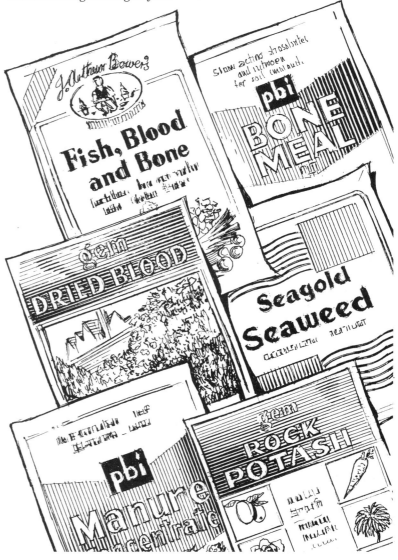

NON-ORGANIC COMPROMISE
Until you can build up the soil to a high
level of fertility by organic methods, you
may think it is worth using a man-made
fertiliser to help in the short term.
    Growmore (which is a formula
rather than a brand) will provide all the
essential major nutrients in a balance
that is likely to suit most plants. You
may want to consider applying this for a
season or two, gradually reducing the
amount each season as the soil fertility
builds up.

quickly. It is expensive, however, which limits its widespread
use outdoors. Hoof and horn is a
slow-acting fertiliser with a
nitrogen content of about 14 per
cent.

■ PHOSPHATE FERTILISERS

Phosphorus is essential for the
healthy development of plant
roots, and it encourages the
development of fruit and seeds.
Lack of phosphorus causes poor
growth, dull green foliage and
poor fruiting.
    Bonemeal is a good source of
phosphorus, but it is a slow-
acting fertiliser. For this reason
it is most useful for herbaceous
plants, bulbs, and shrubs and
trees.

■ MINERAL SUPPLEMENTS

Mineral supplements supply
elements needed in much
smaller amounts than the major
nutrients, such as iron and
magnesium.
    These are most likely to be
needed on problem soils, such as
chalky soils with a high pH,
where the chemistry of the soil
prevents the plant absorbing
them – though they may be
present in the soil, albeit in a
form not readily accessible to the
plant.
    Some of these can be pro-
vided in the form of sequestered
or chelated elements, which
means they are in a form that
will remain available to the
plant even though applied to an
unfavourable soil.
    Foliar feeding is another
way of overcoming trace element
deficiencies caused by the soil
(an Epsom salt solution is sometimes used to overcome magnesium deficiency, for example).
See page 120 for more details.

ORGANIC OR NOT?

Organic
The British Standards definition of an
'organic' fertiliser states that it should
be made up of carbonaceous materials,
mainly of vegetable and/or animal
origin, added to the soil specifically for
the nutrition of plants. Some manufacturers include naturally occurring
minerals such as rock potash in their
description.

Natural
'Natural' is a very vague term, but
manufacturers generally agree that it
means the product has no additive or
man-made chemicals. For example, rock
mined from the earth and crushed
would be a natural fertiliser, but one
produced in a chemical factory would
not – even though both products might
be very similar chemically.

Semi-organic
British Standards describe this term as
useful substances or nutrients that are
of both organic and inorganic origin.

Organic-based
There is no British Standards definition,
but 'organic' organisations consider this
term to be the same as 'semi-organic'.
Manufacturers use the term to describe
products made of organic (biological)
material with chemicals (natural in
origin or otherwise) added to boost the
immediately available nutrients.

Organics
Confusion surrounds this description.
One manufacturer describes its intended
interpretation as being a mixture of
different organic materials that are
biological in origin.

Manure substitutes
These are processed manures intended
as substitutes for garden compost or
well-rotted manure. Many of them claim
to feed plants, but as they are classified
as soil conditioners and not fertilisers,
manufacturers do not have to declare
their nutrient content. It is therefore
difficult to calculate how much you need
to apply.

LIKELY NUTRIENT LEVELS IN ORGANIC FERTILISERS

	%N	%P	%K	NOTES
Blood, fish and bone	4.0	6.0	0.5	fairly fast-acting when finely ground
Bonemeal	2–5	15–32	0	slow-release; most useful for planting trees and shrubs
Dried blood	10–14	trace	0	fast-acting; topdressing for vegetables and lawns
Fish meal	8–10	2–3	trace	fairly fast-acting; contains trace elements
Hoof and horn	14	2–3	0	slow-acting; best as base dressing
Manure concentrate (cow)	1.0–1.5	0.4	0.5–10	slow-release; trace elements
Manure concentrate (poultry)	4.0	3.0	1.5	quick- and slow-release; can scorch plants
Seaweed (meal)	0.5	0.1	1.2	slow-release; trace elements

FEEDING PLANTS: APPLICATION RATES

APPLYING FERTILISERS

Manure should generally be dug into the soil while the plants are dormant (usually late autumn and winter). This will supplement the plant nutrients already present, but will also provide humus and improve the condition of the soil.

Fertilisers can be applied as base dressings before planting or sowing (usually in spring). Apply the fertiliser to the top few inches of soil, following recommended rates of application, and lightly rake or hoe it in.

Apply topdressings during the growing season (usually spring or summer), and spread them evenly, not just around the base of the plant, hoeing into the surface of the soil.

LIQUID FERTILISERS

Liquid fertilisers can be useful to correct deficiencies, as they provide a source of nutrients which is immediately available to your plants. Their main use is for plants in containers. It is better to provide plants in the garden with a good, fertile soil from the outset rather than to try to supplement poor soil with liquid fertilisers, which have only a very short-lived effect.

Some liquid feeds are based on natural organic products such as manure or seaweed; others are based on man-made chemical nutrients (inorganic), but which may contain organic products.

Liquid feeds based on manures and seaweed contain trace elements and can be used as a foliar feed to correct deficiencies of minor nutrients such as manganese (see page 120).

You can make your own liquid feed by half filling a hessian sack with animal manure and submersing this, like a giant tea-bag, in a drum of water. The brew will take about two weeks. The only problem is that because you won't know the nutrient analysis, you will have to experiment with dilution rates. You can also make a liquid fertiliser from comfrey (see below).

HOME-GROWN FERTILISERS

Comfrey leaves break down very quickly and can be used as a quick-release fertiliser for topdressing around crops such as beans, onions, potatoes, tomatoes and soft fruit bushes. Russian comfrey wilted overnight is likely to contain 0.75 per cent nitrogen, 0.75 per cent phosphorus and 1.2 per cent potassium, so, although the nutrient content is quite balanced, you need a 10–15cm (4–6in) layer to achieve good results.

The comfrey leaves can either be dug direct into the soil, laid in potato trenches or applied as a mulch.

To make a liquid feed from comfrey, pack freshly cut leaves into a plastic container which has a tap at the bottom. Top up with water, cover and leave for about four weeks. Then a thick black liquid can be drawn off by tap, diluted and used as a feed. Once the liquid has been extracted from the container,

FEEDING FRUIT

	BLOOD, FISH AND BONE	ROCK POTASH
Apples	150g/sq m	-
Apricots	150g/sq m	-
Blackberries	150g/sq m	-
Black currants	150g/sq m + 150g/sq m [1]	-
Cherries	150g/sq m	-
Damsons	150g/sq m	-
Figs	150g/sq m	-
Gages	150g/sq m	-
Gooseberries	150g/sq m	75g/sq m
Loganberries	150g/sq m	-
Nuts	150g/sq m	-
Peaches	150g/sq m	-
Pears	150g/sq m	-
Plums	150g/sq m	-
Raspberries	150g/sq m	-
Red currants	150g/sq m	75g/sq m
Strawberries	150g/sq m	75g/sq m [2]
Tayberries	150g/sq m	-
White currants	150g/sq m	75g/sq m

Notes
Application rates are for annual spring feeds
[1] Apply second dressing in early summer [2] Apply after picking

FEEDING CONTAINER PLANTS

Before planting, add to the compost a slow-release feed – blood, fish and bone, for example – at about a handful to a bucketful of compost. This should last all season, but be prepared to apply liquid fertiliser in late summer if the plants show signs of deficiencies.

Alternatively, feed plants regularly with a liquid fertiliser throughout the growing season. Start about 4–6 weeks after planting and continue until late August for permanent plants or until the end of the season for annuals.

use the residue as a compost.

Grow comfrey in a sunny position in a bed of its own so that its roots won't have to compete for water and minerals in the soil. If you cut the leaves it will grow again to yield up to five crops in a year.

FEEDING ORNAMENTAL PLANTS

	BASE DRESSING blood, fish and bone	TOPDRESSING blood, fish and bone
Alpines	-	-
Bedding	100–150g/sq m	-
Bulbs	[1]	[1]
Herbaceous	100–150g/sq m	70–140g/sq m [2]
Roses	200–300g/sq m	200–300g/sq m [3]
Lawns	140g/sq m	100–150g/sq m [4]
Trees and shrubs	100–200g/sq m	100g/sq m [5]

Notes
Unless otherwise stated, figures given are for soils of average fertility. All quantities are in grammes per sq m (35g a sq m = 1oz a sq yd)
[1] Apply high potash fertiliser such as rock potash at planting time. At flowering time, feed with a high potash liquid fertiliser such as tomato feed once a week until foliage starts to die down. Very important on poor soils

[2] Apply in March. Can give a repeat application after cutting down first flush of flowers to encourage further flowers. Don't apply after July
[3] Split total amount in half. First application in spring, rest in July
[4] Apply in April or split total amount, giving half in April and rest in July
[5] Poor soils. Apply in February or March for first 2–3 years

FEEDING VEGETABLES

The vegetables listed are those that benefit most from a nitrogen-rich topdressing. Choose one BASE DRESSING from the table. Apply evenly and fork in to a depth of 10–15cm (4–6in) – ideally 10 to 14 days before sowing or planting.

When the crop is actively growing, add extra nitrogen with one of the TOPDRESSINGS (hoof and horn is suitable as a topdressing only if finely ground). The

figures given are total amounts. Divide them by the number of topdressings (usually 2 or 3) to get the figure you apply at each dressing. Keep the fertiliser 5–7cm (2–3in) away from the base of the plant and rake or hoe in lightly. Water if no rain falls.

All quantities are in grammes per sq m (35g a sq m = 1oz a sq yd)

	BASE DRESSING [1]		TOPDRESSING [2]	
	blood, fish, bone	OR hoof and horn [3]	dried blood	OR hoof and horn
Beetroot	100–200g/sq m	50g/sq m	90–140g/sq m	90g/sq m
Broccoli	100g/sq m	25g/sq m	70–115g/sq m	115g/sq m
Brussels sprouts	100–200g/sq m	50g/sq m	115–170g/sq m	115g/sq m
Cabbage (summer and winter) [4]	100–200g/sq m	50g/sq m	115–170g/sq m	115g/sq m
Calabrese	100g/sq m	25g/sq m	70–117g/sq m	115g/sq m
Cauliflower	100g/sq m	25g/sq m	70–115g/sq m	115g/sq m
Kale [4]	100g/sq m	25g/sq m	70–115g/sq m	115g/sq m
Leeks	100–140g/sq m	35g/sq m	75–90g/sq m	75g/sq m
Lettuce	100g/sq m	25g/sq m	75–100g/sq m	75g/sq m
Onions (Japanese) [4]	100–360g/sq m	90g/sq m	120–160g/sq m	120g/sq m
Spinach	100g/sq m	25g/sq m	50–70g/sq m	50g/sq m

Notes
[1] Figures are an approximate guide only. The nitrogen content of organic products varies, so it is difficult to be precise
[2] The figures given are the total amounts. Divide them by the number of topdressings to get the figure you apply at each dressing

[3] Add 35g bonemeal and 70g rock potash to produce a balanced feed
[4] Apply topdressing to overwintered crops in February

FEEDING PLANTS: NUTRITIONAL DEFICIENCIES

RECOGNISING DEFICIENCIES

Although nutritional deficiencies are sometimes difficult to pinpoint, it's useful to know what the tell-tale signs are to look out for:

Boron
Growing points die. Stems and roots turn brown inside. Dry, brittle plants. An excess of boron can cause similar problems. Apply seaweed meal or manure before next crop.

Calcium
General yellowing; young leaves and stems are often stunted and may rot. Growing points may die and root growth is poor. Improve soil with manure.

Iron
Yellowing of younger leaves. Veins remain green. Edges and tips of leaves looked scorched. In severe cases, growing tips die. Most common on alkaline soils. Apply chelated iron.

Magnesium
Pale green or yellowing leaf margins. Shoot tips and veins on older leaves remain green. Leaves die off rapidly. Spray with Epsom salts solution (mix a teaspoonful in a gallon of water).

Manganese
Symptoms vary. Usually stunted growth and yellowing between veins of leaves. Spots of dead tissue on leaves. Use seaweed- or manure-based liquid feed.

Molybdenum
Variable symptoms. Growth reduced. Leaves usually mottled and/or malformed, resulting in strap-like leaf. Use seaweed- or manure-based liquid feed.

Nitrogen
Stunted, yellowish-green plants. Older leaves turn bright yellowish-red along the veins and die off rapidly. Apply dried blood.

Phosphorus
Some plants show no symptoms, but generally growth is poor and lower leaves can turn a dark greenish-purple. Older leaves may die off rapidly. Apply bonemeal.

Potassium
Variable symptoms. Plants are stunted, often bluish-green, and the edges or veins of older leaves look scorched. Brown spots may develop on leaves. Apply rock potash.

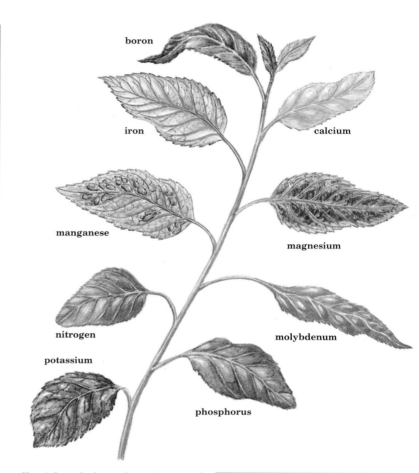

LONG-TERM CURES

Soil deficiencies can be determined only by having your soil analysed, as symptoms can vary a lot from plant to plant. The most likely cause for poor growth is soil that is too acidic or too alkaline for the plants you want to grow. A simple pH test may be enough.

In a soil that contains plenty of organic matter, serious nutrient deficiencies are rare, so look for other causes of poor growth, like pests, disease or drought.

CHAPTER FIFTEEN

BUYING HEALTHY PLANTS

> In a no-chemical garden, it is absolutely essential to buy strong, healthy plants. Follow the advice in this chapter to make sure you get only the best quality plants and don't bring any pests and disease home with you from the garden centre.

Container-grown plants may have to remain in a garden centre for a year or more. To accommodate this, garden centres often get their suppliers to put plants in containers which are large enough to give an extended 'shelf life'. Providing the plants do not become rootbound and are properly looked after, there is nothing wrong with this. But the standard of care varies a lot from garden centre to garden centre.

INSPECTING THE GARDEN CENTRE

DISPLAY BEDS
Container-grown plants should be kept on a free-draining surface – sand, gravel or a slatted bench, say. If they are kept on a surface where water can collect – uneven black polythene, say – the plants may have to stand in water for a long time, which can cause the roots to start rotting. If you suspect this, knock the plants carefully out of their pots as a check.

WATERING
Container plants can dry out within a few hours on warm breezy days, especially those in small pots. Many garden centres have automatic watering systems, but these can have drawbacks. Overhead irrigation can be used only when the garden centre is closed or a section is temporarily shut off. And, if plants have lush foliage, the water might not reach the compost. Capillary watering systems are effective, but the capillary action is broken every time a customer lifts up a plant to inspect it. Supplementary hand watering is often required in summer, and if you see staff doing this it's a sign that plants are well looked after.

SHELTER FOR PLANTS
A good sign that plants are looked after is when a garden centre takes into account the conditions different plants need. For example, plants that like partial shade, such as Japanese maples and ferns, should be kept under netting or lathes so that their foliage does not get scorched. If you visit a garden centre on an exposed site, look for windbreaks that protect the plants. This will reduce the risk of damage to foliage and leaves and help stop the plants from drying out so rapidly.

WINTER CARE
In winter container-grown plants outdoors should be closely packed together. Evergreens should be protected from the wind. In very cold winters the roots of evergreens grown in containers can be killed unless they are protected. However, plants may look perfectly healthy up until April or May and then suddenly die. If buying evergreens in spring following a hard winter, always inspect the roots. Live roots range from white to pale brown; dead roots look black or greyish, often with fungal growth.

Winter damage to evergreens may not become obvious until early summer

Right The larger of these two Leyland cypresses is clearly pot-bound
Below right Avoid plants with discoloured or badly blemished leaves

INSPECTING THE PLANTS

The following points apply to all plants. For buying tips about specific types of plants, see the checklist overleaf.

LABELS

Labels are a good indication of how long plants have been at the garden centre. If the label is faded and almost illegible, it's a strong indication that the plant has been around for a long time and may be pot-bound or starved unless well looked after.

CONTAINERISED OR CONTAINER-GROWN?

If a plant feels loose when you give it a gentle pull and the surface of compost looks quite fresh, it's likely that it has been potted up only recently. You are most likely to find this with roses and fruit bushes. Don't buy plants like this in spring or summer because the compost will fall away when you come to plant them and they may not survive. A few roots growing through the base of the pot and a little moss or liverwort growing on the compost are signs that a plant is well established in its container.

WEEDS

A few weed seedlings on the surface of compost are not serious, but weed-filled pots, like faded labels, are strong indications of neglect.

THE ROOTS

The first test is to pick up the plant. If there are so many roots growing through the container that it's difficult to lift it from the bed, don't buy that plant as it's likely to be pot-bound. As a further test, carefully remove the pot. Look for a rootball that holds together well and which still has some compost for the roots to grow into. Avoid plants that have a solid mass of roots, particularly where the roots have started to grow in circles around the pot. This last point is vital for trees, shrubs and fruit, as the roots will continue growing in circles when planted and they may never get properly established.

With fibrous-rooted plants like azaleas, rhododendrons, heathers, hebes, herbaceous perennials and alpines, don't be too worried about a very dense root system, providing that the top growth looks healthy, as the roots tend not to grow in circles. But with these plants, check the pots for vine weevil grubs. These are white with a brown head and about 1cm (½in) long. If you see them, don't buy the plant as they are very difficult to control.

HOW HEALTHY?

Be wary of starved plants. Undersized leaves, pale-coloured foliage and spindly or stunted growth are the main points to avoid. This is a particular problem with trees, shrubs and fruit, which are commonly kept in the same pots for too long. Also look out for pests and diseases. The

pests you are most likely to find are aphids and whitefly, so check the shoot tips and underneath a few of the young leaves to make sure they are clean.

Ivies and some conifers, particularly dwarf spruces like *Picea albertiana* 'Conica', are prone to red spider mite. Inspect the plants carefully for brown patches on the foliage and for very fine webbing. Mildew is a disease you may come across. Look for white deposits on leaves, but examine plants carefully to make sure these are not remnants of a fungicide treatment or salt deposits from overhead watering. Coral spot is a fungus seen as small orange spots on dead or dying branches of trees or fruit. It's not a serious problem unless it extends right around the main stem, as infected branches can be cut out. But it's a sign that plants have been neglected or badly pruned.

Left Price is not a guide to quality. The Euonymus 'Emerald 'n' Gold' on the right was actually cheaper
Below left For fast-growing shrubs like forsythia, either of these plants would be acceptable

■ WHAT SHAPE?

It's obviously best to go for the most vigorous and bushy plant, but with a number of plants it is not that important. Most deciduous shrubs, for example, will quickly form new shoots to compensate for any lop-sidedness as young plants. Similarly, herbaceous perennials and alpines will quickly make up for any one-sided growth when planted out. The exceptions are with cushion-forming alpines like encrusted saxifrages, which may continue to grow unevenly if you don't buy symmetrical plants.

With some shrubs, achieving a good shape, at least for the first few years, depends on buying a bushy well-balanced plant to start with. This applies to *Choisya* (Mexican orange blossom), *Cotinus* (smokebush), *Elaeagnus, Garrya elliptica, Magnolia, Viburnum tinus* and all slow-growing shrubs.

A well-balanced shape is also important for fruit trees and bushes. Although you can correct defects by pruning, this may mean you have to wait an extra year for the fruit.

Most trees tend to form a single straight stem, and it's important to look for a strong leading shoot. However, there are exceptions. Ornamental crab apples (*Malus*), hawthorns (*Crataegus*) and *Salix matsudana* 'Tortuosa' (tortured willow) all form bushy heads as young trees, so not having a strong leading shoot does not matter too much.

■ BIG OR SMALL?

With trees, shrubs and conifers, small plants tend to become established more quickly than large specimens and often overtake them after a few years. They are also a lot cheaper to buy. If you have a choice between a small and large plant and would prefer the large one for a more instant effect, take a close look at the pots.

Only buy the large plant if it's in a proportionately larger pot and has not become rootbound. With herbaceous plants and alpines, larger plants are often a good buy as they can be divided up to form a number of small plants before planting out.

■ GRAFTED PLANTS

All fruit trees and some ornamental trees and shrubs are grafted on to roots of another variety. The graft will be visible as a small bump, usually near the base of the stem but sometimes, on ornamental plants, near the top. Check that the graft is evenly covered with bark all the way round. If it looks weak or has cracks in the bark, this may lead to the plant snapping off or provide an entry-point for diseases at a later date. Also watch out for vigorous shoots growing from below the graft, which mean that the rootstock rather than the grafted variety could take over.

■ HOW HARDY?

In late summer or autumn be wary of plants with lots of soft new growth, commonly with leaves spaced more widely than normal along the stem. These plants are likely to have been forced in polythene tunnels and will be susceptible to damage in winter and pest and disease attacks.

Forced plants may be susceptible to winter damage and pest and disease attacks

BUYING HEALTHY PLANTS: QUICK CHECKLIST

	LOOK FOR	AVOID	BEST TIME TO BUY
Alpines	large plants that can be divided; good shape for cushion-formers such as encrusted saxifrages	weak-looking plants; yellowing or discoloured foliage; plants becoming bare at the centre; weeds in the pots	Mar–May, when garden centres generally have most choice
Bedding plants	well-spaced plants in strips with fresh, healthy foliage; named varieties (F1s for geraniums)	plants with pale or discoloured foliage; overcrowded or prematurely flowering plants	after frosts; Mar–Apr for hardy types, e.g. antirrhinums
Conifers	young vigorous plants with a good shape and foliage down to soil level; a strong leading shoot is important for upright conifers, but a bad sign for others	plants with yellowing or discoloured leaves; sparse foliage or brown patches; pot-bound plants; over-vigorous shoots on dwarf conifers	Apr–May (esp. in cold areas or on heavy soils) or Sep–Oct
Climbers	fresh healthy growth (or plump buds when not in leaf); several branches near ground level; untangled plants tied to a cane; grafted wisterias	broken or damaged stems (check near base); distorted leaves (mildew); aphids on shoot tips	early spring, or any time if you find a garden centre that doesn't let plants get tangled up
Fruit bushes	for black currants, certified virus-free plants; all branches growing from at or below soil level; well-developed root system. For gooseberries, at least three main branches and a clear main stem at least 15cm (6in) long	plants with few branches, uneven growth or poor roots; swollen buds on currants	bare-rooted plants in autumn
Fruit canes	thick canes with a good root system; certified virus-free summer raspberries	split or spindly canes or those with blotchy bark	bare-rooted plants in autumn
Fruit trees	one- or two-year-old trees with three or four evenly spaced strong branches and a good graft union	branches that form a narrow angle with the main stem; spindly or poorly shaped trees; damaged bark; pot-bound trees	autumn or winter to coincide with pruning
Herbaceous perennials	large plants that can be divided	plants with yellow leaves or with weeds growing in pots	garden centres have best selection in Mar and Apr
Roses	three or four main roots at least 10cm (4in) long with plenty of fibrous roots and at least two strong stems; a good graft union	damaged stems, shrivelled bark, plants not rooted in containers. Buying pre-packed plants can be risky	as bare-rooted plants in autumn
Shrubs, deciduous	healthy foliage but don't worry too much about slightly lop-sided plants or those that are not very bushy unless slow-growing varieties	plants with yellowing or discoloured leaves; weak spindly roots; suckers or reverted shoots on variegated plants	early autumn or any time providing they are kept well watered in dry weather and soil not frozen or waterlogged
Shrubs, evergreen	Symmetrical plants with balanced well-spaced shoots; healthy foliage; healthy roots (white to pale brown)	yellowing or discoloured foliage; brown patches on leaves (wind damage); dead or dying roots (grey or black)	Apr–May (esp. in cold areas or on heavy soils) or Sep–Oct
Trees	well-spaced symmetrical branches; a strong leader (unless tree naturally forms bushy head – see previous page); young vigorous plants	yellowing or discoloured foliage or with brown patches on leaves; pot-bound plants; very large specimens (unless you can carefully nurture them)	Sep–Oct or spring/summer if kept well watered
Vegetables	young, well-spaced plants or plants in individual pots; healthy green foliage; closely spaced leaves on tomatoes, peppers, aubergines and beans	foliage with blue or reddish tinges (frost damage or starvation); pot-bound plants; large plants. All brassicas, as they may introduce clubroot	early spring for hardy vegetables, May–Jun for tender vegetables

TROUBLE-FREE PLANTS

If you are not going to use any chemicals in your garden, you can save yourself a lot of bother by growing plants that suit the soil, position and local climate and don't usually succumb to pests and diseases.

The Tables on pages 126 to 133 list trees, shrubs and perennials that do well on most soils and are reliably hardy throughout most parts of Britain. None of the plants listed are prone to diseases, and they do not usually suffer any serious damage from pests.

Fruit and vegetables with resistance (or tolerance) to at least some pests and diseases are listed in the Tables on pages 134 and 135.

Above left Cotoneaster × watereri
Top Black currant 'Ben Lomond'
Middle Hemerocallis – a tough perennial for any position
Bottom Lettuce 'Malika' is resistant to mildew, root aphids and mosaic virus

TROUBLE-FREE HERBACEOUS PERENNIALS

	FLOWERS	POSITION	SOIL	HEIGHT	PLANTING DISTANCE	NOTES
Acanthus mollis 'Latifolius'	white, purple Jul–Sep	☼ ◑	most	90cm (3ft)	60cm (2ft)	large, deeply cut, spineless leaves
Acanthus spinosus (bear's breeches)	white/purple Jul–Sep	☼ ◑	most	1.2m (4ft)	90cm (3ft)	huge arching leaves deep cut and spiny. A. spinossisimum is smaller
Achillea taygetea 'Moonshine'	pale yellow Jun–Sep	☼	most	60cm (2ft)	45cm (1½ft)	feather-grey foliage, good for cutting and drying
Anemone × hybrida (Japanese anemone)	pink or white Aug–Oct	☼ ●	most	90cm (3ft)	45cm (1½ft)	dislikes disturbance
Asphodeline liburnica	pale yellow Jun–Aug	☼	any	60cm (2ft)	30cm (1ft)	grey-blue grassy leaves
Aster amellus 'Brilliant'	deep pink Aug–Sep	☼	any	60cm (2ft)	45cm (1½ft)	not prone to mildew
Aster amellus 'King George'	violet-blue Aug–Sep	☼	any	60cm (2ft)	45cm (1½ft)	not prone to mildew
Aster amellus 'Violet Queen'	violet Aug–Sep	☼	any	45cm (1½ft)	45cm (1½ft)	mildew-resistant
Aster dumosus 'Lady-in-Blue'	lavender-blue Aug–Sep	☼	any	25cm (1ft)	30cm (1ft)	mildew-resistant
Aster × frikartii 'Moench'	lavender-blue Jul–Sep	☼	avoid dry	90cm (3ft)	45cm (1½ft)	mildew-resistant
Astilbe chinensis 'Pumila'	pink-purple Jul–Aug	☼ ◑	moist	45cm (1½ft)	30cm (1ft)	attractive divided foliage
Astrantia major (masterwort)	green-white, pink Jun–Jul	◑	any	60cm (2ft)	45cm (1½ft)	variegated form good for ground cover
Astrantia maxima	pink Jun–Jul	◑	any	60cm (2ft)	45cm (1½ft)	more showy flowers than A. major
Bergenia cordifolia	pink Mar–Apr	☼ ◑	any	45cm (1½ft)	45cm (1½ft)	choose named varieties
Bergenia stracheyi	pale pink/white Mar–Apr	☼ ◑	any	30cm (1ft)	30cm (1ft)	leaves red/bronze in winter
Brunnera macrophylla	blue Apr–Jun	◑	any	30cm (1ft)	45cm (1½ft)	like forget-me-nots but not mildew-prone
Campanula lactiflora 'Pouffe'	lavender-blue Jun–Aug	☼ ◑	most	23cm (1ft)	45cm (1½ft)	needs no staking
Carex morrowii 'Evergold'	—	☼ ◑	most	30cm (1ft)	45cm (1½ft)	good edging with arching golden grass-like leaves
Chrysanthemum leucanthemum	white Jun–Aug	☼	any	60cm (2ft)	45cm (1½ft)	very tolerant, naturalises in rough areas
Chrysanthemum maximum 'Snowcap'	white Jun–Aug	☼	any	45cm (1½ft)	45cm (1½ft)	flowers don't brown, free-flowering
Chrysanthemum maximum 'Wirral Supreme'	white Jun–Aug	☼	any	90cm (3ft)	60cm (2ft)	reliable double variety
Chrysanthemum rubellum	yellow, pink, red Aug–Oct	☼	most	45cm (1½ft)	60cm (2ft)	smothered with flowers
Convallaria majalis 'Fortins Giant'	white May–Jun	☼ ◑	moist	45cm (1½ft)	60cm (2ft)	large fragrant flowers
Coreopsis grandiflora 'Goldfink'	bright yellow Jun–Sep	☼ ◑	any	20cm (8in)	45cm (1½ft)	longer-lived than other varieties
Crambe cordifolia	white May–Jun	☼	well-drained	1.8m (6ft)	1.8m (6ft)	clouds of small flowers
Dianthus 'Doris'	salmon-pink Jun–Jul	☼	well-drained	45cm (1½ft)	30cm (1ft)	second flush of flowers in September
Diascia rigescens	pink Jun–Aug	☼ ◑	well-drained	45cm (1½ft)	45cm (1½ft)	semi-evergreen
Doronicum plantagineum 'Miss Mason'	bright yellow Apr–Jun	☼ ◑	most	45cm (1½ft)	30cm (1ft)	daisy-like flowers, light green foliage

TROUBLE-FREE HERBACEOUS PERENNIALS

	FLOWERS	POSITION	SOIL	HEIGHT	PLANTING DISTANCE	NOTES
Erigeron aurantiacus 'Darkest of All'	violet-blue Jun–Aug	full sun	moist, well-drained	45cm (1½ft)	30cm (1ft)	daisy-like flowers
Eryngium alpinum (sea holly)	blue Jul–Sep	full sun	well-drained	75cm (2½ft)	45cm (1½ft)	spiky, metallic flower heads
Eryngium variifolium	grey-blue Jul–Sep	full sun	well-drained	90cm (3ft)	45cm (1½ft)	white-veined evergreen leaves
Euphorbia griffithii 'Fireglow'	orange-red May–Jun	light shade / no direct sun	well-drained	75cm (2½ft)	60cm (2ft)	can be invasive on light soils. Sap is an irritant and, together with seeds, is poisonous if digested
Geranium cinereum 'Ballerina'	bright pink May–Oct	full sun / light shade	any	15cm (6in)	30cm (1ft)	good border plant
Geranium endressii 'Wargrave Pink'	pale pink Jul–Aug	full sun / light shade	any	45cm (1½ft)	45cm (1½ft)	good ground cover
Geranium 'Johnson's Blue'	bright blue May–Aug	full sun / light shade	any	30cm (1ft)	60cm (2ft)	good ground cover
Geranium macrorrhizum 'Walter Ingwersen'	pale pink May–Jul	full sun / light shade	any	30cm (1ft)	45cm (1½ft)	good ground cover
Geranium sanguineum	purple-red May–Aug	full sun / light shade	any	30cm (1ft)	45cm (1½ft)	good ground cover
Geum × borisii	orange May	full sun / light shade	any	30cm (1ft)	30cm (1ft)	flowers intermittently to September
Geum chiloense 'Lady Stratheden'	bright yellow Jun–Sep	full sun / light shade	any	60cm (2ft)	45cm (1½ft)	double flowers; divide regularly
Geum chiloense 'Mrs Bradshaw'	bright red Jun–Sep	full sun / light shade	any	60cm (2ft)	45cm (1½ft)	semi-double flowers; divide regularly
Geum 'Georgenberg'	orange Jun–Sep	full sun / light shade	any	30cm (1ft)	30cm (1ft)	single flowers
Hakonechloa macra 'Albo-aurea'	—	full sun / light shade	most	60cm (2ft)	60cm (2ft)	ornamental grass with bright yellow stripes on leaves
Helleborus argutifolius (*H. corsicus*)	yellow-green Mar–Apr	light shade	moist	1.0m (3ft)	60cm (2ft)	can cause allergic reactions
Helleborus foetidus (stinking hellebore)	green, purple Mar–May	full sun / light shade	moist	60cm (2ft)	45cm (1½ft)	unpleasant foliage smell when crushed; invaluable evergreen for shady spots
Helleborus viridis	green Feb–Mar	full sun / light shade	moist	25cm (1ft)	45cm (1½ft)	a native British species; not very striking, small flowers
Hemerocallis	various Jun–Aug	full sun / no direct sun	any	90cm (3ft)	90cm (3ft)	can be invasive; look for named varieties if you want a particular colour
Heuchera 'Palace Purple'	white May–Aug	full sun / light shade	any	60cm (2ft)	45cm (1½ft)	purple maple-like leaves, good foliage bedding
Heuchera sanguinea 'Bressingham Hybrids'	red, pink, white May–Aug	full sun / light shade	any	90cm (3ft)	45cm (1½ft)	plant deeply
Iris pallida 'Dalmatica'	lavender Jun	full sun	most	90cm (3ft)	45cm (1½ft)	worth growing for cream and white leaves

Key

 full sun

☀ light shade or sun for around half the day

● no direct sunlight but not dense shade

Soil

any = will grow in both heavy and free-draining soils, but may be killed by prolonged waterlogging in winter

most = all but very heavy soils or those prone to extended drought

moist = soils which don't dry out in summer; will stand waterlogging unless otherwise specified

TROUBLE-FREE HERBACEOUS PERENNIALS

	FLOWERS	POSITION	SOIL	HEIGHT	PLANTING DISTANCE	NOTES
Liriope muscari	lilac-mauve Sep–Nov	☼ ◐	lime-free	30cm (1ft)	45cm (1½ft)	grassy foliage, grape-hyacinth-type flowers
Macleaya cordata	off-white Jul–Aug	☼ ◐	any	2.1m (7ft)	90cm (3ft)	large rounded leaves, frothy flower heads
Miscanthus sacchariflorus	—	◐	moist	2.7m (9ft)	90cm (3ft)	non-invasive grass with arching foliage
Miscanthus sinensis 'Silver Feather'	pink/brown Sep–Nov	☼ ◐	moist	2.1m (7ft)	90cm (3ft)	fountain-like habit, good focal-point
Paeonia lactiflora 'Duchesse de Nemours'	white Jun	☼ ◐	moist, well-drained	90cm (3ft)	90cm (3ft)	strongly scented, like cold cream
Paeonia mlokosewitschii	creamy-yellow Apr–May	☼	moist, well-drained	75cm (2½ft)	90cm (3ft)	attractive foliage
Physostegia virginiana	white, pink, mauve Jul–Sep	☼	any	60cm (2ft)	60cm (2ft)	snapdragon-like flowers
Polygonatum multiflorum (Solomon's seal)	green-white May–Jun	◐ ●	most	75cm (2½ft)	30cm (1ft)	bell-shaped flowers, attractive arching stems
Polygonum affine 'Donald Lowndes'	rose-red Jun–Oct	☼ ◐	any	23cm (9in)	45cm (1½ft)	good ground cover, evergreen with poker-like flowers
Pulmonaria angustifolia	blue Apr–May	☼ ◐	any	15cm (6in)	30cm (1ft)	plain green leaves
Pulmonaria rubra 'Bowles Red'	coral-red Mar–Apr	☼ ◐	any	30cm (1ft)	30cm (1ft)	white-spotted leaves, a good variety
Pulmonaria saccharata (lungwort)	violet Apr–May	☼ ◐	any	30cm (1ft)	30cm (1ft)	pink buds changing to sky-blue, silver markings on leaves
Rudbeckia fulgida 'Goldsturm'	golden-yellow Jul–Oct	☼ ◐	any	60cm (2ft)	60cm (2ft)	useful for late colour
Salvia × superba 'East Friesland'	violet-blue Jun–Aug	☼ ◐	most	60cm (2ft)	60cm (2ft)	flowers profusely
Saxifraga × urbium (London pride)	pink or red May–Jul	☼ ◐	any	25cm (1ft)	45cm (1½ft)	good ground cover or edging
Sedum roseum 'Ruby Glow'	rose-crimson Jul–Aug	☼	any	25cm (1ft)	45cm (1½ft)	drought-resistant
Sedum × 'Autumn Joy'	deep pink Aug–Oct	☼	any	60cm (2ft)	45cm (1½ft)	drought-resistant
Sempervivum tectorum	bright pink Jul	☼	most	15cm (6in)	30cm (1ft)	drought-resistant
Sidalcea 'Elsie Heugh'	pink Jun–Aug	☼	any	1.2m (4ft)	60cm (2ft)	good alternative to hollyhocks
Stachys lanata 'Silver Carpet'	—	☼ ◐	any	15cm (6in)	30cm (1ft)	ground cover, non-flowering variety
Tolmiea menziesii 'Variegata'	—	☼ ◐	any	25cm (1ft)	45cm (1½ft)	good ground cover or edging

Key

☼ full sun

◐ light shade or sun for around half the day

● no direct sunlight but not dense shade

Soil
any = will grow in both heavy and free-draining soils, but may be killed by prolonged waterlogging in winter
most = all but very heavy soils or those prone to extended drought
moist = soils which don't dry out in summer; will stand waterlogging unless otherwise specified

TROUBLE-FREE TREES AND SHRUBS

	HEIGHT 10 YEARS	SPREAD 10 YEARS	ULTIMATE HEIGHT	ULTIMATE SPREAD	FLOWERS	FOLIAGE	SOIL	POSITION	NOTES
Amelanchier lamarckii 'Ballerina'	5.0m (16ft)	3.0m (10ft)	7.5m (25ft)	6.0m (20ft)	white, Apr	light green, D	any	☼ ◐	orange-red autumn tints
Aucuba japonica 'Crotonifolia'	3.0m (10ft)	3.0m (10ft)	3.0m (10ft)	3.0m (10ft)	–	green/yellow, E	any	☼ ◐	needs no pruning
Berberis candidula	60cm (2ft)	60cm (2ft)	40cm (3ft)	1.2m (4ft)	yellow, May	dark green, silver underneath, E	any	☼ ◐	blue-black fruits in autumn
Berberis darwinii	2.0m (6½ft)	1.5m (5ft)	3.0m (10ft)	3.0m (10ft)	orange, Apr	dark green, spiny, E	any	☼ ◐	blue-black fruits in autumn
Berberis gagnepainii	2.0m (7ft)	2.0m (7ft)	4.0m (14ft)	4.0m (14ft)	yellow, May	dark green, E	any	☼ ◐	blue-black fruits, holly-like leaves
Berberis julianae	2.0m (7ft)	2.0m (7ft)	4.0m (14ft)	4.0m (14ft)	pale yellow, May	olive, spiny, E	any	☼ ◐	blue-black fruits, leaves reddish in autumn
Berberis thunbergii 'Atropurpurea'	1.8m (6ft)	1.2m (4ft)	2.1m (7ft)	2.1m (7ft)	Apr	purple-red, spiny, D	any	☼ ◐	scarlet leaves in autumn
Berberis × stenophylla	1.8m (6ft)	1.8m (6ft)	3.0m (10ft)	3.0m (10ft)	orange/yellow, Apr	green, spiny, small, E	any	☼ ◐	some late autumn flowers
Berberis wilsoniae	1.2m (4ft)	1.2m (4ft)	1.2m (4ft)	1.8m (6ft)	yellow, May	grey/green, D	any	☼ ◐	scarlet leaves in autumn
Betula jacquemontii	9.0m (30ft)	3.5m (12ft)	20.0m (66ft)	10.0m (33ft)	yellow catkins, Mar–Apr	green, D	any	☼ ◐	smooth white bark
Betula pendula 'Youngii'	3.0m (10ft)	4.0m (13ft)	10.0m (33ft)	8.0m (22ft)	green catkins, Mar–Apr	green, D	any	☼ ◐	yellow autumn colour, weeping habit
Betula pendula (*B. verrucosa*, *B.p.* 'Alba')	10.0m (33ft)	3.0m (10ft)	12.0m (40ft)	5.0m (16ft)	green catkins, Mar–Apr	green, D	any	☼	white bark, yellow autumn colour
Buxus sempervirens	1.8m (6ft)	1.8m (6ft)	3.5m (12ft)	3.5m (12ft)	–	dark green, E	any	☼ ●	aromatic foliage
Chaenomeles japonica	1.8m (6ft)	1.8m (6ft)	2.4m (8ft)	2.4m (8ft)	orange/red, Mar–Apr	mid-green, D	any	☼	edible quince fruits
Chaenomeles speciosa 'Nivalis'	2.5m (8ft)	2.5m (8ft)	3.0m (10ft)	3.0m (10ft)	white, Jun–Apr	mid-green, D	any	☼	edible quince fruits
Chaenomeles × superba 'Rowallane'	1.5m (5ft)	1.5m (5ft)	1.5m (5ft)	1.8m (6ft)	crimson, Mar–May	mid-green, D	any	☼	upright habit
Cotoneaster 'Rothschildianus'	2.4m (8ft)	3.0m (10ft)	3.0m (10ft)	4.5m (15ft)	white, Jun	mid-pale green, E	any	☼ ◐	creamy-yellow berries in autumn
Cotoneaster congestus	60cm (2ft)	90cm (3ft)	60cm (2ft)	90cm (3ft)	white, Jun	bright, E	any	☼ ◐	densely branched, mound-forming, red berries
Cotoneaster conspicuus 'Decorus'	90cm (3ft)	1.8m (5½ft)	90cm (3ft)	2.4m (8ft)	white, Jun	dark green, E	any	☼ ◐	orange-red autumn colour, long-lived red berries
Cotoneaster franchetti	3.0m (10ft)	3.0m (10ft)	4.2m (14ft)	4.2m (14ft)	white/pink, Jun	grey/green, SE	any	☼ ◐	orange-red berries in autumn
Cotoneaster franchettii 'Sternianus'	1.8m (6ft)	1.8m (6ft)	3.0m (10ft)	3.0m (10ft)	white/pink, Jun	silver-green, SE	any	☼ ◐	abundant red berries
Cotoneaster horizontalis	60cm (2ft)	1.2m (4ft)	60cm (2ft)	2.4m (8ft)	pink/white, Jun	dark green, D	any	☼ ◐	red leaves and berries in autumn
Cotoneaster horizontalis 'Variegatus'	60cm (2ft)	1.2m (4ft)	60cm (2ft)	1.8m (6ft)	pink/white, May	green/white, D	any	☼ ◐	pink/red foliage in autumn, few berries
Cotoneaster salicifolius 'Repens'	15cm (½ft)	1.5m (5ft)	15cm (½ft)	1.8m (6ft)	white, Jun	dark green, med E	any	☼ ◐	bright red berries
Cotoneaster simonsii	3.0m (10ft)	3.0m (10ft)	4.0m (13ft)	4.0m (13ft)	white, Jun	dark green, SE	any	☼	orange autumn colour, orange-red berries

TROUBLE-FREE TREES AND SHRUBS

	HEIGHT 10 YEARS	SPREAD 10 YEARS	ULTIMATE HEIGHT	ULTIMATE SPREAD	FLOWERS	FOLIAGE	SOIL	POSITION	NOTES
Cotoneaster × 'Hybridus Pendulus'	2.4m (8ft)	1.8m (6ft)	3.0m (10ft)	2.4m (8ft)	white, Jun	dark green, E	any	☀	usually grafted to form a small tree, red berries
Crataegus oxcantha 'Rosea Flore Pleno'	6.0m (20ft)	3.0m (10ft)	6.0m (20ft)	6.0m (20ft)	pink, May	green, D	any	☀ ◐	double flowers, red berries in autumn
Elaeagnus × *ebbingei* 'Limelight'	3.0m (10ft)	3.0m (10ft)	4.5m (15ft)	4.5m (15ft)	white, Oct–Nov	green/yellow, E	any	☀ ◐	wind resistant, good for coasts
Escallonia 'Apple Blossom'	1.5m (5ft)	1.8m (6ft)	2.4m (8ft)	2.1m (7ft)	pink/white, Jul–Oct	dark green, E	well-drained	☀	good for coastal regions
Euonymus fortunei 'Emerald 'n' Gold'	75cm (2½ft)	1.5m (5ft)	90cm (3ft)	3.0m (10ft)	–	green/yellow, E	any	☀ ◐	leaves tinged red in winter
Forsythia 'Lynwood'	2.4m (8ft)	2.1m (7ft)	3.5m (12ft)	2.4m (8ft)	yellow, Mar–Apr	mid-green, D	any	☀ ◐	good for cut flowers
Gleditsia tricanthos 'Sunburst'	5.5m (18ft)	3.5m (12ft)	12.2m (40ft)	5.5m (18ft)	–	yellow, D	any	☀	foliage becomes more green throughout summer
Hebe armstrongii	1.2m (4ft)	2.4m (8ft)	1.2m (4ft)	2.4m (8ft)	–	olive, E	most	☀	whipcord type, salt resistant
Hebe ochracea 'James Sterling'	0.9m (3ft)	1.2m (4ft)	0.9m (3ft)	1.2m (4ft)	white, Jul	gold, E	most	☀	whipcord type, salt resistant
Hebe pinguifolia 'Pagei'	15cm (½ft)	60cm (2ft)	15cm (½ft)	60cm (2ft)	white, May–Jun	blue/grey, E	most	☀ ◐	–
Ilex aquifolium 'J.C. van Tol'	3.0m (10ft)	3.0m (10ft)	4.6m (15ft)	4.6m (15ft)	–	dark green, E	moist, loamy	☀ ◐	female, almost spineless, produces berries without male pollination
Ilex × *altaclarensis* 'Golden King'	3.0m (10ft)	2.4m (8ft)	6.0m (20ft)	4.5m (15ft)	–	green/gold, E	moist, loamy	☀ ◐	female with red berries
Ilex aquifolium 'Silver Queen'	2.4m (8ft)	1.8m (6ft)	6.0m (20ft)	3.0m (10ft)	–	dark green, cream edge, E	any	☀ ◐	pinkish young leaves, male
Ilex crenata 'Golden Gem'	75cm (2½ft)	75cm (2½ft)	1.2m (4ft)	1.5m (5ft)	–	yellow then green, E	well-drained	☀ ◐	female with black berries
Kerria japonica 'Variegata Picta'	75cm (2½ft)	60cm (2ft)	75cm (2½ft)	60cm (2ft)	yellow, Apr–May	green, white-edged, D	any	☀ ◐	cut back after flowering
Lonicera nitida 'Baggesen's Gold'	1.2m (4ft)	1.8m (6ft)	1.8m (6ft)	3.0m (10ft)	–	gold, E	any	◐	leaves may scorch in full sun
Mahonia aquifolium	90cm (3ft)	1.2m (4ft)	1.2m (4ft)	1.5m (5ft)	yellow, Feb–Apr	dark green, E	well-drained	☀ ◐	some leaves turn crimson in winter
Mahonia aquifolium 'Atropurpurea'	1.2m (4ft)	1.5m (5ft)	1.2m (4ft)	1.8m (6ft)	yellow, Feb–Apr	bronzy-green, E	any	☀ ◐	purple leaves in winter
Malus 'Golden Hornet'	6.0m (20ft)	3.5m (12ft)	7.0m (23ft)	5.5m (17ft)	white/pink, May	green, D	any	☀ ◐	bright yellow, long-lasting fruits
Malus 'John Downie'	6.0m (20ft)	3.0m (10ft)	7.0m (23ft)	5.5m (17ft)	pink-white, May	green, D	any	☀ ◐	yellow fruits flushed with crimson
Malus 'Red Jade'	3.5m (12ft)	1.5m (5ft)	4.0m (13ft)	1.8m (6ft)	pink/white, May	green, D	any	☀ ◐	good weeping crabapple with red fruits
Malus 'Royalty'	5.5m (17ft)	3.5m (12ft)	7.0m (23ft)	5.5m (17ft)	pink, purple, May	purple, red, D	any	☀ ◐	small red-purple fruits
Olearia × *haasti*	2.0m (7ft)	2.0m (6½ft)	3.0m (10ft)	3.0m (10ft)	white, Jul–Aug	grey/green, E	well-drained	☀	wind and salt tolerant, but needs winter protection in cold areas
Osmanthus delavayi	1.2m (4ft)	1.2m (4ft)	2.5m (8ft)	2.7m (9ft)	white, Apr–May	dark green, E	any	☀ ◐	needs no routine pruning, may be browned by late frosts, withstands coastal breezes

TROUBLE-FREE TREES AND SHRUBS

	HEIGHT 10 YEARS	SPREAD 10 YEARS	ULTIMATE HEIGHT	ULTIMATE SPREAD	FLOWERS	FOLIAGE	SOIL	POSITION	NOTES
Potentilla arbuscula	50cm (1½ft)	75cm (2½ft)	60cm (2ft)	1.5m (5ft)	yellow, Jun–Oct	mid-green, D	most	☀ ◐	flowers are more prolific in full sun
Potentilla arbuscula 'Beesii'	30cm (1ft)	90cm (3ft)	30cm (1ft)	1.5m (5ft)	yellow, Jun–Oct	grey/green, D	most	☀ ◐	flowers are more prolific in full sun
Potentilla fruticosa 'Farreri'	75cm (2½ft)	1.0m (3ft)	1.2m (4ft)	1.0m (3ft)	yellow, Jun–Oct	light green, D	most	☀ ◐	flowers are more prolific in sun
Prunus cerasifera 'Nigra'	6.0m (20ft)	3.0m (10ft)	7.6m (25ft)	4.6m (14ft)	pink, Mar	purple, D	most	☀	stems dark purple
Prunus laurocerasus 'Marbled White'	3.0m (10ft)	2.4m (8ft)	4.0m (13ft)	3.0m (10ft)	white, Jun	grey/green/white, E	most	☀ ●	conical habit
Prunus laurocerasus 'Otto Luyken'	90cm (3ft)	1.2m (4ft)	1.5m (5ft)	1.5m (5ft)	white, Jun	dark green, E	most	☀ ●	candelabra-like flowers
Prunus lusitanica	3.5m (12ft)	3.5m (12ft)	6.0m (20ft)	6.0m (20ft)	white, Jun	dark green, E	–	☀ ●	can be trimmed as a hedge
Prunus sargentii	5.5m (18ft)	4.0m (13ft)	12.0m (40ft)	7.5m (25ft)	pink, Mar	green, D	–	☀	bronze young foliage, single flowers, orange and scarlet autumn colour
Prunus tenella 'Fire Hill'	1.2m (4ft)	1.2m (4ft)	1.5m (5ft)	1.5m (5ft)	red/pink, Apr	pale green, D	–	☀	watch out for suckers, avoid east-facing site
Prunus × *cistena*	1.0m (3ft)	1.0m (3ft)	1.8m (6ft)	1.8m (6ft)	pale pink, Mar–Apr	purple/bronze, D	–	☀	needs no routine pruning, crimson young foliage
Prunus × *hillieri* 'Spire'	5.5m (18ft)	1.8m (6ft)	7.5m (25ft)	3.0m (10ft)	pale pink, Apr	green, D	–	☀	red autumn foliage, single flowers, coppery young leaves
Pyracantha 'Orange Charmer'	2.4m (8ft)	1.8m (6ft)	4.0m (13ft)	3.0m (10ft)	white, Jun	dark green, E	any	☀ ◐	orange berries Sep–Mar
Ribes sanguineum 'Brocklebankii'	1.2m (4ft)	1.5m (5ft)	1.2m (4ft)	1.5m (5ft)	red, Apr–Jun	yellow, D	any	☀ ◐	attractive blue-black berries
Ribes sanguineum 'King Edward VII'	1.8m (6ft)	1.5m (5ft)	2.4m (8ft)	2.4m (8ft)	red, Apr–Jun	light green, D	any	☀ ◐	attractive blue-black berries
Robinia pseudoacacia 'Frisia'	6.0m (20ft)	4.0m (13ft)	7.6m (25ft)	4.6m (15ft)	–	green/yellow, D	any	☀	leaves bright yellow Apr–Jun
Sambucus racemosa 'Plumosa Aurea'	3.0m (10ft)	1.6m (5ft)	3.0m (10ft)	2.5m (8ft)	yellow/white, Apr–May	yellow, D	any	☀ ◐	retains bright colour longer in shade
Senecio 'Sunshine'	1.2m (4ft)	1.5m (5ft)	1.8m (6ft)	3.0m (10ft)	yellow, Jul–Aug	silver-grey, E	any	☀ ◐	thrives in wind or sea spray, cut back in Mar to keep compact
Skimmia japonica 'Foremanii'	75cm (2½ft)	1.5m (5ft)	1.2m (4ft)	1.8m (6ft)	white, May	mid-green, E	not chalk	☀ ◐	bright red berries if planted with a male variety such as 'Fragrans'
Sorbus aria 'Lutescens'	6.0m (20ft)	3.5m (11½ft)	10.7m (35ft)	6.0m (19½ft)	white, May–Jun	green (grey below), D	most	☀ ◐	young foliage white, orange-red berries in autumn
Sorbus aucuparia	6.0m (20ft)	3.0m (10ft)	11.0m (35ft)	5.5m (18ft)	white, May–Jun	green, D	most	☀ ◐	orange-red berries from Aug, good autumn colour
Sorbus vilmorinii	3.0m (10ft)	1.8m (6ft)	6.0m (20ft)	3.5m (12ft)	white, Jun	deep green, D	most	☀ ◐	red/purple autumn colour, pink and white berries

TROUBLE-FREE TREES AND SHRUBS

	HEIGHT 10 YEARS	SPREAD 10 YEARS	ULTIMATE HEIGHT	ULTIMATE SPREAD	FLOWERS	FOLIAGE	SOIL	POSITION	NOTES
Spiraea × arguta	1.5m (5ft)	1.8m (6ft)	2.1m (7ft)	2.4m (8ft)	white, Apr–May	mid-green, D	most	full sun	arching branches smothered in blossom
Spiraea × bumalda 'Goldflame'	90cm (3ft)	1.2m (4ft)	1.2m (4ft)	1.8m (6ft)	pink/red, Jun–Jul	gold/green, D	most	full sun, no direct sun	foliage becomes greener as summer progresses
Spiraea japonica 'Little Princess'	45cm (1½ft)	75cm (2½ft)	45cm (1½ft)	75cm (2½ft)	pink/red, Jul–Aug	light green, D	most	full sun	abundant flowers
Spiraea thunbergii	1.5m (5ft)	1.8m (6ft)	1.8m (6ft)	2.4m (8ft)	white, Mar–Apr	pale green, D	most	full sun	flowers appear before leaves
Spiraea × vanhouttei	2.0m (6½ft)	1.5m (5ft)	2.0m (6½ft)	2.0m (6½ft)	white, Jun	purple/green, D	most	full sun	plum-coloured autumn foliage
Symphoricarpos orbiculatus 'Albovariegatus'	90cm (3ft)	1.2m (4ft)	1.2m (4ft)	1.5m (5ft)	–	white/green, D	any	full sun	good foliage shrub, rarely produces berries, non-suckering
Symphoricarpos × chenaultii 'Hancock'	60cm (2ft)	60cm (2ft)	1.2m (4ft)	2.0m (6½ft)	–	mid-green, D	any	full sun, no direct sun	purple, pink or red berries, non-suckering
Symphoricarpos × deorenbosii 'Magic Berry'	1.8m (6ft)	1.8m (6ft)	2.5m (8ft)	2.5m (8ft)	–	mid-green, D	any	full sun, no direct sun	abundant rose-pink berries, limited suckering
Syringa microphylla 'Superba'	1.2m (4ft)	1.2m (4ft)	1.8m (6ft)	1.5m (5ft)	rose-pink, May–Oct	mid-green, D	any	full sun, light shade	long-flowering dwarf shrub
Viburnum × bodnantense 'Dawn'	2.4m (8ft)	1.2m (4ft)	2.7m (9ft)	1.8m (6ft)	white/pink, Nov–Mar	mid-green, D	any	full sun	protect from cold winds
Viburnum × burkwoodii	1.5m (5ft)	1.5m (5ft)	2.4m (8ft)	2.4m (8ft)	white, Mar–May	dark green, SE	most	full sun	reddish-brown autumn colour
Viburnum carlesii	1.5m (5ft)	1.5m (5ft)	2.1m (7ft)	2.1m (7ft)	pink/white, Apr–May	grey-green, D	most	full sun	flowers scented, good autumn colour
Viburnum davidii	1.2m (4ft)	1.5m (5ft)	1.5m (5ft)	2.0m (6½ft)	white, May–Jun	dark green, E	most	no direct sun, no direct sun	blue berries if both male and female bushes planted
Viburnum tinus 'Eve Price'	1.5m (5ft)	1.8m (6ft)	2.0m (7ft)	2.5m (8ft)	pink/white, Jan–Apr	dark green, E	most	full sun, no direct sun	pink buds
Vinca major 'Variegata'	20cm (8in)	90cm (3ft)	20cm (8in)	1.8m (6ft)	pale blue, Mar–Jul	green/cream, E	any	light shade, no direct sun	one of least invasive periwinkles
Weigela 'Bristol Ruby'	1.8m (6ft)	1.8m (6ft)	2.2m (7ft)	2.2m (7ft)	ruby-red, May–Jun	mid-green, D	any	full sun, light shade	reliable old variety
Weigela florida 'Foliis Purpureis'	1.5m (5ft)	1.5m (5ft)	1.5m (5ft)	1.5m (5ft)	pink, May–Jun	purple, D	any	full sun, no direct sun	good foliage shrub
Weigela florida 'Variegata'	1.5m (5ft)	1.8m (6ft)	2.1m (7ft)	2.1m (7ft)	pink, May–Jun	green/cream, D	any	full sun, light shade, no direct sun	keeps variegation in the shade
Weigela 'Newport Red'	1.2m (4ft)	1.2m (4ft)	1.5m (5ft)	1.5m (5ft)	dark red, May–Jun	mid-green, D	any	full sun, no direct sun	reliable old variety

Key

full sun

light shade or sun for around half the day

no direct sunlight but not dense shade

Soil

any = will grow in both heavy and free-draining soils, but may be killed by prolonged waterlogging in winter

most = all but very heavy soils or those prone to extended drought

moist = soils which don't dry out in summer; will stand waterlogging unless otherwise specified

TROUBLE-FREE ROSES

	RESISTANCE TO [1]	COLOUR		RESISTANCE TO [1]	COLOUR
LARGE-FLOWERED OR HYBRID TEA ROSES			'Laughter Lines'	blackspot, mildew, rust	pink, light markings
'Alec's Red'	blackspot, mildew, rust	cherry-red	'Lover's Meeting'	blackspot, mildew, rust	orange
'Alexander'	blackspot, mildew, rust	vermilion	'Matangi'	blackspot, mildew, rust	red and white
'Alpine Sunset'	mildew, rust	creamy-yellow peach-pink	'Memento'	blackspot, mildew, rust	light red
			'Mountbatten'	blackspot, mildew, rust	yellow
'Blessings'	blackspot, mildew, rust	coral-pink	'Paul Shiriville'	mildew, rust	pink, yellow at base
'Cheshire Life'	blackspot, mildew, rust	rich orange			
'Congratulations'	blackspot, mildew, rust	reddish-pink	'Princess Alice'	blackspot, mildew, rust	yellow
'Felicia'	blackspot, mildew, rust	light pink	'Queen Elizabeth'	mildew, rust	light pink
'Freedom'	blackspot, mildew, rust	deep yellow	'Sexy Rexy'	blackspot, mildew, rust	rose-pink
'Grandpa Dickson'	blackspot, mildew, rust	pale yellow	'Southampton'	blackspot, mildew, rust	apricot, flushed red
'Just Joey'	blackspot, mildew, rust	coppery-orange			
'Peace'	blackspot, mildew, rust	yellow, pink at edge	'Sweet Magic'	blackspot, mildew, rust	orange and gold
			'The Times'	blackspot, mildew, rust	dark red
'Peudouce'	blackspot, mildew, rust	ivory, pale yellow centre	'Trumpeter'	blackspot, mildew, rust	orange-red
'Pink Favourite'	blackspot, mildew, rust	deep pink	**CLIMBING ROSES**		
'Pink Peace'	blackspot, mildew, rust	reddish pink	'Aloha'	blackspot, mildew, rust	rose and salmon-pink
'Polar Star'	mildew, rust	white			
'Precious Platinum'	blackspot, mildew, rust	bright crimson	'Arthur Bell'	blackspot, mildew, rust	bright yellow
'Rebecca Claire'	blackspot, mildew	copper with pink	'Bobby James'	blackspot, mildew, rust	creamy-white
'Red Devil'	blackspot, mildew	rosy-scarlet	'Compassion'	blackspot, mildew, rust	pink to apricot
'Remember Me'	blackspot, mildew, rust	orange-yellow	'Dortmund'	blackspot, mildew, rust	red, white eye
'Rose Gaujard'	blackspot, rust	red, silver reverse	'Dreaming Spires'	blackspot, mildew, rust	golden-yellow
'Royal Romance'	blackspot, mildew, rust	salmon-peach	'Dublin Bay'	blackspot, mildew, rust	rich red
'Royal William'	blackspot, mildew, rust	deep red	'Galway Bay'	blackspot, mildew, rust	pink
'Silver Jubilee'	blackspot, mildew, rust	salmon-pink, creamy-peach	'Golden Showers'	blackspot, mildew, rust	golden-yellow
'Simba'	blackspot, mildew, rust	yellow	'Hamburger Phoenix'	blackspot, mildew, rust	crimson
'The Lady'	blackspot, mildew, rust	yellow, edged salmon	'Highfield'	blackspot, mildew, rust	light yellow
			'Joseph's Coat'	blackspot, mildew, rust	yellow-orange to red-pink
'Troika'	blackspot, mildew, rust	orange-bronze, shaded red			
			'Maigold'	blackspot, mildew, rust	apricot-yellow
CLUSTER-FLOWERED OR FLORIBUNDA ROSES			'Meg'	blackspot, mildew, rust	light pink/apricot
'Amber Queen'	blackspot, mildew, rust	amber			
'Anisley Dickson'	blackspot, mildew, rust	reddish-pink	'Mme Gregoire Staechelin'	blackspot, mildew, rust	clear pink
'Anne Harkness'	blackspot, mildew, rust	apricot-yellow			
			'New Dawn'	blackspot, mildew, rust	pearl-pink
'Baby Bio'	blackspot, mildew, rust	yellow	'Phyllis Bide'	blackspot, mildew, rust	light yellow and pink
'Beautiful Britain'	blackspot, mildew, rust	tomato-red			
'Bonica'	blackspot, mildew, rust	pink	'Rambling Rector'	blackspot, mildew, rust	cream
'Bright Smile'	blackspot, mildew, rust	yellow	*Rosa banksiae* 'Lutea'	blackspot, mildew, rust	pale yellow
'Chanelle'	blackspot, mildew, rust	cream, flushed buff and pink			
			Rosa filipes 'Kiftsgate'	blackspot, mildew, rust	creamy-white
'City of Belfast'	blackspot, mildew, rust	scarlet			
'Escapade'	blackspot, mildew, rust	mauve and white	'Seagull'	blackspot, mildew, rust	white
			'Sympathie'	blackspot, mildew, rust	deep red
'Fragrant Delight'	blackspot, mildew, rust	light salmon-pink	'Wedding Day'	blackspot, mildew, rust	cream
'Invincible'	blackspot, mildew, rust	red			
'Korresia'	blackspot, mildew, rust	yellow			

[1] Information on resistance to diseases is based on the experiences of the Royal National Rose Society. Even varieties that show disease-resistance may succumb to diseases in bad years

TROUBLE-FREE FRUIT

	VARIETY	RESISTANT TO	MAIN EATING PERIOD	NOTES
Apple (cooking and dessert)	'Belle de Boskoop'	scab, canker	Dec–Apr	large, with yellow flesh
Apple (cooking and dessert)	'Charles Ross'	scab	Oct–Dec	large, pale yellow fruit; better than most on chalk
Apple (cooking and dessert)	'Crawly Beauty'	scab	Dec–Feb	late-flowering, so good for cold areas
Apple (cooking)	'Lord Derby'	mildew, scab	Nov–Dec	large green fruit; good for baking
Apple (cooking)	'Newton Wonder'	scab	Dec–Mar	juicy; ripens to a moderately good eater
Apple (dessert)	'Baker's Delicious'	mildew, scab	Aug–Sep	aromatic cox-like flavour
Apple (dessert)	'Christmas Pearmain'	scab	Nov–Jan	small fruit with an aromatic flavour
Apple (dessert)	'Duke of Devonshire'	scab	Jan–Mar	yellow, firm and sweet fruit
Apple (dessert)	'Fortune'	scab	Sep–Oct	crops well only in alternating years
Apple (dessert)	'Heusgen's Golden Reinette'	scab	Feb–Apr	late-flowering, so good for cold areas
Apple (dessert)	'King of the Pippins'	scab	Oct–Dec	good aromatic flavour
Apple (dessert)	'Lord Hindlip'	scab	Dec–Mar	creamy, very juicy aromatic flesh
Apple (dessert)	'Sunset'	scab	Oct–Dec	good cox-type apple
Apple (dessert)	'Winston'	scab	Jan–Mar	small fruit, excellent for storing
Apricot	'Helmskerk'	die-back	Jul–Aug	the hardiest variety, good flavour
Blackcurrant	'Ben Lomond'	mildew	Jul	large fruit, good flavour; late-flowering
Blackcurrant	'Malling Jet'	mildew	Jul–Aug	very high yields, not strong on flavour
Blackcurrant	'Ben More'	mildew	Jul–Aug	heavy yields, acidic fruit
Gooseberry	'Keepsake'	mildew	Jul	good flavour, cooking variety
Gooseberry	'Invicta'	mildew	Jun	fair to good flavour, eat cooked or raw
Hybrid berry	'Josterberry'	mildew	Jun–Jul	like an improved version of 'Worcesterberry' on spineless bush
Hybrid berry	'Worcesterberry'	mildew	Jun	like small purple gooseberry
Pear	'Beurre Hardy'	scab	Oct	good flavour, heavy cropping
Pear	'Dr Jules Guyot'	scab	Sep	yellow fruit, reasonable flavour
Pear	'Jargonelle'	scab	Aug	good flavour, but unreliable cropper
Raspberry	'Autumn Bliss'	some resistance to aphids	Aug–Sep	best autumn-fruiting variety
Raspberry	'Glen Moy'	some resistance to aphids	Jul	susceptible to leaf-spot virus
Raspberry	'Glen Prosen'	some resistance to aphids	Jul–Aug	spineless canes
Raspberry	'Malling Joy'	grey mould, some resistance to aphids	Jul–Aug	large fruit, very heavy cropping
Raspberry	'Malling Leo'	cane spot, spur blight, some resistance to aphids	Jul–Aug	heavy cropping
Strawberry	'Cambridge Favourite'	mildew	Jun–Jul	heavy cropping; viruses can be a problem
Strawberry	'Cambridge Late Pine'	mildew	Jul	good flavour
Strawberry	'Harvester'	verticillium wilt	Jun–Jul	large fruit, but flavour can be poor
Strawberry	'Montrose'	grey mould	Jul	heavy cropping, good flavour
Strawberry	'Red Gauntlet'	grey mould	Jun–Jul	very large fruit, flavour only fair
Strawberry	'Saladin'	mildew, red core and some strains of grey mould	Jul	fruit may be naturally misshapen
Strawberry	'Silver Jubilee'	grey mould, mildew, red core	Jul	very good flavour and a good garden variety
Strawberry	'Tantallon'	grey mould, red core	Jun–Jul	firm flesh and above-average flavour
Strawberry	'Troubadour'	mildew, red core, verticillium wilt	Jul	high yields, but average flavour
Strawberry	'Tyree'	grey mould	Jul	holds its shape well in the freezer
Strawberry	'Honeoye'	mildew	Jun	can grow in heavy shade
Tayberry	'Medana'	virus-free strain	Jul	heavy cropping, mild sweet flavour

TROUBLE-FREE VEGETABLES

	VARIETY	RESISTANT TO	MAIN CROPPING PERIOD	NOTES
Aubergine	'Dusky'	tobacco mosaic virus	Aug–Sep	standard purple aubergine
Aubergine	'Elondo'	tobacco mosaic virus	Aug–Sep	standard purple aubergine
Beetroot	'Avon Early', 'Boltardy'	bolting	Jun–Oct	good for early sowings
Brussels sprout	'Rampart'	mildew, ringspot	Dec–Jan	tall, with large sprouts
Brussels sprout	'Troika'	mildew	Dec–Feb	very uniform sprouts
Calabrese	'Dixie'	clubroot-tolerant	Oct–Nov	contracts clubroot, but yields not greatly affected
Carrot	'Nandor'	carrot fly	Jul–Oct	quick-maturing variety
Cucumber	'Burpless Tasty Green'	mildew	Aug–Sep	climbing outdoor type
Cucumber	'Carmen'	leafspot, mildew, scab	Aug–Sep	all-female, greenhouse variety
Cucumber	'Fembaby'	mildew	Aug–Sep	all-female, greenhouse variety
Cucumber	'Mildana'	mildew	Aug–Sep	all-female, greenhouse variety
Cucumber	'Pepinex'	cucumber mosaic virus, leafspot	Aug–Sep	all-female, greenhouse variety
Lettuce	'Avoncrisp'	mildew, root aphid	Sep–Oct	good for autumn cropping
Lettuce	'Avondefiance'	mildew, root aphid	Nov–Dec	butterhead – good for late sowing
Lettuce	'Malika'	lettuce mosaic virus, mildew, root aphid	Jun–Sep	medium-sized crisphead
Lettuce	'Musette'	mildew, root aphid	Jun–Sep	medium-sized butterhead
Lettuce	'Sabine'	mildew	Jul–Aug	large butterhead
Parsnip	'Avonresister'	canker	Nov–Feb	bulbous-rooted good for poor soils
Parsnip	'Tender and True'	canker	Nov–Feb	long variety with very little core
Pea	'Hurst Green Shaft'	fusarium, mildew	Jun–Jul	grows to 60cm (2ft), good yields
Pea	'Kelvedon Wonder'	mildew	Sep–Oct	sow in June for autumn crop
Pea	'Pioneer'	mildew	Sep–Oct	sow in June for autumn crop
Pepper	'Midnight Beauty'	tobacco mosaic virus	Sep–Oct	early variety with deep purple fruit
Potato	'Cara'	blight, eelworm	Jun–Jul	maincrop, good for baking
Potato	'Kirsty'	potato blackleg	Jun–Jul	drought-resistant maincrop; does poorly in north
Potato	'Maris Piper'	blight, eelworm	Sep	maincrop, good all-rounder
Potato	'Pentland Javelin'	eelworm, scab	Jun–Jul	early, with waxy texture
Potato	'Ulster Sceptre'	blight	Jun–Jul	drought-resistant
Potato	'Golden Wonder'	blight	Sep	needs a light and well-manured soil
Potato	'Estima'	blight	Jul–Aug	drought-resistant early, good for baking
Potato	'Maris Peer'	scab	Jul–Aug	second early, good for salads
Potato	'Wilja'	blight, scab	Jul–Aug	second early, good in salads
Swede	'Chignecto'	clubroot	Nov–Feb	recent introduction
Swede	'Marian'	clubroot, mildew	Nov–Feb	high yields, good texture
Tomato	'Arasta'	cladosporium	Jul–Sep	standard greenhouse variety
Tomato	'Cumulus'	tobacco mosaic virus	Jul–Sep	standard greenhouse variety
Tomato	'Curabel'	cladosporium, fusarium, tobacco mosaic virus	Jul–Sep	standard greenhouse variety
Tomato	'Dona'	fusarium, tobacco mosaic virus, verticillium	Jul–Sep	beef-steak type
Tomato	'Estrella'	cladosporium, fusarium, verticillium, tobacco mosaic virus	Jul–Sep	standard greenhouse variety
Tomato	'Grenadier'	leafmould, fusarium	Jul–Sep	standard greenhouse variety
Tomato	'MM Super'	cladosporium	Jul–Sep	similar to 'Moneymaker'
Tomato	'Money Cross'	leafmould	Jul–Sep	similar to 'Moneymaker'
Tomato	'Piranto'	brown root rot, tomato mosaic virus	Jul–Sep	standard greenhouse variety
Tomato	'Shirley'	cladosporium, fusarium, tobacco mosaic virus	Jul–Sep	standard greenhouse variety

SOURCES OF SUPPLY

BIOLOGICAL CONTROLS

FOR APHIDS IN THE GREENHOUSE
Aphid predators are available from English Woodlands, Natural Pest Control and Thompson & Morgan

FOR CATERPILLARS
Bacillus thuringiensis is sold as:
Bactospeine (from Chase Organics, Dig 'n' Delve, Henry Doubleday Research Association and Unwins Seeds)
BT4000 (from Cumulus Organics)
Dipel (from English Woodlands)

FOR CODLING MOTHS
Pheromone traps are sold as:
Pagoda (from Oecos)
Trappit (from Chase Organics, Dig and Delve, Henry Doubleday Research Association and Steel & Brodie)

FOR MEALY BUGS IN THE GREENHOUSE
Suppliers as for aphid controls

FOR RED SPIDER MITES IN THE GREENHOUSE
Predators are available from English Woodlands, Natural Pest Control, Henry Doubleday Research Association and Thompson & Morgan

FOR WHITEFLY IN THE GREENHOUSE
Suppliers as for red spider mites

PEST BARRIERS

FOR CABBAGE ROOTFLY
Ready-made collars, sold as Fyba Brassica Collars, are available from Cumulus Organics and also shops and garden centres

FRUIT TREE GREASE AND GREASE-BANDS (for ants and winter moths)
Sold as:
pbi Boltac greasebands (from Chase Organics; also shops and garden centres)
Synchemicals Fruit Tree Grease (from shops and garden centres)

SPUN POLYPROPYLENE FLEECE (for flying insects and frost protection)
Sold as:
Agriframes Spun Web Mulch (from Agriframes)
Agryl p17 (from Chase Organics, Dobies, Henry Doubleday Research Association, Suffolk Herbs)
Nortène Harvest Guard (from shops and garden centres); Enviromesh (from Agralan) is similar
You may also find it sold under other names from other suppliers

FERTILISERS AND MINERAL SUPPLEMENTS

ORGANIC FERTILISERS AND TRACE ELEMENTS
Joseph Bentley and Chempak sell a large range of fertilisers and mineral supplements
Chase Organics, Cumulus Organics, Dig 'n' Delve Organics and Henry Doubleday Research Association sell a range of organic fertilisers

SEQUESTERED (CHELATED) IRON
Sold as:
Maxicrop Sequestered Iron (from shops and garden centres)
Murphy Sequestrene (from shops and garden centres)

ORGANICALLY APPROVED PESTICIDES

ALUMINIUM SULPHATE-BASED SLUG KILLERS
(not approved of by all organic growers). Brands include **Ferto-san** (did well in *Gardening from Which?* trials)

DERRIS (dust)
Sold as:
Murphy Derris Dust
Synchemicals Corry's Derris Dust

DERRIS (liquid)
Sold as:
pbi Liquid Derris
pbi Bio Friendly Insect Spray

PYRETHRUM (dust)
Sold as:
Synchemicals Py Garden Insect Killer Powder

PYRETHRUM (liquid)
Sold as:
Synchemicals Py Garden Insect Killer
ICI Bug Gun

SOFT SOAP SOLUTION
Sold as:
Phostrogen Safer's sprays
pbi Bio Friendly Pest Pistol

MULCHES
Woven polypropylene mulch is available from Agriframes

See overleaf for suppliers' mail order addresses

MAIL-ORDER SUPPLIERS

Agriframes Ltd, Charlwoods Road, East Grinstead, West Sussex RH19 2HG (fleece and woven polypropylene mulches)

Agralan, The Old Brickyard, Ashton Keynes, Swindon, Wiltshire SN6 6QR (products for organic gardeners)

Joseph Bentley Ltd, Beck Lane, Barrow-on-Humber, South Humberside DN19 7AQ (fertilisers and soil conditioners)

Chase Organics (GB) Ltd, Addlestone, Surrey KT15 1HY (seeds, including green manures, and products for organic gardeners)

Chempak Products, Geddings Road, Hoddesdon, Hertfordshire EN11 0LP (wide range of fertilisers)

Cumulus Organics, Ninevah Farm, Idlicote, Shipston-on-Stour, Warwickshire CV36 5EH (manure concentrates, fertilisers and organic sundries)

Dig 'n' Delve Organics, Fen Road, Blo'Norton, Diss, Norfolk IP22 2JU (products for organic gardeners)

Samuel Dobie and Son Ltd, Broomhill Way, Torquay, Devon TQ2 7QW (general seedsmen, but also sell sundries, including fleece)

English Woodlands Ltd, Hoyle Depot, Graftham, Petworth, West Sussex GU28 0JR (biological controls)

Henry Doubleday Research Association, National Centre for Organic Gardening, Ryton-on-Dunsmore, Coventry, West Midlands CV8 3LG (seeds, including green manures, and products for organic gardeners)

Natural Pest Control Ltd, Yapton Road, Barnham, Bognor Regis, West Sussex PO22 0BQ (biological controls)

Oecos, 130 High Street, Kimpton, Hertfordshire SG4 8QP (Pagoda pheromone traps)

Steel & Brodie, Stevens Drive, Houghton, Stockbridge, Hampshire SO20 6LP (manufacturers of Trappit pheromone traps)

Suffolk Herbs, Sawyers Farm, Little Cornard, Sudbury, Suffolk CO12 0NY (sells mainly seeds of herbs and less common vegetables, and some sundries, including fleece)

Thompson & Morgan, London Road, Ipswich, Suffolk IP2 0BA (general seedsmen, but sells green manures and some sundries for organic gardeners and biological controls)

Unwins Seeds Ltd, Mail Order Department, Histon, Cambridge CB4 4LE (general seedsmen, but sells some sundries for organic gardeners)

SOCIETIES AND ORGANISATIONS

Bats Group of Britain, c/o Zoological Society of London, Regent's Park, London NW1 4RY. Information on bats and their conservation

British Trust for Ornithology, Beech Grove, Tring, Hertfordshire HP23 5NR

The Centre for Alternative Technology, Machynlleth, Powys SY20 9AZ. Advice on ecological gardens

Flora and Fauna Preservation Society, c/o Zoological Society of London, Regent's Park, London NW1 4RY. Advice on conservation

Henry Doubleday Research Association, National Centre for Organic Gardening, Ryton-on-Dunsmore, Coventry, West Midlands CV8 3LG

Royal Society for Nature Conservation, The Green, Nettleham, Lincoln LN2 2NR. Can supply details of local groups which operate frog spawn distribution schemes

Royal Society for the Protection of Birds, The Lodge, Sandy, Bedfordshire SG19 2DL

Soil Association, 86 Colston Street, Bristol BS1 5BB. Advice on organic gardening (mainly concerned with professional growers)

St Tiggiwinkles Wildlife Hospital Trust, 1 Pemberton Close, Aylesbury, Buckinghamshire HP21 7NY. Advice on safeguarding hedgehogs

INDEX